Mauro Borgo · Alessandro Soranzo
Massimo Grassi

MATLAB for Psychologists

Mauro Borgo
Via Marosticana 168
Dueville (VI), Italy

Massimo Grassi
Department of General Psychology
University of Padova
Padova, Italy

Alessandro Soranzo
School of Social Science & Law
University of Teesside
Middlesbrough, UK

ISBN 978-1-4614-2196-2   e-ISBN 978-1-4614-2197-9
DOI 10.1007/978-1-4614-2197-9
Springer New York Dordrecht Heidelberg London

Library of Congress Control Number: 2012931943

Printed on acid-free paper

Springer is part of Springer Science+Business Media (www.springer.com)

*To my three women: my wife, Tatiana,
my mother, Angelina, and my grandmother
Emilia*

–Mauro Borgo

To my father

–Alessandro Soranzo

To Viola and Ruggero

–Massimo Grassi

Preface

Psychological researchers should possess several skills, and one of them is surely creativity. Creativity is needed at several key points of the research process, such as in creating experimental stimuli and planning and designing an experiment. Creativity drives good data analysis, so that numbers can reveal their full potential.

Much of this creativity is now expressed through a computer program. For example, in planning and designing a psychological experiment and in analyzing data, we use specific software that has been dedicated to that particular job. This software might, however, be a hindrance to creativity, preventing it from permeating research. This is because in the majority of cases, software is designed to satisfy the average user and it is not flexible enough to meet specific needs.

In this sense, MATLAB is exactly the other side of the coin. When we first open the software, the lack of a graphical interface may be frustrating: at a first glance, the program may seem difficult to use. This book is aimed at helping users in their first approaches to this software, to aid them in programming their psychological experiments and consequently in liberating their creativity. And this is MATLAB's major advantage: we do not have to adapt our needs to the software; it is the software that adapts to our needs.

MATLAB is an extremely powerful research tool. By means of this single software tool we can control every step of our research. We can create stimuli of any kind (e.g., pictures, sounds), and we can program psychological experiments, calculate statistics, run simulations, and do any kind of signal or biosignal processing. In brief, the flexibility of this software lets us to control and customize every conceivable step of our research requiring a computer program. Moreover, knowledge of MATLAB will help you to find a postdoc in experimental psychology after completing the Ph.D. In many cases, research groups look for researchers with good MATLAB programming skills.

The current text is written to help the newcomer in using MATLAB for research in experimental psychology. However, the content can be transferred to any application. The reader can find the scripts written in this book at the following web page: http://www.psy.unipd.it/~grassi/matlab_book.html

A final recommendation for the reader: do not begin to work with MATLAB without a goal. Our teaching experience suggests that having a goal greatly accelerates your learning. Therefore, think immediately about the amazing custom code you need to complete your state-of-the-art research. That code is here in this book, waiting to be written by you.

Dueville (VI), Italy   Mauro Borgo
Middlesbrough, UK   Alessandro Soranzo
Padova, Italy   Massimo Grassi

Acknowledgments

Thanks to Professor Silvano Pupolin for his support.

Contents

Chapter 1
Basic Operations

This chapter gives an overview of MATLAB and compares MATLAB with a scientific calculator. The chapter gives also an overview of basic arithmetic operations and functions as well as a short introduction to matrices and matrix manipulation.

It is supposed that you have already installed MATLAB on your computer. When you start MATLAB, the MATLAB desktop opens, as shown in Fig. 1.1 (or something similar, depending on your MATLAB version). In this first chapter we refer only to the Command Window, where the special >> prompt appears. The other windows have the following meaning:

- The Workspace Window contains a list of variables that are in use in the working session.
- The Command History contains the list of all commands you have typed in the command window.
- The Current Folder window shows the list of the files contained the folder you are working on.

When the prompt >> is visible, this means that MATLAB is waiting for a command. You can quit MATLAB at any time in either of the following ways:

1. Select Exit MATLAB from the desktop File menu.
2. Enter `quit` or `exit` after the command window prompt >>, and press the Enter key.

Alternatively, select File with the mouse from the top menu bar, and then exit MATLAB.

Observe that the tab above the Workspace shows the Current Directory Window. For example, in the Windows operating system, the path might be as follows: C:\MATLAB\Work, indicating that directory "Work" is a subdirectory of the main directory "MATLAB," which is installed in drive C. Clicking on the arrow in the Current Directory Window shows a list of recently used paths. Clicking on the button to the right of the window allows the user to change the current directory. Knowing which is the current path is fundamental: from the Command Window you

M. Borgo et al., *MATLAB for Psychologists*,
DOI 10.1007/978-1-4614-2197-9_1, © Springer Science+Business Media, LLC 2012

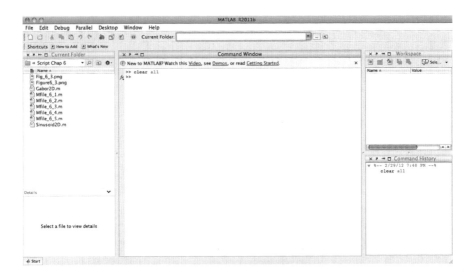

Fig. 1.1 The MATLAB desktop. MATLAB release 2011b

have access to the file stored in the given directory. It is, of course, possible to change your working directory.

Before continuing our introduction to MATLAB, we want to highlight a very useful window: the HELP Window. This window is the most useful window for beginning MATLAB users—and for expert users as well: select Help▶ PRODUCTHELP from the top bar menu. The Help Window has most of the features you would see in any web browser, including clickable links, a back button, and a search engine. All MATLAB commands and functions are explained with examples: you have simply to search for the desired word.

Now let us begin with a description of the MATLAB language. The word "MATLAB" is the concatenation of the words MATrix LABoratory, meaning that MATLAB is an interactive software system for numerical computation, especially designed for computations with matrices. Before going into the details of matrix computations, let us first see how to use MATLAB to do simple arithmetic operations: Type 1+1 after the >> prompt, followed by Enter; that is, press the Enter key, as indicated by <ENTER>

```
>> 1+1          <ENTER>
```

MATLAB gives its quick answer by displaying the following message:

```
ans =
    2
```

You can perform other arithmetic operations, such as multiplication, subtraction, and division, and MATLAB always returns the correct result. If such is not the case, there is certainly something wrong with what you typed. For example, you can try the following operations (type the operation after the >> prompt followed by Enter):

To TYPE after prompt >> followed by Enter	MATLAB answer	Meaning of the operation
35*12	ans = 420	Multiplication
2/45	ans = 0.0444	Division
4-1	ans = 3	Subtraction
2^3	ans = 8	Exponentiation

Note that to type numbers such as the Avogadro's number 6.023×10^{23}, you can either write the *expression* 6.023*10^23 or you can *represent* the number in *scientific notation*. To enter Avogadro's number in scientific format, type 6.023e23, where 6.023 is the mantissa and 23 is the exponent. Mantissa and exponent must be separated by the letter e (or E):

```
>>  6.023*10^23          <ENTER>
ans =
    6.0230e+023
```
```
>>  6.023e23             <ENTER>
ans =
    6.0230e+023
```

Such numbers are also defined to be *floating point*.

MATLAB warns you in the case of in invalid operation or "unexpected" results. What do you think MATLAB will show us if we type 12/0 or 0/0? Let's try it:

To TYPE after prompt >> followed by Enter	MATLAB answer	Meaning of the answer
12/0	ans = Inf	You should not divide by zero, but if you do, the result is **Infinity**
0/0	ans = NaN	Unable to find the answer, so the result is **NaN = Not a Number**
11+	??? 11+ | Error: Expression or statement is incomplete or incorrect	If you want to perform this operation, you must complete the expression with another term

As you can see, MATLAB is unable to "stay quiet." It quickly answers your commands by displaying something in the command window. In the previous cases, the answer was a special value such as Inf *(Infinity)* or NaN *(Not a Number)*. You can use these special values on their own, typing, for example:

```
>>  12/Inf              <ENTER>
ans =
    0
```

MATLAB can be used as a scientific calculator, combining several operations in one expression. The computation of the expression is based on well-known mathematical rules. In particular, some operations are performed before others, based on precedence rules, which are given in the following table:

Precedence	Operator
1	Parentheses (round brackets)
2	Exponentiation, left to right
3	Multiplication and division, left to right
4	Addition and subtraction, left to right

If you want to know the result of the operation $\{2+[5*3/(7-5)^2]/3\}$ you have to type:

```
>> (2+(5*3/(7-5)^2)/3)              <ENTER>
ans =
     3.2500
```

In this example, MATLAB first calculates $(7-5)=2$, then it squares $2^2=4$, then it performs the multiplication $5*3=15$ (multiplication left to right), and then divides the result by the previously computed result, i.e., $15/4=3.75$. The result in brackets is divided by 3 ($3.75/3=1.25$) and then added to 2, giving the result. Note that in MATLAB, parentheses are always given by round brackets.

MATLAB was developed for scientists, and for this reason you can find built-in operations and functions that are more advanced than the ones we have just looked at. Considering MATLAB as a sort of scientific calculator, you can engage the "cosine button" simply by typing:

```
>> cos(36)                <ENTER>
ans =
    -0.1280
```

Other common functions are reported in the following table. Type the operation after the >> prompt followed by Enter:

To TYPE after prompt >> followed by Enter	MATLAB answer	Meaning of the operation
cos(12)	ans = 0.8439	Cosine of the element in parentheses
sin(12)	ans = -0.5366	Sine of the element in parentheses
tan(4)	ans = 1.1578	Tangent of the element in parentheses
exp(3)	ans = 20.0855	Exponential of the element in parentheses
log(10)	ans = 2.3026	Natural logarithm of the element in parentheses
log10(12)	ans = 1.0792	Base-10 logarithm of the element in parentheses

We will see in the rest of the book the possibility using many other functions. Just to introduce some: statistical functions, interpolation functions, linear-algebraic functions, functions for images and sound elaboration, and last but not least, your own custom-created functions!

We conclude by giving some hints on creating and editing command lines:

- You can select (and edit) previous commands you have entered using the up-arrow and down-arrow keys. Remember to press Enter to execute the command.
- MATLAB has a useful editing feature called *smart recall*. Just type the first few characters of the command you want to recall, e.g., type the characters lo and press the up-arrow key—this recalls the most recent command starting with lo. The result might be, for example, log(10) or log10(12) .

Variables

Thus far, we have seen the use of MATLAB as a scientific calculator. However, MATLAB is much more than a calculator, and the main difference is the possibility to use "variables." In a scientific calculator we can save and recall a single number only. In MATLAB, in contrast (as in other programming languages), we can store and recall virtually an infinity of different values called *variables*. A *variable* is a sort of box, having a certain shape, a certain dimension, with a label naming it. In such a box you can put the (virtual) item you need, for example a number, an image, and so on.

Suppose you want to save a number representing your age. You can create your own variable and store it by simply typing the following command:

```
>> age=22            <ENTER>
age =
    22
```

The symbol age is the variable name (the box name), which contains the number 22. Each time you recall (type) such a name, the content of the variable is used; in this simple case, it is displayed. Type again the *variable* name:

```
>> age            <ENTER>
age=
    22
```

You can define other variables, for example the number of your friends. Just type:

```
>> Nfriends = 132            <ENTER>
Nfriends =
    132
```

At this stage, you may wonder about the shape of the box or its volume. The answer is not straightforward. However, by typing the `whos` command, MATLAB prompts all the variables currently active in the working session:

```
>> whos            <ENTER>

Name       Size    Bytes  Class     Attributes
age        1×1         8  double
Nfriends   1×1         8  double
```

The `whos` command gives you a list of all the variables created in the workspace together with their characteristics. In order to understand the meaning of such characteristics, consider the analogy between variable and box, as presented in the following table:

Variable	Box	Visual interpretation
Name	Name of the box	
Size	Number of objects you have put in (in the previous case, just one object, i.e., 1 × 1).	
Bytes	Total volume of the box. This is the number of objects multiplied by the dimension of each (to store a number you need 8 bytes)	
Class	Type of object you can put inside the box (in the previous case, it is a number stored with *double precision*)	
Attributes	Other information	

Note that the variables list obtained using the command `whos` can readily be seen in the Workspace Window (see Fig. 1.1).

One nice thing that MATLAB does when you create a variable is that it automatically selects the most suitable type of box for the variable. You need, however, to know a few simple rules about variable names:

1. The variable name must start with a letter.
2. It may consist only of the letters a–z, the digits 0–9, and the underscore (_). You cannot have a name with spaces or others symbols (such as +, ^, *).
3. MATLAB is case-sensitive, which means that it distinguishes between upper- and lowercase letters. So `age` is different from `AgE` or `Age`.

Try to create the following variables by typing them after the >> prompt followed by Enter: `N-friends=12`, `$aDay=60`, `3rd_classified=11`. What happens, and why? MATLAB gives you the following error:

```
??? $aDay=60
    |
Error:The input character is not valid in MATLAB statements or expressions.
```

Obviously, in these examples we didn't follow the aforementioned rules (use of the character—and $, beginning the name with a number).

MATLAB has a few predefined variable names. Some of these are presented in the following table:

To TYPE after prompt >> followed by Enter	MATLAB answer	Value contained in the variable
`Pi`	`ans = 3.1416`	π
`Esp`	`ans = 2.2204e-016`	Floating-point relative accuracy, i.e., the distance from 1.0 to the next largest double-precision number
`j`	`ans = 0 + 1.0000i`	Imaginary unit, i.e., sqrt(−1), used to enter complex numbers
`I`	`ans = 0 + 1.0000i`	Imaginary unit, i.e., sqrt(−1), used to enter complex numbers
`NaN`	`ans = NaN`	Not a number
`Inf`	`ans = inf`	Infinity

You can redefine a variable by simply assigning it a new value:

```
>> pi=12                    <ENTER>
pi =
   -12
>> pi                       <ENTER>
pi =
   -12
```

Once you have inserted a new value, you cannot recall the previous one. However, in the special case of predefined variables, you can clear the redefined variable, and the predefined variable is restored. To clear variables you use the command `clear` followed by the variable name (or a list of them). Let's try:

```
>> clear pi                 <ENTER>
```

MATLAB doesn't give you an answer. However, the command has been executed. Type the *pi* variable again, and MATLAB will return the value of π:

```
>> pi                       <ENTER>
ans =
   3.1416
```

The command `clear` can be followed by the specification `all`, and all the variables
stored in the workspace are deleted. To test whether this is indeed the case, type the
`whos` command:

```
>> clear all            <ENTER>
>> whos                 <ENTER>
>>
```

Note that you receive no answer from MATLAB because there is nothing to display.
At the same time, you can see that the Workspace Window (Fig. 1.1) is empty.

With variables you can type complex expressions and store the result. Let's try:

```
>> number=13;                       <ENTER>
>> a=14;                            <ENTER>
>> c=pi*((number+a/2)/10);   <ENTER>
```

MATLAB doesn't give an answer because you ended the command with the
semicolon (;) which prevents the value of `number` from being echoed on the screen.
However, `number` still has the value 13, as you can see by entering its name without
a semicolon (or looking at the Workspace Window):

```
>> number               <ENTER>
number =
    13
>> c                    <ENTER>
c =
    6.2832
```

Thinking in a Matrix Way

Our first question about matrices is, "What is a Matrix?" We are not talking about
the film, the sequels, the comic books, or the video games. For us, a matrix isn't a
complex computer simulation that you have to do battle with to save humanity.
However, you can choose to continue to read the book (in analogy to the blue pill in
the film that allows you to lead your normal life) to learn how use MATrix
LABoratory to create innovative experiments, thereby changing the world with your
discoveries.

In MATLAB, a matrix is a rectangular array of numbers, as shown in the following Fig. 1.2.

The horizontal lines of a matrix are called rows, and the vertical lines are called
columns. The numbers in the matrix are called entries. A matrix with m rows and n
columns is called an $m \times n$ matrix. A matrix one of whose dimensions equals one is
often called a vector. An $m \times 1$ matrix (one column and m rows) is called a column
vector, and a $1 \times n$ matrix (one row and n columns) is called a row vector.

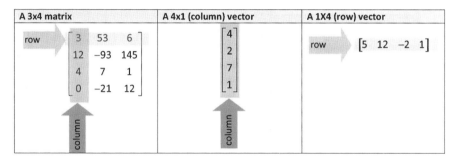

Fig. 1.2 Matrices of various dimensions

If you are familiar with the spreadsheet software Excel, you can imagine each Excel worksheet as a matrix, with rows and columns.

Now let's try to define some matrices and vectors in MATLAB. Type the following statements as written:

```
>> a=[3,5,7,8]                    <ENTER>
a =
       5    12    -2    1
>> b=[4;2;7;1]                    <ENTER>
b =
       4
       2
       7
       1
>> c=[3, 53,6;12,-93,145;4,7,1;0,-21,12]          <ENTER>
c =
       3    53      6
      12   -93    145
       4    7       1
       0   -21     12
>> whos                           <ENTER>
    Name      Size         Bytes         Class        Attributes

     a        1x4           32           double
     b        4x1           32           double
     c        4x3           96           double
   number     1x1            8           double
```

As you can see, after the command whos, each variable is displayed together with its size expressed in rows × columns. (Note: if you have used other variables previously, your list of variables could be different). Note that a scalar value, like the variable number, can be considered a 1×1 matrix.

Sometimes we need to know the size of the variables only, instead of the full list of their properties. In this case, the function `size(c)` returns the number of rows and columns of the variable c:

```
>> size(c)
ans =
     4    3
```

Another useful function is `length(c)`, which returns the length of the vector c. If c is a matrix, the function `length` returns the number of rows only:

```
>> length(c)
ans=
     4
```

To put data into a matrix, you must type the values within square brackets, separated by *spaces* or *commas* for different elements in a row, while the *semicolon* (;) is used to indicate the end of the row. Note that the number of elements must be the same in each row:

```
>> x=[ 1 2 3; 2 5 7]            <ENTER>
x =
     1    2    3
     2    5    7
```

If you have not put the same number of elements in each row, MATLAB displays an error:

```
>> x = [2 3; 2 5 7];
??? Error using ==> vertcat
CAT arguments dimensions are not consistent.
```

As you can see, MATLAB is not a wizard who tries putting the missing element in the right place. MATLAB does not know whether you want to put the element 2 and 3 in the first and second columns or in the second and third columns respectively.

You can use a matrix or a vector to implement another variable. For example, type in the following statements:

```
>> x = [3 2 1];                 <ENTER>
>> y = [6,7,8];                 <ENTER>
>> z1 = [x -y];                 <ENTER>
>> z2 = [x; -y];                <ENTER>
```

Can you work out what `z1 and z2` will look like before displaying them? In the following table we present other examples showing how to use variables already implemented to create new variables:

Mathematical representation	MATLAB (type after the prompt >> followed by Enter)	Dimension
$M = \begin{bmatrix} 3 & 12 & \pi \end{bmatrix}$	`M=[3,12,pi];`	1×3 Row vector

$N = \begin{bmatrix} 3 & 12 & \pi \\ 8 & 9 & 10 \end{bmatrix}$	`N=[3,12,pi; 8,9,10];`
	 Or equivalently, if you have already inserted M:
	 `N=[M; 8,9,10];`
		2×3 Matrix

$P = \begin{bmatrix} 4 \\ 2 \\ -1 \end{bmatrix}$	`P=[4;2;-1]`	3×1 Column vector

$Q = \begin{bmatrix} 4 & -4 \\ 2 & -2 \\ -1 & 1 \end{bmatrix}$	`Q=[4, -4;2, -2;-1, 1];`
	 Or equivalently, if you have already inserted P:
	 `Q=[P;-P];`
		3×2 Matrix

If you do not specify any variable content (i.e., any values inside the square brackets), MATLAB creates a variable of size zero with no value, or more precisely, a matrix of dimension 0×0 with no value in it.

```
>> y = [ ];                    <ENTER>
>> whos y                      <ENTER>
Name          Size         Bytes         Class         Attributes

y             0x0          0                           double
```

The Workspace Browser in the desktop provides a handy visual representation of the workspace. By clicking a variable in the Workspace Browser, we open the Array Editor, which can be used to view and change values.

The entry that lies in the ith row and the jth column of a matrix is typically referred to as the (i,j), or (i,j)th entry of the matrix. For example, the (3,2) entry of matrix Q in the table above is 1. In mathematical format, it is usually written as $Q_{3,2}$, while in MATLAB you can access to the matrix entries in this way:

```
>> Q(3,2)                      <ENTER>
ans =
       1
```

Note the use of parentheses. For indexing you use parentheses, whereas to define a matrix, you use square brackets; otherwise, you get an error:

```
>>Q[2,3]
??? Q[2,3]
     |
Error: Unbalanced or unexpected parenthesis or bracket.
```

In the following table you can find other examples:

Mathematical representation	MATLAB (type after the prompt >> followed by Enter)
$Q_{3,1}$ is equal to -1	```>>Q(3,1)
ans=
-1```
$N_{2,2}$ is equal to 9	```>> N(2,2)
ans=
9```
$M_{1,3}$ is equal to π	```>> M(1,3)
ans=
3.1416```
$P_{2,1}$ is equal to 2	```>> N(2,1)
ans=
2```

If P and M are two vectors, it is possible to refer to their entries by referencing only their single dimension, i.e., you can type M(3) instead of M(1,3), and N(2) instead of N(2,1).

If you refer to an element in a nonexistent position, MATLAB gives you an alert:

```
>> Q(3,3)                    <ENTER>
??? Index exceeds matrix dimensions.
```

What happens if you want to address more than one element at time? This is possible in MATLAB using a vector (or a matrix) in the indexing place to express the selected rows or columns:

```
>> Q([1,3],2)                <ENTER>
ans =
    -4
     1
```

How many values do you expect MATLAB to display when you type Q([1,3],[1,2]) ? Two or Four? Let's try:

```
>> Q([1,3],[1,2])            <ENTER>
ans =
     4    -4
    -1     1
```

The answer is four, because MATLAB shows the values in the positions given by each combination of the specified rows and columns, i.e., Q_{11}, Q_{12}, Q_{31}, Q_{32}.

Now suppose you have a large matrix from which you want to extract elements going from the ith row to the jth row in the second column. MATLAB offers a very efficient way to this, namely the colon (:) operator. Before seeing how it works, let us generate a new matrix:

```
>> x=[1 2 3; 4 5 6; 7 8 9; 10 11 12; 13 14 15]    <ENTER>
```

```
x =
      1      2      3
      4      5      6
      7      8      9
     10     11     12
     13     14     15
```

Now type:

```
>> i=2; j=4;                    <ENTER>
>> x(i:j,2)                     <ENTER>
ans =
      5
      8
     11
```

Note that more than one command has been typed on the first line. This can be done by separating commands with a semicolon. In addition, note that MATLAB displays exactly the values from the second row to the fourth row in the second columns. This is equivalent to:

```
>> x([2 3 4],2)                 <ENTER>
ans =
      5
      8
     11
```

As a matter of fact, using the colon operator is equivalent to generating a vector going from a given value to another one, possible using a prescribed increment (step). The rule is:

Start:Step:Stop

Type the following commands:

To TYPE after prompt >> followed by Enter	MATLAB answer	Meaning of the operation
2:5:25	ans = 2 7 12 17 22	Generate a vector going from 2 to 25 incremented by 5. Note that $22+5=27$, which is greater than 25. MATLAB will generate numbers until it reaches or exceeds the Stop value (i.e., 25)
i:j	ans = 2 3 4	Generate a vector going from 2 to 4. Here the step value is not specified, and MATLAB uses the default value 1
10:-3:-5	ans = 10 7 4 1 -2 -5	Generate a vector going from 10 to –5, increasing the first value by –5. This is equivalent to generating a vector of decreasing values

You now have three equivalent ways of accessing the third-row entries of x:

```
>> x(3,[1 2 3])                    <ENTER>
ans =
      7    8    9
>> x(3,1:3)                        <ENTER>
ans =
      7    8    9
>> x(3,:)                          <ENTER>
ans =
      7    8    9
```

In the last case, you do not need to specify the start and stop values when you use the colon operator. MATLAB assumes that you mean the entire row. Analogously, if you need the first column only, you can type either x([1,2,3,4,5],1) or x([1:5],1) or x(:,1);

By using the colon operator together with the empty array, we are able to delete entire rows or entire columns. For example, to delete the entire second column of x and then its third and fourth rows, type:

```
>> x(:,2) = [ ]                    <ENTER>
x =
      1     3
      4     6
      7     9
     10    12
     13    15
>> x([3,4],:) =[ ]                 <ENTER>
x =
      1     3
      4     6
     13    15
```

Note that you cannot delete a single entry in a matrix because that would lead to an ambiguity in its dimensions. So a statement like x(1,2)=[ ] returns an error:

```
>> x(1,2)=[ ]
??? Subscripted assignment dimension mismatch.
```

We conclude this paragraph by mentioning a way to create a matrix using indexing. In contrast to other computer languages, in MATLAB we do not need to declare a variable (i.e., tell to MATLAB what type of variable, how large it is, etc.) before using it. MATLAB creates the variable on the fly. So if you want to insert the response time to the stimulus number 10, you can simply type:

```
>> AnsTime(10)=1.34
AnsTime =
            0     0     0     0     0     0     0     0
   0    1.3400
```

MATLAB automatically creates the variable called AnsTime and put the number you have entered in position 10. The unspecified values are filled with zeros by default.

Operations

There are operations that can be applied to modify the contents of a matrix without changing the number of elements. These operations are *matrix addition, scalar multiplication*, and *transposition*. These form the basic techniques for dealing with matrices, as displayed in the following table:

Operation	Definition	Math example	Matlab example
Addition (subtraction)	The result of **A + B** or (**A−B**) is calculated entrywise, i.e., the element $B_{i,j}$ is added to (subtracted from) the element in $A_{i,j}$	$A = \begin{bmatrix} 1 & 5 \\ 2 & 3 \end{bmatrix}, B = \begin{bmatrix} 2 & 3 \\ 4 & 1 \end{bmatrix}$ $A + B = \begin{bmatrix} 3 & 8 \\ 6 & 4 \end{bmatrix}$ $A - B = \begin{bmatrix} -1 & 2 \\ -2 & 2 \end{bmatrix}$	`>>A=[1,5;2,3];` `>>B=[2,3;4,1];` `>>A+B` `ans =` 3 8 6 4 `>> A-B` `ans =` -1 2 -2 2
Scalar multiplication	The multiplication of a scalar (= number) s by a matrix **C** is obtained by multiplying every entry of **C** by s	$C = \begin{bmatrix} 3 & 2 \\ 4 & 1 \end{bmatrix}, s = 4$ $s \cdot C = \begin{bmatrix} 12 & 8 \\ 16 & 4 \end{bmatrix}$	`>>C=[3,2;4,1];` `>>s=4;` `>>s*C` `ans =` 12 8 16 4
Transposition	The transpose of an m×n matrix **D** is an n×m matrix denoted by D^T obtained by turning rows into columns and columns into rows	$D = \begin{bmatrix} 3 & 12 & 2 \\ 8 & 9 & 10 \end{bmatrix}$ $D^T = \begin{bmatrix} 3 & 8 \\ 12 & 9 \\ 2 & 10 \end{bmatrix}$	`>> D=[2,12,2;8,9,10];` `>> D'` `ans =` 3 8 12 9 2 10

Multiplication of a matrix by another matrix is more complicated. *Multiplication of two matrices is well defined only if the number of columns of the left-hand matrix is the same as the number of rows of the right-hand matrix.* Matrix multiplication may seem complex, and perhaps you will not use it very often. However, it turns out to be useful when one of the matrices is a vector, so we give you the following definition:

If **A** is an *m×n* matrix and **B** is an *n×p* matrix, then their *matrix product* **AB** is the *m×p* matrix whose entries are given by the following equation.

$$(AB)_{i,j} = \sum_{r=1}^{n} A_{i,r} B_{r,j}$$

Fig. 1.3 Visual interpretation of matrix product

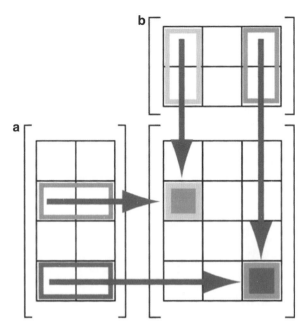

The equation means that each element of the ith row of **A** is multiplied successively by each element of the jth column of **B**. In Fig. 1.3 you can see a visual interpretation of the previous equation.

We reiterate that a matrix product can be performed only if the number of columns in the first matrix (**A**) is equal to the number of rows of the second matrix (**B**). For example, using the matrices entered in the previous table, it is not possible to perform the product **DC** (try to verify this with MATLAB):

```
>> D*C
??? Error using ==> mtimes
Inner matrix dimensions must agree.
```

However, you can compute the product CD. The result is a matrix having the same number of rows as the first matrix (**C**) and the same number of columns as the second matrix (**D**). We see, then, that in general, for two matrices $\mathbf{CD} \neq \mathbf{DC}$, and indeed, one of these products might not even be defined. But even if **C** and **D** are square matrices, it is generally the case that $\mathbf{CD} \neq \mathbf{DC}$:

```
>> C*D                         <ENTER>
ans =
      22    54    26
      16    57    18
```

An element-by-element operation similar to matrix summation is also available in MATLAB. Let's say that we want to multiply the elements of **A** in position i,j by the elements of **B** in the same i,j position using the *element-by-element operators*, as shown in the following table:

Description	MATLAB operator	Example

Element-by-element Multiplication	.*	`>> A.*B`
		`ans=`
		`     2    15`
		`     8     3`

Element-by-element Right division	./	`>> A./B`
		`ans =`
		`     0.5000    1.6667`
		`     0.5000    3.0000`

Element-by-element Left division	.\	`>> A.\B`
		`ans =`
		`     2.0000    0.6000`
		`     2.0000    0.3333`

Element-by-element Exponentiation	.^	`>> A.^B`
		`ans =`
		`     1    125`
		`    16      3`

For those who are familiar with matrix equations, MATLAB has a huge number of other possible operations. Here are some of the basic functions: The inverse function *inv(A)*, the determinant function *det(A)*, the eigenvalue function *eig(A)*, the singular value decomposition function *svd(A)*, the LU factorization *lu(A)*.

Summary

- MATLAB can be thought of as a scientific calculator: you can perform operations from simple to complex, simply by typing them into the command line of the command window; operations are calculated immediately.
- The six arithmetic operators for scalars are + − * \ / and ^. They operate according to rules of precedence. Parentheses have the highest precedence.
- To store numbers or operation results you need variables.
- Variable names consists only of letters, digits, and underscores, and must start with a letter. MATLAB interprets uppercase and lowercase as different letters (e.g., AgE is different from age).
- The command whos lists the variable in the workspace. To delete variables use clear followed by the name of variables, or alternatively, clear all to clear every variable.

- MATLAB refers to all variables as matrices:
  - An N×M matrix is an array having N rows and M columns.
  - A vector can be a 1×N matrix (row vector) or an N×1 matrix (column vector)
  - A scalar is a 1×1 matrix
- Vectors and matrices are entered in *square brackets*. Elements are separated by spaces or commas. Rows are separated by semicolons.
- An element of a matrix is referred to by a pair of numbers in *parentheses* indicating its position. An element of a vector can be referenced using simply a number. A range of elements can be referred to using vectors instead numbers in parentheses.
- The Colon operator is equivalent to generating a vector going from one value to another, possibly using a specified increment (step): start:step:stop
- Pay attention when using Matrix operations especially to the dimensions of the matrices involved.
- The basic matrix operations are addition (+), scalar multiplication (*), and transposition (').
- Element-by-element operations between matrices of the same dimension can be carried out using the operators ./ .\ .* and .^ .

Exercises

1. Evaluate the following expressions:

Mathematical expression	Solution (to type after prompt >> followed by Enter)	Result
$2 \cdot 4/12 * 2$	`2*4/12*2^2`	`ans=2.6667`
$2 \cdot 3+5/2-7.$	`2*3+5/2-7.5`	`ans=1`
$\sqrt{16}$	`sqrt(16)`	`ans=4`
$\dfrac{13 \cdot 3}{12-4}$	`(13*3)/(12-4)`	`ans=4.875`
$\dfrac{(2\pi+4)-2\cdot\sin\left(\dfrac{\pi}{2}\right)}{12-3}$	`((2*pi+4)-2*sin(pi/4))/(12-3)`	`ans=0.9854`
$\dfrac{22+12}{12/3+4}$	Try by yourself. The result must be the same	`ans=4.2500`
$\sqrt{(2+3)^2 -2}$	Try by yourself. The result must be the same	`ans=4.7958`

2. Create in MATLAB the following variables:

Mathematical expression	Solutions (to type after prompt >> followed by Enter)
$Mat1 = \begin{bmatrix} 3 & 4.56 & 8 & 7 \\ 12 & 2 & 1 & 3 \\ \pi & 34 & 2 & 3 \end{bmatrix}$	`Mat1=[3, 4.56, 8, 7; 12, 2, 1, 3;` `   pi, 34, 2, 3];`

$Mat2 = \begin{bmatrix} 1 & 0 & 0 \\ 0 & 0 & 0 \\ 0 & 0 & 0 \\ 0 & 0 & 3 \end{bmatrix}$	`Mat2=[1, 0, 0; 0, 0, 0; 0, 0, 0;`
	`   0, 0, 3];`
	or
	`Mat2=1;`
	`Mat2(4,3)=3;`

$Mat3 = \begin{bmatrix} 2 & 4 & 6 & 8 & 10 & 12 & 14 \\ 3 & 6 & 9 & 12 & 15 & 18 & 21 \end{bmatrix}$	`Mat3=[2,4,6,8,10,12,14;`
	`   3,6,9,12,15,18,21];`
	or
	`Mat3=2:2:14;`
	`Mat3(2,:)=3:3:21;`

3. c is a variable containing the second and the third elements of the third row of
   Mat1.
   - b is a variable containing the first and second elements of the second row of
     Mat3.
   - Create a matrix called bbcc with b on top of c.
   - Use the first column of Mat1 and the transpose of the last row of Mat2 to cre-
     ate a new matrix called nice. Multiply the result by the third element in the
     first row of Mat3.
   - SubMat1 is a matrix obtained from the second and fourth columns of Mat3.
   - SubMat2 is a matrix obtained from the first and last columns of Mat3.
   - NewMat is a 2x4 matrix obtained by using SubMat1 in the first two columns,
     and SubMat2 in the second two columns.

Solutions:

To type after prompt >> followed by Enter	Display by MATLAB

`c=Mat1(1,2:3)`
or
`c=Mat1(1,[2,3])`
	`c =`
	`    4.5600      8.0000`

`b=Mat3(2,1:2)`	`b =` `    3    6`
`REsuLT=(b+c)*4`	`REsuLT =` `   30.2400     56.0000`

`bbcc=[b;c]`	`bbcc =`
	`    3.0000      6.0000`
	`    4.5600      8.0000`

`nice=[Mat1(:,1), (Mat2(4,:))']*Mat3(1,3)`	`nice =`
	`   18.0000           0`
	`   72.0000           0`
	`   18.8496     18.0000`

(continued)

(continued)

To type after prompt >> followed by Enter	Display by MATLAB

`SubMat1=Mat3(:,[2,4])`	SubMat1 =
	       4 8
	       6 12

Try by yourself	SubMat1 =
	       2 14
	       3 21

Try by yourself	NewMat =
	       4 8 2 14
	       6 12 3 21

4. Calculate the sum of b and c and multiply the result by 4. Put the result in the matrix REsuLT.
   - Create a matrix Mol obtained from element-by-element multiplication between SubMat1 and SubMat2.
   - Change the element in position (2,2) of Mol to 5;

To type after prompt >> followed by Enter	Display by MATLAB
`REsuLT=(b+c)*4`	REsuLT = 30.2400 56.0000

`Mol=SubMat1.*SubMat2`
 	
PAY ATTENTION: MATLAB can also compute the product Mol=SubMat1*SubMat2. However, that is not the element-by-element product
	Mol =
	       8 112
	      18 252

`Mol(2,2)=5`	Mol =
	       8 112
	      18 5

A Brick for an Experiment

In this section of the book we illustrate, step by step, a MATLAB program implementing a behavioral experiment together with the graphical interface for running the program and the statistical analysis for analyzing the data. The experiment we are implementing is a classic experiment in audiovisual perception by Sekuler et al. (1997). The effect showed by these authors is one of the most compelling examples of interaction between audition and vision. It can be observed by comparing the post coincidence trajectories of two moving objects. The objects are perceived as bouncing off each other or as streaming through each other according to whether a sound is presented (or not) when the objects overlap during the motion (Sekuler et al. 1997; Watanabe and Shimojo 2001; Remijn et al. 2004; Kawabe and Miura 2006; Kawachi and Gyoba 2006; Zhou et al. 2007; Grassi and Casco 2009, 2010; Grove and Sakurai 2009). The effect is based on a motion display originally proposed by Metzger (1934). Metzger's display shows two identical objects (e.g., two discs) that move along the azimuth with uniform rectilinear motion and opposite directions: discs start their motion, overlap and stop at the other disc's starting point with uniform rectilinear motion. This simple two-dimensional display is a complex inverse optics problem for the visual system (Marr 1982). The display is equally representative of two different events in the real three-dimensional world. In both events the two objects are placed at different depths so that the retinal images of both have identical size. In one event, the objects start their motion, overlap (i.e., one object occludes the other), then stream past one another. In the other possible event, in contrast, after the occlusion, the objects reverse their motion and return to their original starting positions. In brief, the motion of the discs is bistable because both the streaming and bouncing percepts are compatible with the proximal stimulus. However, the streaming percept is usually predominant if the motion display is silent, whereas the bouncing is predominant when the sound is presented. We strongly suggest that the reader read the cited paper to have a clearer idea about the experiment we are going to implement in the "brick" section.

Here, we implement the original experiment by Sekuler et al. (1997). The experiment is a 2 (motion type) by 2 (sound condition) experiment. In the experiment, a disc's motion can be continuous, or it can stop for a certain number of frames when the discs overlap. In addition, the discs' motion can be accompanied (or not) by a brief sound that is presented when the discs overlap. The subject's task is to report whether s/he perceived the discs as streaming or as bouncing. Usually, in this type of experiment, the experimenter records the proportion of bounce responses as a function of the various experimental conditions (the number of streaming responses is, of course, the reciprocal of the number of bounce responses).

The experiment by Sekuler et al. (1997) is a classic "fixed stimuli" experiment. In other words, we know before the subject participates in the experiment what and how many stimuli we are going to present.[1] This is an advantage, because we can prepare many things in advance. For example, a wise thing to do in such cases is to write an event table, i.e., a table in which we write the exact experimental condition we are going to present to the subject trial after trial. In the event table all events will be represented in numbers.

In this chapter we limit ourselves to writing few variables that will turn out to be useful later. First of all, let's write one variable containing the two factors we are manipulating in the experiment. We will symbolize each factor/condition in numbers.

```
>> conditions = [1, 1; 1, 2; 2, 1; 2, 2];
```

if you visualize the content of this variable, it looks like this:

```
>> conditions
conditions =

     1     1
     1     2
     2     1
     2     2
```

---

[1] This is not the case of adaptive psychophysical procedures in which the stimuli presented are selected trial by trial as a function of the subject's response.

The left column codes as a number the video display we are presenting (e.g., 1 = continuous motion; 2 = discontinuous motion), the right column codes as a number the sound associated with the display (1 = no sound; 2 = sound). However, usually in psychological experiments stimuli are presented more than once, i.e., they are presented with a certain number of repetitions (say, 20 times each).

```
>> repetitions = 20;
```

we can now begin to write the event table:

```
>> EventTable = [];
>> EventTable = [EventTable; conditions];
>> EventTable = [EventTable; conditions];
>> EventTable = [EventTable; conditions];
```

You should repeat the command `EventTable=[EventTable; conditions];` 20 times (i.e., the number of repetitions) in order to obtain the complete event table. In a later chapter we will show how to generate repetitive commands automatically.

Now let's add to the left of the `EventTable` a new column with the trial number (note the use of the apostrophe, which transposes the array we are creating, so that `EventTable` becomes a matrix of a few columns but several rows, one row for each trial of the experiment):

```
>> TotalNumberOfTrials = length(EventTable(:, 1));
>> TrialNumber = (1:TotalNumberOfTrials)';
>> EventTable = [TrialNumber, EventTable];
```

Now let's look at the content of the table matrix. At trial number 12, for example, we know that we are going to present the display 2 (the discontinuous motion) together with the sound (i.e., 2). At trial number 37, we will present the display 1 (the continuous motion) and no sound (i.e., 1), and so on. However, in the current experiment, as in the majority of experiments in psychology, we want the stimuli to be randomized within the block of trials the subject performs. In this way, we avoid possible unwanted effects such as the serial effects that could arise if we were using, for example, a fixed sequence of trials. We can do this by shuffling the trial sequence by means of `randperm`, which is a MATLAB function that generates a random permutation of integers from 1 to n, i.e., the input the user has to pass to the function. (Note that we will transpose the output of the `randperm` function so that we have an array with one column and several rows.) Now we substitute the trial sequence column by the shuffled trial sequence column:

```
>> RandomTrialSequence = randperm(TotalNumberOfTrials)';
>> EventTable(:, 1) = RandomTrialSequence;
```

Now let's sort the `EventTable` content by the shuffled trial number in the first column:

```
>> EventTable = sortrows(EventTable, 1);
```

If you now echo in the command window the content of the `EventTable` matrix, you will see that the stimuli presentation list is now nicely randomized.

A part of the commands we have shown will be included in a script that automatically generates the event table in the desired form. This will be shown in Chap. 3.

References

Grassi M, Casco C (2009) Audiovisual bounce-inducing effect: attention alone does not explain why the discs are bouncing. J Exp Psychol Hum Percept Perform 35:235–243

Grassi M, Casco C (2010) Audiovisual bounce-inducing effect: when sound congruence affects grouping in vision. Atten Percept Psychophys 72:378–386

Grove PM, Sakurai K (2009) Auditory induced bounce perception persists as the probability of a motion reversal is reduced. Perception 38:951–965

Kawabe T, Miura K (2006) Effects of the orientation of moving objects on the perception of streaming/bouncing motion display. Percept Psychophys 68:750–758

Kawachi Y, Gyoba J (2006) Presentation of a visual nearby moving object alters stream/bounce event perception. Perception 35:1289–1294

Marr D (1982) Vision: a computational investigation into the human representation and processing of visual information. W. H. Freeman, New York

Metzger W (1934) Beobachtungen über phänomenale Identität. Psychol Forsch 19:1–60

Remijn GB, Ito H, Nakajiama Y (2004) Audiovisual integration: an investigation of the "streaming-bouncing" phenomenon. J Physiol Anthropol Appl Human Sci 23:243–247

Sekuler R, Sekuler AB, Lau R (1997) Sound alters visual motion perception. Nature 385:308

Watanabe K, Shimojo S (2001) When sound affects vision: effects of auditory grouping on visual motion perception. Psychol Sci 12:109–116

Zhou F, Wong V, Sekuler R (2007) Multi-sensory integration of spatio-temporal segmentation cues: one plus one does not always equal two. Exp Brain Res 180:641–654

Suggested Readings

Some of the concepts illustrated in this chapter can be found, in an extended way, in the following books:

Gilat A (2008) MATLAB: an introduction with applications. Wiley, Mahwah, N.J.

Hunt BR, Lipsaman RL et al (2006) A guide to MATLAB: for beginners and experienced users, 2nd edn. Cambridge University Press, Cambridge, United Kingdom

Kattan PI (2008) MATLAB for beginners: a gentle approach, Revised edn. Lulu.com, Raleigh, NC, United States

Rosenbaum DA (2007) MATLAB for behavioral scientists. Lawrence Erlbaum Associates, Hoboken, N.J.

Chapter 2
Data Handling

MATLAB stores numbers, strings, and logical values into variables. Variables can be either simple, i.e., referring to one data type only, or complex, i.e., referring to different data types at the same time. Furthermore, variables can be imported, exported, and manipulated at will.

Types of Variables (Logical Values, Strings, NaN, Structures, Cells)

In the previous chapter we saw how to store and operate with numbers; however, sometimes we need to deal with other types of data such as strings, logical values, and so on. MATLAB can be used to deal with these types of variables as well.

Logical Variables

Logical data (or simply *logical*) represent the logical TRUE state and the logical FALSE state. Logical variables are the variables in which logical data are stored. Logical variables can assume only two states:

- False, always represented by 0;
- True, always represented by a nonzero object. Usually, the digit 1 is used for TRUE. However, MATLAB treats any nonzero value as TRUE.

There are two ways to create a logical variable. The first is to explicitly declare it using the `logical(X)` function; this function converts the elements of the array X into logical data types.

M. Borgo et al., *MATLAB for Psychologists*,
DOI 10.1007/978-1-4614-2197-9_2, © Springer Science+Business Media, LLC 2012

```
>> clear all;¹
>> Test_Logic_Var = logical(1);
>> x = [0,1,2,3];
>> x_becomelogic = logical(x)
x_becomelogic =
      0      1      1      1
>> whos
   Name                  Size     Bytes    Class       Attributes
   Test_Logic_Var        1x1          1    logical
   ans                   1x4          4    logical
   x                     1x4         32    double
   x_becomelogic         1x4          4    logical
```

By typing whos at that MATLAB prompt, you can see that Test_Logic_Var is a 1×1 matrix (a scalar value) of logical values. Vector x contains numbers different from 0 and 1. When the logical function is applied to the vector x, the nonzero values are marked as 1, that is, TRUE values.

We can also create logical variables indirectly, through logical operations, such as the result of a comparison between two numbers. These operations return logical values. For example, type the following statement at the MATLAB prompt:

```
>> 5 > 3
ans =
      1
>> 10 > 45
ans =
   0
```

Since 5 is indeed greater than 3, the result of the comparison is true; however, 10 is not greater than 45, and hence the comparison is false. The operator > is a *relational* operator, returning logical data types as a result.

When a vector or a matrix is involved in a logical or relational expression, the comparison is carried out *element by element*. Therefore, if we are checking whether the content of an array is greater than 5, the comparison is made for each element of the array, and the resulting logical array has the same length as that of the array we are checking. The following example shows how this works:

```
>> clear all;
>> a = [1,3,5,9,11];
>> b = [3,4,5,8,10];
>> c = a > 3;
>> D = a > b;
>> whos a b c d
```

¹Ccommand examples are intended followed by the <ENTER> key, i.e.:
```
>> clear all
```
means: Type clear all after the >> prompt, and press the Enter key.

```
Name        Size        Bytes       Class       Attributes
a           1x5         40          double
b           1x5         40          double
c           1x5         5           logical
d           1x5         5           logical
```

Using the command `whos` you can see that the vectors c and d are logical vectors. They are not considered by MATLAB as numeric vectors but as vectors of logical values.

The following table lists the relational operators used by MATLAB.

MATLAB operator	Description	Example	Meaning

>	Greater than	>> c = a > 3
		c =
		   0 0 1 1 1
		>> d = a > b
		d =
		   0 0 0 1 1
			c shows which values of **a** are greater than 3
			
			d shows which values of **a** are greater than the values in the same position of **b**

>=	Greater than or equal to	>> e = a >= 3
		e =
		   0 1 1 1 1
		
		>> f = a >= b
		f =
		   0 0 1 1 1
			e shows which values of **a** are greater than or equal to 3
			
			f shows which values of **a** are greater than or equal to the values in the same position of **b**

<	Less than	>> g = b < 3
		g =
		   0 0 0 0 0
		
		>> h = a < b
		h =
		   1 1 0 0 0
			g shows which values of **b** are less than 3.
			
			h shows which values of **a** are less than the values in the same position of **b**

<=	Less than or equal to	>> i = b <= 3
		i =
		   1 0 0 0 0
		
		>> j = a <= b
		j =
		   1 1 1 0 0
			i shows which values of **a** are less than or equal to 3
			
			j shows which values of **a** are less than or equal to the values in the same position of **b**

==	Equal to	>> k = a == 9
		k =
		   0 0 0 1 0
		
		>> l = a == b
		l =
		   0 0 1 0 0
			k shows which values of **a** are equal to 9
			
			l shows which values of **a** are equal to the values in the same position of **b**
			
			Note: the logical operator == is different from the assign operator= ! Pay attention when you use it: a=b **is different from** a == b

~=	Not equal to	>> k = a ~= 9
		k =
		   1 1 1 0 1
		
		>> l = a ~= b
		l =
		   1 1 0 1 1
			k shows which values of **a** are equal to 9
			
			l shows which values of **a** are equal to the values in the same position of **b**

Logical operators are useful in different occasions, such as in preliminary data analysis. Let's say you need to calculate the average of a data set that includes some outliers, and you want to have the average calculated without them. In this case, you can use the logical operators to average only the data you want to include and according to a cutoff value of your choice (later in the text you will see more examples).

MATLAB uses several logical operators such as &, |, and ~. The following table shows their use by considering the vectors a, b, c, and d implemented above.

MATLAB operator	Description	Truth table	Example	Meaning

&	Logical AND	<table><tr><td>A</td><td>B</td><td>A&B</td></tr><tr><td>0</td><td>0</td><td>0</td></tr><tr><td>0</td><td>1</td><td>0</td></tr><tr><td>1</td><td>0</td><td>0</td></tr><tr><td>1</td><td>1</td><td>1</td></tr></table>	`>> m = a & b`
			`m =`
			`1 1 1 1 1`
			`>> n= c & d`
			`n =`
			`0 0 0 1 1`
				m contains the element-by-element AND of the vectors **a** and **b**. The values of **a** and **b** are all different from zero, that is, they are TRUE values. The result is a vector of 1s
				
				n contains the element-by-element AND of the logical vectors **c** and **d**

		Logical OR	<table><tr><td>A</td><td>B</td><td>A|B</td></tr><tr><td>0</td><td>0</td><td>0</td></tr><tr><td>0</td><td>1</td><td>1</td></tr><tr><td>1</td><td>0</td><td>1</td></tr><tr><td>1</td><td>1</td><td>1</td></tr></table>	`>> o = a	b` `o =` `1 1 1 1 1` `>> p = c	d` `ans =` `0 0 1 1 1`	**o** contains the element-by-element OR of vectors **a** and **b**. The values of **a** and **b** are all different from zero; they are TRUE values **p** contains the element-by-element OR operation of the logical vector **c**.

~	Logical NOT	<table><tr><td>A</td><td>~A</td></tr><tr><td>0</td><td>1</td></tr><tr><td>1</td><td>0</td></tr></table>	`>> q = ~a`
			`q =`
			`0 0 0 0 0`
			`>> r = ~c`
			`r =`
			`1 1 0 0 0`
				q contains the element-by-element NOT. Values in **a** are all different from zero; they are TRUE values. The result is a vector of 1s
				
				r contains the element-by-element NOT logical operation of the logical vector **c**

In many cases we need to perform multiple comparisons at once. This is, of course, possible in MATLAB, but we need to follow the MATLAB rules if we do not want to get the wrong result. To show this, let's test whether a variable x falls within the range from 0 to 2. We might be tempted to prompt: $0 < x < 2$. However, using this syntax leads to an incorrect result. Indeed, if, let's say, x is equal to 3, hence outside our range, MATLAB returns 1, which is TRUE.

```
>> x = 3;
>> 0 < x < 2
ans =
       1
```

Why does MATLAB return an incorrect result? Because MATLAB makes the comparisons in succession. It first compares x with 0, and because 3 greater than 0, the result of the comparison is true, i.e., 1. Then MATLAB compares the result, i.e., 1, with 2. Because 1 is less than 2, the result of the operation is true. So we need to use a different syntax to obtain the correct result. Multiple comparisons like the previous one have to be written in the following way:

```
>> (0 < x) & (x < 2)
ans =
       0
```

Let us see how to use logical values to target different positions in a vector. We have already seen in Chap. 1 that the elements of a vector can be referenced by means of another numeric vector; we can access some of the vector's elements using another vector to point to the positions we want. For example, if we want the elements in the third and fifth positions of a vector **a** of size 5, we can use another vector **b** as an index vector pointing to the positions we need:

```
>> clear all
>> a=[3, 4, 7, 9, 11];
>> b=[3,5];
>> a(b)
a=
       7       11
```

When programming, we use logical index vectors in several contexts. Let's say that we have a numeric vector and we want to store in a second vector only the values outside the range 6–2. We can do so in this way:

```
>> clear all;
>> a = [1, -2, 5, 7, 3, 26];
>> c = (a>=7) | (a<2)
c =
       1   1   0   1   0   1
>> d=a(c)
d =
       1   -2   7   26
```

d contains those values stored in **a** that are TRUE according to **c**. Note, however, that logical vectors, such as **c**, can be used to index another vector only when their sizes are identical. Indexing through logical vectors is a very practical way to remove elements from a vector. So we can create the vector d with the following simple command line:

```
>> d = a( (a>=7) | (a<2) )
d =
      1    -2     7    26
```

Logical indexing is very useful when one variable is used to categorize a second variable. Let's suppose we have collected some data in the following experiment, which is based on the Posner cueing paradigm (Posner 1980). Subjects are asked to react as fast as possible to the appearance of a target that can appear to either the left or the right of a central fixation point. Before the target appears, a cue indicates its location, but this cue has a limited validity (e.g. 70% of the trials).

The cue's validity (or invalidity) can be represented with 1s (or 0s) in the CueValidity vector. Subjects' response times, in seconds are stored in the vector RT. And these are the data we have collected so far:

```
>> RT           = [0.90, 0.55, 1.01, 0.33, 0.442, 0.51, 0.85, 0.44];
>> CueValidity = logical([0 , 1, 0, 1, 1, 1, 0, 1]);
```

Response time can be categorized according to cue validity in the following way:

```
>> RTvalid = RT(CueValidity)
RTvalid =
      0.5500   0.3300   0.4420   0.5100   0.4400

>> RTinvalid = RT(~CueValidity)
RTinvalid =
      0.9000   1.0100   0.8500
```

MATLAB has a number of *logical functions* operating on scalars, vectors, and matrices. Some examples are given in the following table. The examples use the following vectors:

```
>> clear all
>> a=[1 3 6 3 1 7];
>> b=a>5;
>> d=[ ];
```

MATLAB function	Description	Example 1	Example 2
any(x)	Return the logical 1 (true) if any element of the vector is a nonzero number. For matrices, any(x) operates on the columns of x, returning a row vector of logical 1s and 0s	>> any(a) ans = 1	>> any(b) ans = 1

(continued)

(continued)

MATLAB function	Description	Example 1	Example 2

all(x)	Return the logical 1 (true) if all the elements of the vector are nonzero. For matrices, all(x) operates on the columns of x, returning a row vector of logical 1s and 0s	>> all(a)
		ans =
		    1
			>> all(b)
			ans =
			    0

exist('A')	Check whether variables or functions are defined. 0 if A does not exist, 1 if A is a variable in the workspace	>> exist('c')
		ans =
		    0
			>>
			exist('a')
			ans =
			    1

isempty(x)	Return the logical 1 (true) for the empty array	>> isempty(a)
		ans =
		    0
			>>
			isempty(d)
			ans=
			    1

Strings

A string is a variable containing characters instead of numbers. Strings can be used to record subjects' names or any other type of textual information. A string is assigned to a variable by enclosing it within apostrophes as in the following example:

```
>> nameStr = 'Anne';
>> whos name
   Name      Size    Bytes    Class     Attributes
   nameStr   1x4         8    char
```

The string 'Anne' is composed of four characters, and the variable nameStr is a 1×4 row vector of characters. The second letter of the name can be accessed in the following way:

```
>> name(2)
ans =
    n
```

If you want to include a string containing an apostrophe, the apostrophe must be repeated:

```
>> sentence='Anne''s dog is Buddy'
sentence =
Anne's dog is Buddy
```

Because strings are vectors, they may be linked with square brackets, e.g.,

```
>> name ='Andrea';
>> surname = 'Palladio';
>> fullname=[name,' ',surname]
```

```
fullname =
Andrea Palladio
>> whos name surname fullname
   Name        Size    Bytes   Class   Attributes
   fullname    1x15       30    char
   name        1x6        12    char
   surname     1x8        16    char
```

Note that we have put a space character between the name and the surname to separate them. The result is a vector of 15 characters: 6 characters belong to the name, 8 to the surname, and 1 for the space.

Now let's suppose you want to create an array of names, each row for one name. Because names can differ in length, we need to use the char function. Indeed, if we implement the variable NameList in the following way, we get an error.

```
>> NameList=['John', 'Milly', 'Giovanni'];
??? Error using ==> vertcat
CAT arguments dimensions are not consistent.
```

Function char() overcomes the problem:

```
>> NameList2=char('John','Milly','Palladio')
NameList2 =
John
Milly
Palladio
```

MATLAB has many functions for working with strings, which are listed in the following table. Use the string MyString='Vision Search', str1='hello' and str2='help' to get some practice with them:

Function	Description	Example
int2srtr(n)	Convert numeric arguments into a string	>> IntStrIng=int2str(25);
num2str(n)	Convert numeric arguments into a string	>> numString=num2str(23.4);
lower(S)	Convert a string into a lowercase string	>> lower(MyString) ans = vision search
upper(S)	Convert a string into an uppercase string	>> upper(MyString) ans = VISION SEARCH
strcmp(S1,S2)	Compare the strings S1 and S2 and return true (1) if strings are identical, and false (0) otherwise	>> strcmp(str1,str2) ans = 0

(continued)

(continued)

Function	Description	Example
strrep(S1,S2,S3)	Replace all the occurrences of the string S2 in the string S1 with the string S3	>> strrep(str1,'llo','avy') ans = heavy
findstr(S1,S2)	Return the starting indices of any occurrences of the shorter of the two strings in the longer	>> findstr(str1,'l') ans = 3 4

strmatch(S1,CAR)	Look through the character array CAR to find strings beginning with the string contained in S1, returns the matching row indices	>> strmatch('he',str3)
		ans =
		   1
		   2

disp(S1)	Displays the array S1, without printing the array name	>> disp(str3);
		hello
		help
		>> disp([1 2; 3 4]);
		   1 2
		   3 4

To create formatted strings there is another useful function: `sprintf(format, variables)`. Let us see an example. Type the following commands:

```
>> RTmean=[0.431,0.321];
>> Pos=char('left', 'right');
>> sprintf('The RT for objects in %s position is %1.1f sec.',...
Pos(1,:),RTmean(1))
ans =
The RT for objects in left position is 0.4 sec.

>> sprintf('The RT for objects in %s position is %1.3f sec.',...
Pos(2,:),RTmean(2))
ans =
The RT for objects in right position is 0.321 sec.
```

Note that the three ellipsis points ... allow you to continue the command in the next line.

The function `sprintf()` contains the format argument and some variables. The format argument is a string containing ordinary characters and conversion specifications. A conversion specification controls the notation, the alignment, the significant digits, the field width, and other aspects of the output format. Conversion specifications begin with the % character. There are also special characters beginning with the / character. Some of these are presented in the following table; however, for a complete list of them, refer to the MATLAB help.

Conversion specification and special characters	Description	Example

`%c`	Single character	`>> sprintf('character: %c','c')`
		`ans =`
		`character: c`

`%d`	Decimal notation (signed). There is an implicit conversion from number to string without use the int2str function	`>>sprintf('integer: %d',12)`
		`ans =`
		`integer: 12`

`%f`	Fixed-point notation. A decimal number can be inserted between the % and f symbols to specify the size of the integer part and the fractional part, respectively	`>> c=5.12345;`
		`>>sprintf('float: %3.1f',c)`
		`ans =`
		`float: 5.1`
		`>>sprintf('float: %3.3f',c)`
		`ans =`
		`float: 5.123`

`%s`	String of characters	`>> s='test';`
		`>> sprintf('string: %s',s)`
		`ans =`
		`string: test`

`\n`	New line	`>> sprintf('go to \n new line')`
		`ans =`
		`go to`
		`new line`

`\t`	Horizontal tab	`>> sprintf('Test the \t tab \t tab')`
		`ans =`
		`Test the    tab    tab`

Another useful function is `input()`. It waits for input from the keyboard, ending with the ENTER key. Type the following:

```
>> input('How old are you? ')
How old are you? 35
ans =
     35
```

By default, `input()` takes numbers as its argument. If we need strings instead, we need to add the optional argument 's' to the `input` call:

```
>> input('How old are you? ','s')
How old are you? thirtyfive
ans =
thirtyfive
```

NaN

NaN means *Not a Number*. This variable type is used for missing data. For example, let's suppose you need to calculate the mean of the elements of a vector but there are some missing values:

```
>> Meanex=[2 NaN 12 4 NaN 3 NaN]

Meanex =
      2    NaN    12    4    NaN    3    NaN
>> nanmean(Meanex)
ans =
     5.25
```

MATLAB has few built-in functions for working with NaNs. However, not all standard MATLAB functions can deal with NaNs. To overcome this limitation we need to use logical operators. The function isnan(X) finds where the NaNs are. It returns a logical array containing 1s wherever the elements of X are NaNs. To calculate the mean of a vector using the standard mean () function, we need to use the following syntax:

```
>> S=mean(Meanex (~(isnan(Meanex))))
S =
    5.25
```

Note that if you don't use logical operators, the result you get is a NaN:

```
>> S=sum(Meanex)
S =
    NaN
```

Structures

MATLAB can manage complex variables, that is, variables that are of different types, at the same time. These variables are called *structures*. A structure collects different types of elements under the same name. The elements are called *fields*. For example, to store the information about the participant of an experiment, we can create a structure variable called SubjectTest and assign different values to the various fields as follows:

```
>> SubjectTest.name='Nelson';
>> SubjectTest.surname='Cowan';
>> SubjectTest.age=24;
>> SubjectTest.TestDone=[1,2,3,6,12];
>> SubjectTest.Response=[12.3, 11.2, 14.3, 12.2,12.4];
>> SubjectTest.CorrectConduction=logical([1,1,0,1,1]);
```

```
>> SubjectTest
SubjectTest =
                 surname: 'Cowan'
                    name: 'Nelson'
                     age: 24
                TestDone: [1 2 3 6 12]
                Response: [12.3000 11.2000 14.3000 12.2000 12.4000]
       CorrectConduction: [1 1 0 1 1]
```

The structure name is SubjectTest, while name, surname, age, TestDone, Response, CorrectConduction, are the fields. Fields are addressed using the structure name followed by a dot and then the field name. Hence, the second element of the Response field can be addressed as follows:

```
>> SubjectTest.Response(2)
ans =
      11.2000
```

Structure fields are case-sensitive; this means that MATLAB creates additional fields if we do not type the field name correctly. It is also possible to combine structures to create a matrix of structures. This is useful, for example, when you need to save the results of different participants. For example, the data of a second participant can be added to the structure in the following way:

```
>> SubjectTest(2).name='Johan';
>> SubjectTest(2).ResponseTime=[11.9, 11.1, 14.1, 11.8,12.0];
>> whos SubjectTest
   Name           Size   Bytes   Class      Attributes
   SubjectTest    1x2    1045    struct
```

As you can see from the whos command, SubjectTest is a 1×2 row vector of struct:

```
>>SubjectTest(2).Name = 'Johan'
SubjectTest =
1x2 struct array with fields:
    surname
    name
    age
    TestDone
    Response
    CorrectConduction
    ResponseTime
    Name
```

If you want to address the second element of the matrix, you can type:

```
>> SubjectTest(2)
ans =
```

```
         surname: []
             name: 'Johan'
              age: []
         TestDone: []
         Response: []
CorrectConduction: []
     ResponseTime: [11.9000 11.1000 14.1000 11.8000 12]
             Name: 'Johan'
```

As you can see, some fields are empty; this is because they haven't been filled for the second participant. It is possible to fill them in later. To do this, type:

```
>> SubjectTest(2).surname= 'Baptist'
>> SubjectTest(2).age= 31
>> SubjectTest(2)
ans =
         surname: 'Baptist'
             name: 'Johan'
              age: 31
         TestDone: []
         Response: []
CorrectConduction: []
     ResponseTime: [11.9000 11.1000 14.1000 11.8000 12]
             Name: 'Johan'
```

Let's see how to access an element of a vector that is a field of a structure while the structure is simultaneously a member of a matrix of structures. To do this, we have to type the structure name, the index of the structure within parentheses, followed by a point and finally the field name within parentheses. For example, let's suppose you want to display the last of John's response times:

```
>> SubjectTest(2).ResponseTime(5)
ans =
     12
```

Dynamic Field Names

Another way to access structure data that are embedded in a vector is to use *dynamic field names*. Dynamic field names express the field as a string variable. For example, to extract all the surnames in the vector, you have to type:

```
>> StrField='surname'
>> SubjectTest.(StrField)
ans =
Cowan
ans =
Baptist
```

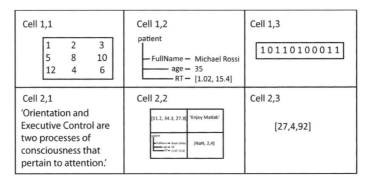

Fig. 2.1 An example of cell array

You can remove a given field from a structure embedded within a structure array using the rmfield() function:

```
>> rmfield(SubjectTest,'TestDone')
ans =
1x2 struct array with fields:
    age
    ResponseTime
    CorrectConduction
    surname
    name
```

Cells

A *cell* is a variable containing different types of data; it is therefore similar to a structure, but cells are more general and have notational differences as well. A cell can contain any data type, from a simple number to a structure or another cell. You can have even a *cell array*, i.e., a matrix in which each element is a cell.

In Fig. 2.1 is reported an example schema which should clarify the concept by showing a 2×3 cell array. In the first row and first column, the cell array contains a matrix of numbers, while in the first row and second column, the cell array contains a structure, and in the second row and second column, the cell array contains another cell array, and so on.

Let's see how to create cell arrays and how to insert and retrieve data from them. Be aware of the notational differences between simple arrays, such as numeric and character arrays, and cell arrays, because they can be source of confusion (and errors!).

To create a cell array there are two methods, called "Cell indexing" and "Content indexing":

- Cell Indexing:

```
>> SoundInf={'sine','square','Sting'}
SoundInf =
    'sine' 'square' 'Sting'
>> whos SoundInf
  Name        Size    Bytes    Class    Attributes
  SoundInf    1x3     210      cell
```

Here the curly braces { } are on the **right-hand side,** and indicate the cell contents. This is a *cell array* of strings, which is different from an *array* of strings; indeed, strings stored in cell arrays can have different numbers of characters. Let's add additional values to the cell:

```
>> SoundInf(2,3) = {[5, 6; 7, 8] }
SoundInf =
    'sine'    'ramp'    'sting'
    []        []        [2x2 double]
```

The parentheses on the left-hand side of the assignment refer, in the normal way, to elements in a cell array, while on the right-hand side the curly braces indicate the content of a cell.

Let's see how content indexing differs from cell indexing.

- Content Indexing:

```
>> SoundInf{2,3}=5
SoundInf =
    'sine'      'ramp'    'sting'
    []          []        [        5]
>> SoundInf{3,3}=[2 3; 7 8]
SoundInf =
    'sine'      'ramp'    'sting'
    []          []        [        5]
    []          []        [2x2 double]
```

Here, the **index of the cells within curly braces { }** and the content are specified in the standard way after the assignment sign.

You can access the content of a cell by indexing:

```
>> PreferArtist = SoundInf{1,3}
PreferArtist =
Sting
>> whos PreferArtist
  Name           Size    Bytes   Class  Attributes
  PreferArtist   1x5        10   char
```

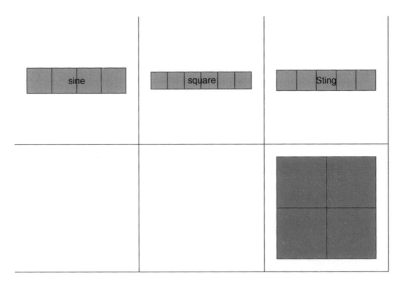

Fig. 2.2 Output of the cellplot command

To access an element of an array stored in a cell you have to concatenate curly braces and parentheses as follows:

```
>> SoundInf{2,3}(2,2)
ans =
      8
```

The `celldisp()` function recursively displays the contents of a cell array. The function `cellplot` draws a visualization of a cell array, as shown in Fig. 2.2. Nonempty array elements are shaded.

```
>> cellplot SoundInf
```

We have seen that both *structures* and *cell arrays* can contain different element types. The main difference between them is reported in the following table:

Structures	Cell arrays
Structures are different data type collections, **organized in fields having their own names**	Cell matrices can contain different data types. **Each cell is indexed by numbers**

Import/Export

In this section we see how to save and load the variables that have been created and used in a working session. If we do not save the variables, MATLAB automatically clears them from the working space when you quit the program. The `save` command followed by a filename saves all the variables that are in the workspace.

In the following example we create a file named test1 containing the vector a, the number b, and the string f:

```
>> clear all;
>> a=[4,2,1,43; 2,5,1,6];
>> b= sin(a)+5;
>> f='test';
>> save test1
```

If we clear all the variables by means of clear all, we will see that these variables no longer exist in the workspace:

```
>> clear all;
>> whos
>>
```

However, we can retrieve them by means of the load command, followed by the filename:

```
>> load test1
>> whos
  Name   Size   Bytes   Class     Attributes
   a      2x4      64    double
   b      2x4      64    double
   f      1x4       8    char
```

If you want to save only a subset of the variables you have created, you have to type the list of variables, separated by blanks (not by commas), that you want to save after the filename:

```
>> save prova2 b f
>> clear all
>> load prova2
>> whos
  Name   Size   Bytes   Class     Attributes
   b      2x4      64    double
   f      1x4       8    char
```

By default, MATLAB saves the variables in a .mat file. However, other extensions can be given such as ASCII (save the information in ASCII format so that the file can be editable from a standard text editor) or TAB (delimited with tabs).

The commands save and load can be seen as functions. The argument of these functions is a string. The first argument is the filename, the others are the variable names. Let's suppose you have the matrices RT1 = [0.34, 0.45] and RT2 = [0.23, 0.39]:

```
>> save('test1','RT1');
```

MATLAB provides some built-in functions that can import/export numbers and characters from and to different file formats. In the following table the most common of these formats are presented.

File format	File content	Extension	Functions
MATLAB formatted	Saved MATLAB workspace	.mat	load, save
Text	Text	.txt	textread
	Comma-separated numbers	.csv	Csvread csvwrite
Extended markup language	XML-formatted text	.xml	Xmlread xmlwrite
Spreadsheet	Excel worksheet	.xls	Xlsread xlswrite

There are other built-in functions that enable importing images or sound files, and they will be described in the following chapters. If you don't want to type the function in the command window, you can simply use the MATLAB Import Wizard by selecting *Import Data* in the MATLAB *File* menu, or equivalently, by typing `uiimport` at the MATLAB command line prompt.

Summary

- Logical variables can assume only two values: true (not equal to 0) and false (equal to 0).
- Logical and relational operators are used to assess whether a statement is true or false.
- Logical variables can be defined using the function `logical (variablename)`.
- Logical variables are the results of element comparison.
- Logical variables can be used to select or remove elements from a matrix. Logical variables are also useful in categorizing elements.
- Strings are arrays in which each element represents one character. Because strings are arrays, all the rows must have the same number of columns.
- Strings are defined using apostrophes'.
- There are many functions operating on strings to compare them, display them, etc.
- `sprintf` is a useful function to write formatted text.
- NaN means *Not a Number.* It is useful for representing missing data.
- *Structures* are collections of different data types, organized in fields.
- A *cell matrix* contains different data types, from simple numbers to structures or even other cell arrays. Each cell is indexed by numbers.
- There are two ways to insert data into a cell: *Cell indexing* (Index the cell array with the content in *curly braces { }*) and *content indexing* (the *indices of the cells are in curly braces { }*; the content is specified in standard way after the = sign).
- To store data in files, use the `save` command; to retrieve data from files, use the `load` command. There are other commands for importing or exporting data in specific formats including xml and xls.

Exercises

1. Categorize the elements of the vector x = [−2 3 0 2 −6 1 −2 0 0 −13 12] as positive, negative, and zero and store them in three separate vectors. Count the number of elements in each vector.

   Solution:

   ```
   >> pos=x(x>0); neg=x(x<0); zer=x(x==0);
   >> npos=length(pos); nneg=length(neg); nzeros=length(zer);
   ```

   or equivalently:

   ```
   >> npos=sum(x>0); nneg=sum(x<0); nzeros=sum(x==0);
   ```

   where the `sum(Z)` function calculates the sum of the elements in the vector Z.

2. Define the following cell matrix:

   ```
   NAMES=char('John','Robert','James','Michael'...
   ```

   ```
   'Mary', 'Tatiana','Jenny', 'William');
   ```
   and evaluate the following questions:

Question	Solution	Result
How many names start with the letter 'J'?	`>> sum(NAMES(:,1)=='J')`	ans = 3
Substitute the string 'es' with the string 'iroquai' in the third name	`>> strrep(NAMES(3,:), ...` `'es','iroquai')`	ans = Jamiroquai
Is the first name equal to the third?	`>>strcmp(NAMES(1,:),` `NAMES(2,:))`	ans = 0
Convert the names in the odd rows to uppercase	`>> odds=[2:2:length(NAMES)];` `>> NAMES(odds,:)=...` `upper (NAMES(odds,:))`	NAMES = Joh ROBERT James MICHAEL David MARY Tatiana JENNY William
Display the formatted string 'The best is' followed by the name of the seventh name	`>> sprintf('The best is %s,'` `NAMES(7,:));`	ans = The best is Tatiana
Delete the names starting with J	`>> NAMES(NAMES(:,1)=='J',:)=[]`	NAMES = Robert Michael David Mary Tatiana William

A Brick for an Experiment

Read the Results

We are still in the introductory chapters, and during this brick we will realize a program to run a quite complex experiment. In order to use the concepts we have learned so far, for the brick we need to hypothesize that the experiment is over and that the data file has been safely stored onto the hard drive. In the current brick we will see how to analyze the data.

Before showing how to use the concepts learned so far for the current brick, we need to give you some detail about the data file we will write in the successive chapters. Moreover, we have to inform you about how the data will be stored into this data file. At the end of the experiment we will save a tab-delimited text file. This file will be organized in rows and columns. The first row of the file contains the header, that is, a set for strings identifying the content of the column. The data file will contain on the left text data and on the right numeric data. From left to right, the columns of our data file will contain the subject name, the subject sex, a text note about the subject, the subject number, the subject age, the block number, the trial number, the motion condition (coded as 1 for continuous motion, 2 for the stop at overlap), the sound condition (coded as 1 for the no sound condition and 2 for the sound condition), and the subject's response, which will be coded as 0 (streaming response) or 1 (bouncing response).

The first thing we have to do is to import the data written in the data file into MATLAB. As we have seen, MATLAB offers several command line options to do this. In order to perform this particular operation, a very convenient (and simple) option is that of using the MATLAB import wizard. If you click on the MATLAB file menu you will see the import data function. An alternative way to call the wizard is to type `uiimport` at the MATLAB prompt. In both cases, MATLAB asks you where the file you want to import can be found. You have now to browse your computer and look for the file. Let's suppose that the file is placed in the same folder where we have run the experiment. Once you have selected the data file,[2] you should see a graphical interface similar to the following (Fig. 2.3).

MATLAB shows you a preview of the file content. Click next. At the top of the import wizard interface there are several options you can select. For example, in our case, we need to tell MATLAB that the file content is tab delimited (but MATLAB should recognize this). On the right you can tell MATLAB the number of header rows in the file. Our data file has one header row. In importing this particular data file, MATLAB will store two variables. One cell type variable and one double type variable. The reason is simple: our data file contains numbers as well as strings. MATLAB recognizes the first columns as strings (those containing the subject's name, sex, and note). However, the successive columns are recognized as numbers

---

[2] You can download this file from the book website (http://www.psy.unipd.it/~grassi/matlab_book. html). The filename is data.txt.

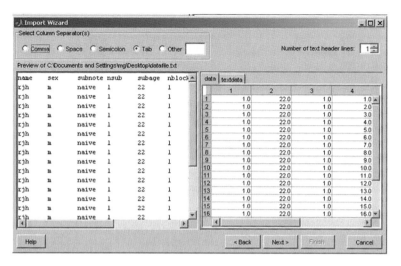

Fig. 2.3 Graphical interface to import data

(the subject's age, the subject number, and so on) and are therefore stored into a matrix of type double.

The first thing you may want to do is to have a preliminary look at the data, such as a set of descriptive statistics. For example, we may want to see whether bounce responses are predominant in the sound condition as well as when the discs stop at the overlap point. The following commands are sufficient to highlight the rows where MATLAB can find the conditions under which we presented the sound and where the discs stopped at the overlap:

```
>> data(:, 5)==1; % continuous motion
>> data(:, 5)==2; % motion with stop
>> data(:, 6)==1; % sound absent
>> data(:, 6)==2; % sound present
```

Note the presence of the % character. It is used for comments in MATLAB when you write an M-script (see Chap. 3). MATLAB takes no action when the % character is encountered, and it ignores everything that follows it.

If we want to compute the mean separately for these four conditions, we need to use the above rows of code when we call for the function `mean`. In detail, we need to tell MATLAB to calculate the mean of the column in which we have stored the dependent variable (i.e., the last column) and to calculate the mean in particular when the conditions outlined by the independent variables are satisfied. To do the calculation we have to write as follows:

```
>> mean(data(data(:, 5)==1, 7)); % continuous motion
>> mean(data(data(:, 5)==2, 7)); % motion with stop
>> mean(data(data(:, 6)==1, 7)); % sound absent
>> mean(data(data(:, 6)==2, 7)); % sound present
```

If we substitute the command `mean` with the command for the standard deviation (i.e., `std`), we can also obtain the standard deviations of the four conditions. The same command lines can be used as well for other descriptive statistics such as min and max.

Reference

Posner MI (1980) Orienting of attention. Q J Exp Psychol 32:3–25

Suggested Readings

Some of the concepts illustrated in this chapter can be found, in an extended way, in the following book:

Hahn BD, Valentine DT (2009) Essential MATLAB for engineers and scientists, 4th edn. Elsevier/ Academic Press, Amsterdam
Higham DJ, Higham NJ (2005) MATLAB guide. Siam, Philadelphia
Kattan PI (2008) MATLAB for beginners: a gentle approach, Revised edn. Lulu.com, Raleigh, NC, United States
Rosenbaum DA (2007) MATLAB for behavioral scientists. Lawrence Erlbaum Associates, Mahwah, N.J.

Chapter 3
Plotting Data[1]

MATLAB can display data in high-quality graphs. There are many built-in functions for creating scatter plots, 2D and 3D bar graphs, pies charts, line graphs, etc. MATLAB makes it possible to control each characteristic of a graphical object, so that the resulting graph shows exactly what you want to show in the way you want to present it.

Plot Data

Data can often be better understood if they are represented in a graphical format rather than in a numerical format. MATLAB is a powerful tool for plotting data, either in 2D or 3D form. Graphs can be created, edited, and saved for later modification or exported as graphics files.

The simplest way to draw a graph is to use the `plot` function. The following code creates a plot of the sine function:

```
>> x=[0:0.2:7];
>> y=sin(x);
>> plot(x,y);
```

If no other figure is open, the window is automatically named *Figure 1,* and in Fig. 3.1 it is reported how it looks like.

MATLAB assigns a progressive number to the figures, so that it is easy to refer to the different figures. The figure window contains buttons, such as the zoom in/zoom out buttons, and above all, the edit button. This button allows you to select the graph and edit its characteristics such as its color and width. The edit button provides a graphical and intuitive way to modify the graph. However, it is often better

---

[1] Note that, although the book figures are black and white, the commands reported in the current chapter generate color figures.

M. Borgo et al., *MATLAB for Psychologists,*
DOI 10.1007/978-1-4614-2197-9_3, © Springer Science+Business Media, LLC 2012

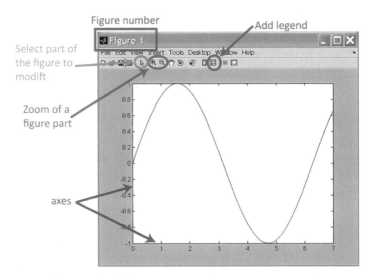

Fig. 3.1 Layout of the plot function

to modify a figure's appearance using MATLAB code. This is because once the code is saved, it can be used again to draw similar graphs with different data.

The main function for plotting 2D figures is `plot`, and it takes many arguments. The following table shows some examples. Before running the examples, make sure you have saved in the workspace the x and y variables as implemented above.

Syntax and description	Example	Graphical result
`plot(Y)` Plot the columns of Y versus the Y vector indexes	`Plot(y)`	
`plot(X1,Y1,…)` Plot all lines defined by the Xn-Yn pairs	`plot(x,y,x,cos(x))`	

(continued)

(continued)

Syntax and description	Example	Graphical result
`plot(X1,Y1,LineSpec,…)` Plot all lines defined by the Xn- Yn, LineSpec triplets. LineSpec is a string specifying the line type, marker symbol, and color of the plotted lines	`plot(x,y,'-.ro')`	

Let us see in more detail how to use the LineSpec string, which is the argument specifying the property of the line drawn in the plot. The following table lists all the LineSpec options.

Color		Marker						Line style	
Charact.	Description	Charact.	Description	Charact.	Description	Charact.	Description	Charact.	Description
B	Blue	m	Magenta	.	Point	*	Star	–	Solid
G	Green	y	Yellow	o	Circle	s	Square	:	Dotted
R	Red	k	Black	x	x-mark	d	Diamond	-.	Dashdot
C	Cyan			+	Plus	V	Triangle (down)	--	Dashed
						^	Triangle (up)		
						<	Triangle (left)		
						>	Triangle (right)		

Note that `plot()` generates a graph that connects the x-y coordinates written in the input vectors with a line. Therefore, the graphic result is not necessarily a continuous graph. In the first example the sinusoidal curve appears continuous because the x points were very close to each other; however, the following example shows that the line can be fragmented if the coordinates are not contiguous:

Example	Graphical result	Description

`>> x=[1,4,2,6,5];`
`>> y=[2,3,1,8,4];`
`>> plot(x,y);`
		The first point coordinates are 1 and 2; it is connected to the second point, having as coordinates 4 and 3. Then this second point is connected to a third one having coordinates 2 and 1, and so on

It is possible to add curves to the same figure by freezing the figure. This can be done using the `hold on` command. Once `hold on` has been activated, the plot commands add curves to the same figure. For example, the following lines add one curve to another one:

```
>> plot(x,y)
>> hold on;
>> plot(x,cos(x));
```

The same result can be obtained by means of the following complex line:

```
plot(x,y,x,cos(x));
```

MATLAB also has a function enabling plotting two curves with different y-axes within the same figure. This function is called `plotyy`:

```
>> plotyy(x,sin(x),x, 2*cos(x));
```

Here, the cosine is multiplied by 2. If you plot the graph, you will see that the left y-axis ranges from −1 to +1, whereas the right y axis ranges from −2 to +2.

Control the Plot's Objects: Labels, Legend, Title…

When a `plot` is made, the axes are automatically scaled to include the minimum and the maximum values. However, it is possible to customize the axes limits using `axis([xmin, xmax, ymin, ymax])`. For example, type:

```
>> axis([1, 6, -1.5, 1.5]);
```

The command `axis` has other specifications, such as the command `axis equal`, which makes unit increments along the *x*- and *y*-axes of the same length. If you do not need the axes, you can turn them off using the command `axis off`. To turn the axis on again, use the command `axis on`.

There are other useful functions enabling the customization of the plots: it is possible to add labels, titles, legend, text, and so on. The most frequently used of these functions are listed in the following table:

Function	Description	Examples
`xlabel(STR)` `ylabel(STR)` `zlabel(STR)` `xlabel(STR,'FontSize',fs)` `ylabel(STR,'FontSize',fs)` `zlabel(STR,'FontSize',fs)`	Add the content of the string STR along the X, Y, Z axes. The font size is set by the `fs` value if the property `'FontSize'` is specified	`xlabel('time')` `ylabel('record level')` `xlabel('time','FontSize',16)`
`title(STR)` `title(STR,'FontSize',fs)`	Add the content of the string STR at the top of the graph. The font size is set by `fs` if the property `'FontSize'` is specified	`title('Sine experiment)` `title('Sine experiment' 'FontSize',18)`

(continued)

(continued)

Function	Description	Examples
`text(posx,posy,STR)`	Write the content of the string STR at the point specified by `posx` and `posy`. Note that `posx` and `posy` relate to the current axis	`text(2,3,'very nice exp!');`
`gtext(STR)`	Write the content of the string STR in the graphics window at the position pointed to by the mouse	`gtext('A comparison');`

`legend(S1, S2,... SN)`
 	
`legend(S1,S2,...`
`    'location',LOC)`
	Add a legend to the graph using the specified strings as labels. The association of the strings with the curves follows the order in which the curves were plotted
	
	Sometimes it is useful to specify the legend position with respect to the axes. This can be done using the specification `'Location'` and then a string LOC such as `'Best'`
	
	For further details see the help
		`legend('sine','cosine')`
		
		`legend('sin','cos',...`
		`    'location','Best')`

`Grid`	Add/remove the grid to/from the current graph	`grid;`

Let's plot a sine and a cosine function ranging from 0 to 12 with step 0.2; then we shall add a legend, a title, and labels:

Example	Graphical result

`>> x=[0:0.2:12]; y1=sin(x);`
`y2=cos(x);`
`>> plot(x,y1,'r',x,y2,'b:');`
`>> xlabel('time','FontSize',16);`
`>> ylabel('Value');`
`>> axis([0,12,-1.5,1.5]);`
`>> grid;`
`>> legend('sine','cosine',`
`'location',...`
`'North');`
`>> title('Sine and cosine`
`comparison',... 'FontSize',18);`
`>> text(2.5,0.75,'sine');`
`>> text(5,0.1,'cosine');`
	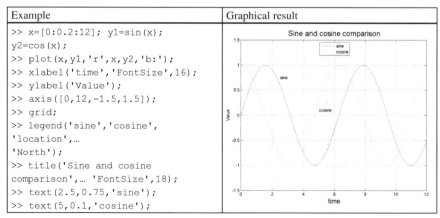

If you want to close a figure, you use close followed by the figure number. Alternatively, if you want to close all the figures, you use close all.

To open an empty window in which to add graphical data, use the command figure. It is a good idea to open a new window before creating a plot. If you don't, every time you plot new data, the new data are plotted on the existing figure, overwriting the previous data.

Subplot: Multiple Plots in One Figure

It is possible to display multiple plots within the same figure using subplot(Nrows,Ncolumns,CurSub). This function divides the figure into Nrows rows and Ncolumns columns. Each part of the figure is identified by the CurSub value; this value increases by row (top to bottom) and from left to right. For example, if your figure has four subplots, two at the top and two at the bottom, number 1 identifies the top-left graph, number 2 identifies the top-right one, number 3 the bottom-left, and number 4 the bottom-right graph, as in Fig. 3.2.

Let's suppose we want two rows and three columns of subplots. We want to plot in row 1, column 3 a sine wave ranging from 0 to 6. Moreover, we want to plot in row 2, column 2 a cosine wave ranging from 6 to 9. This is how it can be done:

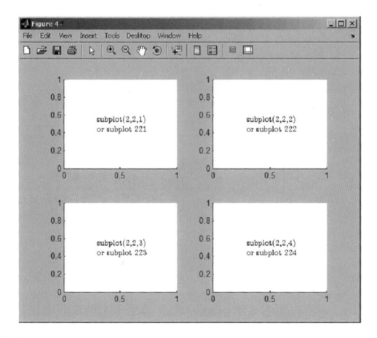

Fig. 3.2 Subplot layout

Example	Graphical result

```>> xs=[0:0.2:6];```
 ```>> xc=[6:0.2:9];```
 ```>> figure;```
 ```>> subplot(2,3,3);```
 ```>> plot(xs,sin(xs));```
 ```>> xlabel('time');```
 ```>> title('Sine test');```
 ```>> axis([0 6 -1.2 1.2]);```
 ```>> subplot(2,3,5);```
 ```>> plot(xc,cos(xc));```
 ```>> xlabel('time in seconds');```
 ```>> title('test the subplot');```
 ```>> axis([6 9 -1.2 1.2]);```
	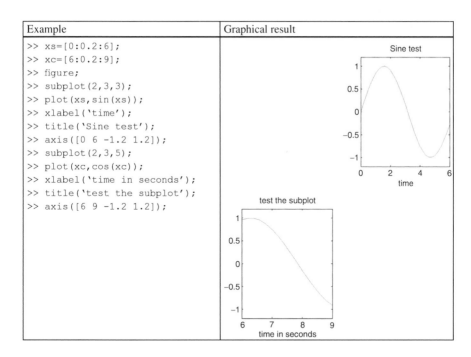

Each time you use `subplot`, all the commands you write refer to the part of figure identified by `CurSub`. A common mistake is to use two consecutive subplot commands with different numbers of rows and columns. If you do so, everything you have plotted after the first subplot command is overwritten by the second one.

The subplots within a figure do not need to be all of the same size. For example, you can have one plot that extends over the space of two (or more) subplots. To do this, pass a vector to `CurSub`. The following table shows how to divide the figure into three parts, in which the length of one graph occupies the same amount of space as the other two combined.

Example	Graphical result

```>> xs=[0:0.2:6];```
 ```>> figure;```
 ```>> subplot(2,2,[1 2]);```
 ```>> plot(xs,sin(xs));```
 ```>> title('Sine');```
 ```>> subplot(2,2,4);```
 ```>> plot(xs,cos(xs));```
 ```>> title('Cosine');```
 ```>> subplot(2,2,3);```
 ```>> plot(rand(1,30));```
 ```>> title('Random ');```
	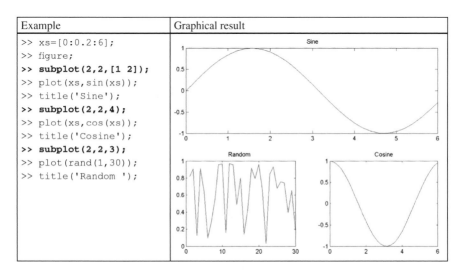

As can be seen from the table, CurSub is a vector telling MATLAB that the first subplot spans from position 1 to position 2.

Although plot is a useful function, MATLAB is provided with additional functions to represent data. The following table lists the most common types of graphs together with the functions used to draw them. Since we do not have data here, we have used the useful rand function to create them. The command rand(r,c) creates a, r by c matrix with uniformly distributed random numbers. There is also randn(r,c), which creates an r by c matrix with normal Gaussian distributed random numbers.[2]

Function	Description	Examples
bar(X,Y,W) barh(X,Y,W)	Draw the columns of the M by N matrix Y as M groups of N vertical bars. X gives the position of the values in Y. If X is omitted, the default value of X=1:M is used. W specifies the width of the bars (0.8 by default) bar(…,'stacked') produces a vertical stacked bar chart barh is the same as bar but plots the bars horizontally	>> bar(rand(10,5),'stacked'); >> colormap(cool);

errorbar(X,Y,Err,
'LSp')
	Plot Y versus X with error bars [Y−Err Y+Err]. Here 'LSp' is a string specifying the line style as for the plot function and can be omitted	x=[1,4,5,8];
		RT=[1.2,1.4,1.9,2.3];
		SD=[0.1,0.15,0.25,0.4];
		bar(x,RT,'w'); hold on;
		errorbar(x,RT,SD,'.k');

(continued)

---

[2] The functions rand and randn will be documented more fully in the chapter on statistical analysis.

(continued)

Function	Description	Examples

`[Nel,xc]=hist(y);`
`[Nel,xc]=hist(y,Ndiv);`
	`[N,xc]=hist(y)` places the elements of y into ten equally spaced containers and returns in `Nel` the number of elements in each container. In `xc` can be found the positions of the bin centers
	
	Once we obtain the number of events of each bin and the bin center using hist, the distibution of events can be plotted using `bar` or `plot`
		`Ages=[22,25,23,22,45,12,34,33,21];`
		`[N,xc]=hist(Ages,3);`
		`bar(xc,N);`

`pie(X)`
`pie(X,explode)`
`pie(…,labels)`
	PIE draws a pie chart of the normalized data in the vector X. `explode` is a (logical) vector of the same size as X, specifying which slices have to be pulled out from the pie. The cell array `labels` contains strings. The number of cells must be equal to the size of X
	
	`explode` and `labels` can be omitted
		`x=[2 4 6 3 5];`
		`pie(x,[0 0 1],…`
		`{'Tom','Anne','Milly'});`
		`colormap(spring);`

`colormap(CM);`
`colormap(srt);`
	Set the color lookup table. You can set up a color map matrix CM on your own. CM may have any number of rows, but it must have exactly three columns (the RGB color combination; see Chap. 5). In any case, you can use the predefined `colormap` (e.g., str='cool') or create one using the function `colormapeditor`
	
	For more details on `colormap` refer to Chap. 5
		`x=[2,5]; y= rand(2,3);`
		`barh(x,y, 0.9);`
		`colormap([1 0 0; 1 0.5 0.5; 0,1,0]);`

3-D Plots

MATLAB can also handle 3-D plots, including lines and various types or surfaces. For a 3-D plot you need three dimensions; therefore, you need to pass to the function data points with three coordinates. The basic command is `plot3`. It works like `plot`, except that it takes three vectors instead of two, one for the x-coordinate, one for the y-coordinate, and one for the z-coordinate.

Here we report an example of a 3-D a line connecting five points:

Example	Graphical result
>> x=[1,4,5,1,3]; >> y=[2,6,2,4,3]; >> z=[1,2,3,4,2]; >> plot3(x,y,n); >> axis square; >> grid on; >> xlabel('X'); >> ylabel('Y'); >> zlabel('N');	

In the example, the first point has coordinate $x = 1$, $y = 2$, and $z = 1$. Note that you can add a label for the z-axes using the command `zlabel`.

MATLAB can also display 3-D surfaces using the commands `mesh` and `surf`: the `mesh` function gives a transparent "mesh" surface, whereas `surf` gives an opaque shaded surface.

Usually a 3-D surface is a set of `z` values associated to a set of `(x,y)` coordinates. For example if we have a set of coordinates

$$(x, y) = \begin{pmatrix} 1,1 & 1,2 & 1,3 & 1,4 \\ 2,1 & 2,2 & 2,3 & 2,4 \\ 3,1 & 3,2 & 3,3 & 3,4 \\ 4,1 & 4,2 & 4,3 & 4,4 \end{pmatrix},$$

the (x, y) pairs can be split into two matrices:

$$x = \begin{bmatrix} 1 & 1 & 1 & 1 \\ 2 & 2 & 2 & 2 \\ 3 & 3 & 3 & 3 \\ 4 & 4 & 4 & 4 \end{bmatrix} \qquad y = \begin{bmatrix} 1 & 2 & 3 & 4 \\ 1 & 2 & 3 & 4 \\ 1 & 2 & 3 & 4 \\ 1 & 2 & 3 & 4 \end{bmatrix}$$

MATLAB provides a function called `meshgrid` that can be used to simplify the generation of `x` and `y` matrix arrays used in 3-D plots. It is invoked using the form

[X,Y]=meshgrid(a,b), where a and b are vectors that specify the region in which the coordinates, defined by element pairs of the matrices x and y, will lie. To obtain the x, y matrix you can do as follows:

```
>> a=[1:4];
>> b=[1:4];
>> [x,y]=meshgrid(a,b)
x =
     1     2     3     4
     1     2     3     4
     1     2     3     4
     1     2     3     4
y =
     1     1     1     1
     2     2     2     2
     3     3     3     3
     4     4     4     4
```

Now it is simple to obtain the z=f(x,y) values as a function of each (x,y) pair as shown in the following example:

Example	Graphical result

`>> a=[-3:0.25:3];`
`>> b=[-3:0.25:3];`
`>> [X,Y]=meshgrid(a,b);`
`>> Z= X.*exp(-X.^2-Y.^2);`
`>> surf(X,Y,Z);`
	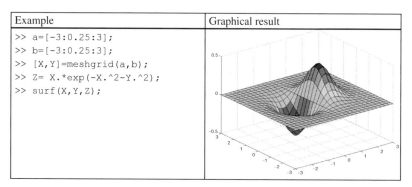

MATLAB has equivalent 3-D functions to obtain 3-D bar graphs and 3-D pie charts. Here we show an example of these functions. For further details, please refer to online help.

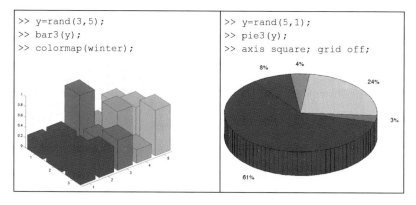

Printing and Saving Images

Figures can be saved or printed by means of the `print` function. The structure of the function is `print -dformat fileName -options`, where `-dformat` stands for the specified graphics format (such as JPEG) and `filename` is the filename.

The following table lists some of the formats that can be used to print and save figures.

Example	Description
`print -dmeta`	Saves the active figure in the clipboard. This command is equivalent to the copy command that can be used via the mouse or keyboard
`print -dpng pippo`	Saves the active figure in the file named pippo.png The file is saved in the Portable Network Graphics (png) format
`print -depsc pluto`	Saves the active figure in the file named pluto.eps. The file is saved in the Encapsulated Postscript Color (epc) format
`print -djpeg83 Minnie`	Save the active figure in the file `Minnie.jpg`. The file is saved in jpeg format with quality 83%. To obtain a different quality (=compression), the last number can be changed: e.g., print `-djpeg25 Minnie2` saves a jpeg image named `Minnie2.jpg` with quality 25%

Handle Graphics

In this chapter we have seen the MATLAB functions that enable the production of simple graphs and how to set many parameters such as the color of the axes, the line thickness, the position of the plot, the font size, and so on. However, MATLAB allows us to control many of the graph's characteristics by getting and setting some of the properties for each object in the figure window (lines, axes, text, surfaces, etc.).

Each object in the figure window has a unique identifier (a number) called a *handle*. The handle is used with the commands `get` and `set` to read the current properties of the object and to change and set these properties according to your needs.

Everything will be clarified by the following example:

Example	Graphical result

```>> figure;```
```>> x=[0:0.1:2*pi];```
```>> h=plot(x,cos(x),'r.-');```
```>> hl=xlabel('time [s]');```
	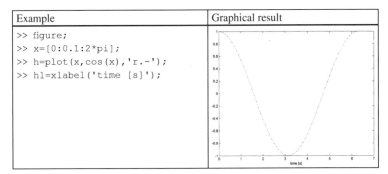

Here h is the handle of the line object, while h1 is the handle of the axes object. Now, if you type the following get commands, you obtain a list of the line properties and a list of the axes properties:

Example 1	Example 2
`>> get(h)`	`>> get(h1)`
Color: [1 0 0]	BackgroundColor = none
EraseMode: 'normal'	Color = [0 0 0]
LineStyle: '-'	EdgeColor = none
LineWidth: 0.5000	EraseMode = normal
Marker: '.'	Editing = off
MarkerSize: 6	Extent = [3.12 −1.21 0.69 0.09]
MarkerEdgeColor: 'auto'	FontAngle = normal
MarkerFaceColor: 'none'	FontName = Helvetica
XData: [1x63 double]	FontSize = [10]
YData: [1x63 double]	FontUnits = points
ZData: [1x0 double]	FontWeight = normal
BeingDeleted: 'off'	HorizontalAlignment = center
ButtonDownFcn: []	LineStyle = -
Children: [0x1 double]	LineWidth = [0.5]
Clipping: 'on'	Margin = [2]
CreateFcn: []	Position = [3.48 −1.13 1.00]
DeleteFcn: []	Rotation = [0]
BusyAction: 'queue'	String = time [s]
HandleVisibility: 'on'	Units = data
HitTest: 'on'	Interpreter = tex
Interruptible: 'on'	VerticalAlignment = cap
Selected: 'off'	
SelectionHighlight: 'on'	BeingDeleted = off
Tag: ''	ButtonDownFcn =
Type: 'line'	Children = []
UIContextMenu: []	Clipping = off
UserData: []	CreateFcn =
Visible: 'on'	DeleteFcn =
Parent: 158.0052	BusyAction = queue
DisplayName: ''	HandleVisibility = off
XDataMode: 'manual'	HitTest = on
XDataSource: ''	Interruptible = on
YDataSource: ''	Parent = [158.005]
ZDataSource: ''	Selected = off
	SelectionHighlight = on
	Tag =
	Type = text
	UIContextMenu = []
	UserData = []
	Visible = on

You can change each property using the command set. For example, let's try to change the font size of the xlabel object and the size of the line object by typing the following commands:

```
>> set(h1,'FontSize',18);
>> set(h, 'LineWidth',3);
```

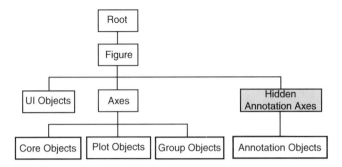

Fig. 3.3 MATLAB graphical object hierarchy

The way to use the set function is the following: the first argument of the function is the handle (a number that refers to the specific object), and the second argument is the property name (in our case the "FontSize"),[3] and finally the third argument is the value that is assigned to the property.

To really understand how to manage the MATLAB graphical objects, you must know that they are arranged according to the hierarchy shown in Fig. 3.3.

The object immediately above another is called a parent, and the objects below another are called children. In general, children inherit their handle graphics properties from their parent. For example, the position of a line on a plot depends on the position of the axes, which, in turn, depends on the position of the figure window. The Root object is the computer screen, and there can only be one Root object.

The UI objects are graphical user interface elements that are discussed in Chap. 8 of this book.

A parent can have any number of children. For example, the *Root* can have many *Figures*, a *Figure* can have many *Axes*, and a set of *Axes* can have many plot objects, such as *lines*, *surfaces*, and so on. If a parent has many children, one of them is designated to be the current one. For example, the current set of axes is the one that will be updated the next time you run a command. You can also make an object current by clicking on it with the mouse. The following functions return the handles of the current object:

Function	Description
Gcf	Return the handle of the current figure. The current figure is the last figure created, modified, selected or clicked on
Gca	Get the handle of the current *axes*. The current *axes* is typically the last *axes* used for plotting or the last *axes* clicked on by the mouse. Pay attention: do not confuse axes with the command axis
Gco	Get the handle of the current graphics object, which is the last graphics object created, modified or clicked on

(continued)

---

[3]This property and the associated value are listed by MATLAB using the command get.

(continued)

Function	Description
h=findobj('PropName',PropVal)	Return the handles of all graphics objects having the property *PropName*, set to the value *PropValue*. You can specify more than one property/value pair, in which case, findobj returns only those objects having all specified values

We have no wish to describe every MATLAB object's property here. The properties can be viewed using the online MATLAB help. We want to call your attention to the fact that every object's properties can be changed at will. The following example shows a few of the possible changes.

Example	Graphical result

```>> figure;```
```>> plot(1:6,10:10:60)```
```>> set(gca,'XTick',[1,3,5])```
```>> set(gca,'XTickLabel',…```
```   {'one' ,'three','five'})```
```>> set(gca,'XMinorTick','on')```
```>> set(gca,'Xgrid','on')```
```>> set(gca,'YTick',[17,27,37,54])```
```>> h=findobj('Type','line');```
```>> set(h,'color','k')```
```>> set(h, 'LineWidth',3);```
```>> set(gca,'FontSize', 20);```
	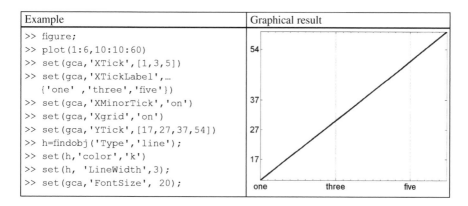

As you can see, there are many ways to change the appearance of a figure. As we wrote at the beginning of the chapter, it is possible also to change all a figure's properties by clicking "edit" in the figure menu bar and then by selecting one of the alternatives (Figure Properties, Axes Properties, etc.), or clicking on the arrow button in the figure menu and selecting the desired item (line, axis, title, etc.). However, in the long run, the possibility of writing a short code to create a figure and edit the figure's characteristics turns to be useful for researchers.

Summary

- plot is the basic function for 2-D plots.
- Graphs can be customized with text, title, xlabel, ylabel, grid, etc.
- Axes limits are implicitly calculated. However, they can be modified using the axis function.
- Multiple graphs can be obtained using subplot.
- hist, bar, errorbar, pie, are other functions to plot 2-D graphs.
- plot3, bar3, surf, surfc, mesh, meshc, are the functions to plot 3-D graphs.
- meshgrid is useful to define the x-y points for 3-D plots.

- Figures can be printed in files or directly to printer output using the command `print`.
- A handle is a number associated to a graphical object. It is used with the `set` and `get` commands to obtain or change an object's properties.
- The handles can be obtained when an object is created or by using one of the following commands: `gcf` (gets the handle of the current picture), `gca` (gets the handle of the current axes), `gco` (gets the handle of the current object).

Exercises

1. Create a vector x of values from 1 to 10. Then create a vector y containing the squares of the elements of x. In vector z put the values of x multiplied by 9.

   (a) In Figure 1 plot the vector y versus x using a red line with squares as markers.
   (b) In Figure 5 plot the vector z versus x using a black dash-dot line having triangles as markers.
   (c) In Figure 3, plot the vector y versus x using a green line and the vector z using a magenta line. Provide a title and a legend.

2. Create the figure of a hypothetical perceptual learning experiment divided in two graphs. At the top, plot the performance (i.e., the threshold) vs. the session number using the circle symbol. The session number goes from 1 to 100. The threshold is given by the following command: `th=1000*[1:100].^(-1/4)+randn(1,100)/5;` Set the y-axis to display values from 0 to 10. On the bottom part, plot the histogram of thresholds, subdividing the data intp 40 bins. Add legends, a title, and grids.

Solution	Graphical result

`th=10*[1:30].^(-1/4)+randn(1,30)/5;`
`figure;`
`subplot(2,1,1);`
`plot(th,'o');`
`axis([1 30 0 10]);`
`ylabel('Participant''s threshold');`
`xlabel('Session number');`
`grid;`
`title('Perceptual learning`
`curve','FontSize',14);`
`subplot(2,1,2);`
`hist(th,20)`
`xlabel('Threshold');`
`title('Threshold distribution',…`
`     'FontSize',12);`
	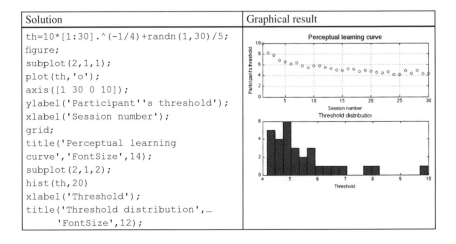

3. Create a figure divided into two parts. On the left side, display five horizontal bars with the following values: horbarValue=[34,12,45,41,55]. On the right side, display two graphs. The upper part will contain a 3-D pie, with three pieces named "left," "center," "right," with values val=[12, 45, 23]. In the bottom part place an error bar. The mean is equal to mv=[3,2,5], and the standard deviation is equal to stdval=[0.4, 1.1, 0.8].

Solution	Graphical result

```>> horbarValue = [34,12,45,41,55];```
```>> val=[12, 45, 23];```
```>> mv=[3,2,5];```
```>> stdval=[0.4, 1.1, 0.8];```
```>> figure;```
```>> subplot(2,2,[1 3]);```
```>> barh(horbarValue);```
```>> subplot(2,2,2)```
```>> pie(val,[0 0 1],```
```{'Left','Center','Right'});```
```>> subplot(2,2,4);```
```>> errorbar(mv,stdval,'xr');```
	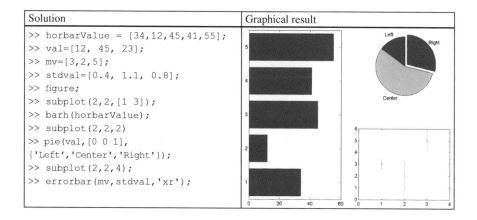

4. Given the 4×5 matrix Temp=[2 3 5 7 8; 20 23 28 25; 14, 13, 12, 7; 6 2 -3 2], display its values using a 3-D bar graph. Title the figure "Season Temperature." Place on the y-axis the labels 'Spring', 'Summer', 'Autumn', 'Winter'. Label the x-, y-, and z-axes "Season," "Measures," and "Temperature."

Solution	Graphical result

```>> Temp = [2, 3, 5, 7, 8; …```
```   20, 23, 28, 25, 22; …```
```   14, 13, 12, 7, 8; …```
```   6, 2, -3, -1, 2];```
```>> bar3(Temp)```
```>> set(gca,'yTickLabel',…```
```{'Spring','Summer','Autumn','Winter'});```
```>> ylabel('Seasons','FontSize',15)```
```>> xlabel('Measures','FontSize',15)```
```>> zlabel('Temperatures',```
```'FontSize',15)```
```>> title('Season Temperature',```
```'FontSize',20)```
	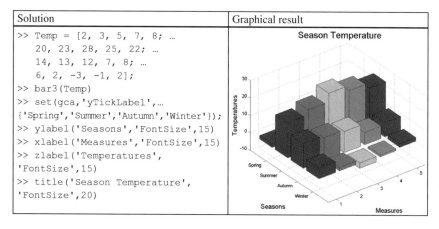

5. Display the function y=tan(sin(x))-sin(tan(x)), where x=-pi:pi/10:pi. Change the color line to red, use stars (*) as a marker, with a marker size equal to 10. Set the graph background color to green. Set the axis font size to 20.

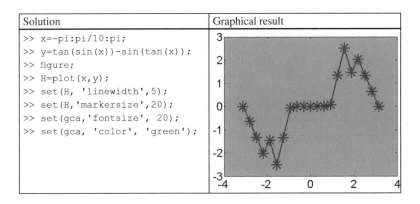

Solution	Graphical result
| ```
>> x=-pi:pi/10:pi;
>> y=tan(sin(x))-sin(tan(x));
>> figure;
>> H=plot(x,y);
>> set(H, 'linewidth',5);
>> set(H,'markersize',20);
>> set(gca,'fontsize', 20);
>> set(gca, 'color', 'green');
``` | |

A Brick for an Experiment

Plot the Results

MATLAB is a powerful tool for graphics. However, this brick requires a relatively simple graph. Usually, the results of experiments like that of Sekuler et al. (1997) are represented with bar graps. Here too we will represent the results with a bar graph. We will draw a plot where the discs' motion (continuous versus with stop) is represented along the x-axis and bars are grouped by presence (or absence) of sound.

First, we need to get the means and the standard errors of the data we want to represent. We proceed as in the previous chapter. But first, we store the number of subjects we have run within the variable N.

```
>> N = 10;
>> m=zeros(2, 2);
>> m(1, 1) = mean(data(data(:, 5)==1 & data(:, 6)==1, 7)); %
continuous motion no sound
>> m(1, 2) = mean(data(data(:, 5)==1 & data(:, 6)==2, 7)); %
motion with stop
>> m(2, 1) = mean(data(data(:, 5)==2 & data(:, 6)==1, 7)); % sound
absent
>> m(2, 2) = mean(data(data(:, 5)==2 & data(:, 6)==2, 7)); % sound
present
>> err=zeros(2, 2);
>> err(1, 1) = std(data(data(:, 5)==1 & data(:, 6)==1, 7))/
sqrt(N); % continuous motion
>> err(1, 2) = std(data(data(:, 5)==1 & data(:, 6)==2, 7))/
sqrt(N); % motion with stop
```
```

```
>> err(2, 1) = std(data(data(:, 5)==2 & data(:, 6)==1, 7))/
sqrt(N); % sound absent
>> err(2, 2) = std(data(data(:, 5)==2 & data(:, 6)==2, 7))/
sqrt(N); % sound present
```

The brick plot will be made using a function that can be freely downloaded from MATLAB central. The function is called barweb.[4] The reason for using barweb is the following: this function combines within the same function two different functions: bar and errorbar. In other words, barweb simplifies the creation of a bar graph with error bars. We can now fill all the necessary fields and have a final look at the data:

```
>> barweb(m, err, [], {'without stop', 'with stop'}, [], {'kind
of motion'}, {'percent bouncing'}, [], [], {'no sound',
'sound'})
```

Finally, you may want to export the figure as a graphic file. This can be done as follows. In the file menu of the plot figure you can "save as" the figure as a jpg, tif, gif, PostScript, or one of various other graphics formats. Alternatively, you can use the print option at the MATLAB prompt. For example:

```
>> figure(1);
>> print -depsc finalresult.eps
```

Reference

Sekuler R, Sekuler AB, Lau R (1997) Sound alters visual motion perception. Nature 385:308

Suggested Readings

Some of the concepts illustrated in this chapter can be found, in an extended way, in the following book:

Marchand P, Holland OT (2003) Graphics and GUIs with MATLAB. CRC press. Boca Raton, FL
Siciliano A (2008) MATLAB: data analysis and visualization. World Scientific, Singapore
Wallisch P, Lusignan M, Benayoun M, Baker TI, Dickey AS, Hatsopoulos NG (2009) MATLAB for neuroscientists: an introduction to scientific computing in MATLAB. Elsevier/Academic Press, Amsterdam

---

[4]You can also download the file from the book website.

Chapter 4
Start Programming

This chapter outlines the Basic programming concepts in MATLAB such as loop generation and program flux control. Programming *style and debugging techniques are also presented.*

M-Scripts and Functions

When we manage long and complex lists of operations, it is inconvenient to type them directly into the MATLAB prompt. It is preferable in such cases to write scripts, which are text files containing lists of commands. Because scripts are text files, they can be written in any text editor. However, MATLAB provides a built-in text editor that offers many advantages over conventional text editors. For example, the MATLAB editor highlights the commands, automatically indents the script, shows where loops start and end, identifies rows with numbers to aid in locating errors, etc. This editor can be opened by typing `edit` at the MATLAB prompt or by selecting File->New -> M-file.

The Fig. 4.1 highlights some of the key icons of the MATLAB editor [1] (e.g., open a file, create a new script, save a script, run). Type into the editor the script shown in the figure (it is also presented in the text) and save it with the name MyFirstProgram.m (do not type the numbers, they refer to the script lines).

Listing 4.1

```
1  % MyFirstProgram
2  %
3  % This is my first program. These lines are used as comment
4
5  x=5;
6  y=cos(x);
7  STR=sprintf('The cosine of %2.2f is %2.2f',x,y);
8  disp(STR);
```

---

[1] The appearance of the window can differ depending on Matlab version you are using.

M. Borgo et al., *MATLAB for Psychologists*,
DOI 10.1007/978-1-4614-2197-9_4, © Springer Science+Business Media, LLC 2012

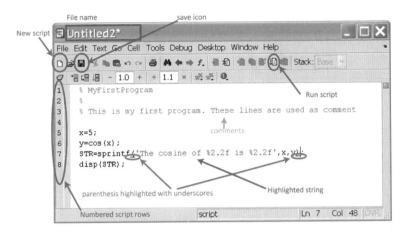

Fig. 4.1 MATLAB editor window

The semicolon after each command prevents MATLAB from echoing the command output in the command window. This echoing can be annoying, especially when the echoed content is large. To insert comments in your script, just type % at the beginning of the line you want to comment; this line is not executed by MATLAB. Note that comments are colored green in the MATLAB editor. Comments can also be written in the same row of a MATLAB command, as in the following case:

```
>> a=1; % the comment can be written at the right of a MATLAB command
```

Once you have written a script, you can save it with any name you like. However, we recommend saving scripts with meaningful filenames. Moreover, we recommend starting the script with some comments explaining what the script does. These comments are very useful especially when you open the script after a period of time. MATLAB scripts (M-scripts) are saved with the *.m* extension in the directory where you are working. Once the script is saved, the script name appears in the editor window title.

To run/test the M-script, press the run icon or the F5 key of the keyboard. The example above should output in the command window the following text:

```
The cosine of 5.00 is 0.28
```

It is possible to run a script directly from the command window by typing the filename of the script. In our case we should type:

```
>> MyFirstProgram
The cosine of 5.00 is 0.28
```

An M-script can be saved in any directory of your computer; however, to run the script from the MATLAB prompt you need either to be in the directory where you saved the script or to tell MATLAB where to find your M-script. MATLAB looks for scripts within the directory where you are working and within any directories defined in the search path. There are two possible ways to add the directory where you are working to the MATLAB default search path:

1. Click on the FILE menu, and then select the SET PATH option.
2. By means of the `path` command from the MATLAB command window or within an M-script file. The `path` command uses the following syntax: `path(path,'newpath')` (for example `path(path,'C:\myFiles')`).

Let's see how to write an M-script file that draws a graph so that every time we want to plot the same type of graph we do not need to retype all the commands. We do this in the following example. Save the script with the name plotLC in the current directory.

Listing 4.2

```
1    % plotLC
2    % Plot the learning curve.
3
4    close all;
5    clear all;
6    x=[1:10];
7    y=10./exp(x);
8    figure;
9    plot(x,y,'rd-');
10   xlabel('trials');
11   ylabel('ErrorRate');
12   grid;
13   MyFirstPrograms;
```

At the beginning of the script we have inserted the commands `close all` and `clear all` to close all figures and then to be sure that no variable can affect the script behavior. After this script is run, a figure appears, and the sentence `The cosine of 5.00 is 0.28` appears in the MATLAB command window.

MATLAB is provided with an excellent debugger to warns us if we have made any errors. Let's suppose, for example, that at line 7 of the script we have forgotten to add the dot after the number 10, in this way:

```
7    y=10/exp(x);
```

In this case, MATLAB returns the following error:

```
??? Error using ==> mrdivide
Matrix dimensions must agree.
Error in ==> PlotLR at 7
y=10/exp(x);
```

The debugger explains what type of error terminated the script prematurely, the filename of the corrupted script, and the line where the error is located (unfortunately, errors are not always so easy to pinpoint).

Control Flow Statements

In the previous scripts (i.e., Listing 4.1 or 4.2), MATLAB executed the instructions as they were typed directly in the command window. This programming style, however, is not always efficient. For example, it does not solve such problems as the execution of repetitive tasks and the control of operation flow. MATLAB, like other programming languages, has flow control statements, which we now explain.

Cycles and Conditionals: If

The `if` command is used to control the execution of a script or a function (see later in this chapter). Frequently, the `if` command is used together with the `else` command in the following form:

```
if condition
      DoSomething
else
      DoSomethingElse
end
```

The `if` command checks whether `condition` is satisfied (i.e., whether it is true or false). If the condition is true, MATLAB executes `DoSomething`, while if the condition is false, MATLAB executes `DoSomethingElse`, which represents the alternative statements. Note the indentation of the text. The indentation helps in visualizing the scope of the *if – else – end* structure. Let's see an example with the following script:

Listing 4.3

```
1  % Test the if statement
2
3  a = 0;
4  if a > 1
5      disp('true')
6  else
7      disp('false')
8  end
```

Save the script with the name TestIf1 and run it (by typing the name in the command window or by clicking the Run button in the editor window); the word "false" appears in the command window:

```
>> TestIf1
false
```

Because 0 is smaller than 1, the comparison between the variable a and the number 1 returns the value false. The condition of an if command very often contains a combination of relational and logical operators (see Chap. 2), which returns a logical result: true or false.

Now, try to replace line 4 with the following statement and run the script again:

```
4    if 1
```

the result is also "true." Why this counterintuitive result? We have to keep in mind that the condition after the if statement is a logical value (true or false). In MATLAB, every numerical value different from zero is interpreted as true (see Chap. 2). Therefore, the condition "if 1" is always true. By the same token, the condition becomes false if you replace "1" with "0".

In many circumstances you can have more than two conditions to test. In such cases you can use elseif:

```
if condition1
     Statements1
elseif condition2
     Statements2
elseif condition3
     Statements3
else
     Statements4
end
```

if *condition1* is false, MATLAB tests *condition2*. If it is false, MATLAB tests *condition3*, etc.

As we wrote in the previous chapter, be careful when you want to verify whether a value is within a certain range. For example, if you want to display the string 'mean score' when the MemoryScore variable is between 50 and 100, you cannot write the if statement as follows:

```
1    MemoryScore = 10;
2    if 50 < MemoryScore <100
3         disp('mean score');
4    end
```

If you save and run the above script (use the TestIf2 name), the result is

```
>> TestIf2
mean score
```

which is wrong. As we have seen in the previous chapters, the statement in line 2 is always true (the output of 50<MemoryScore can be either 0 or 1, which are both less than 100). The appropriate way to write the statement is the following:

```
2  if (50 < MemoryScore) & (MemoryScore < 100)
3      disp('mean score')
4  end
```

Or alternatively, you can write the script in a *nested* way:

```
2  if 50 > MemoryScore
3      if MemoryScore < 100
4          disp('mean score');
5      end
6  end
```

In this nested structure, when the first if statement is true, everything between if and end is executed. Then at line 3, there is another if. In case of a true condition, everything between the if (on line 3) and the associated end (on line 5) is executed, and so on. On the other hand, in the case of a false condition, MATLAB skips to the line after the end on line 5, which is the end on line 6.

Switch Case

An alternative to the *if – else* form is the *switch – case* form. The advantage of the *switch – case* form is that in some situations, it yields a code that is more readable. The *switch – case* form has the following syntax:

```
switch condition
    case fact1
        Statements1
    case fact2
        Statements2
    case fact3
        Statements3
    otherwise
        StatementsOtherwise
end
```

the condition after the switch command is evaluated and compared successively with *fact1, fact2,* etc. When a comparison is true, the corresponding statement is executed. Then MATLAB skips to the first line after the end. If no match is found among the case statements, then MATLAB skips to the otherwise statement, if present, and executes StatementsOtherwise or else to the end statement. Note that the otherwise statement is optional.

Let's see an example. Write the following M-script and save it with the name ArrOrder.

Listing 4.4

```
1   % The M script displays a different string on
2   % the command window.
3   % according to the integer value of i (to be set before
4   % the script execution.)
5   %
6   % Author: Borgo, Soranzo, Grassi 2012
7
8   switch k
9       case 1
10          disp('First! Good job!');
11      case 2
12          disp('Second!');
13      case 3
14          disp('Third, nice result!');
15      otherwise
16          disp('Next time is going to be better!');
17  end
```

Now let's test the how the script works by typing the following:

```
>> clear all
>> k = 27
>> ArrOrder
Next time is going to be better!
```

Note that if you do not define the variable k (in the command window or inside the M-script) MATLAB returns an error:

```
>> clear all
>> ArrOrder
??? Input argument "k" is undefined.
Error in ==> ArrOrder at 7
switch k
```

Multiple expressions can be handled in a single *case* by enclosing the fact to compare within a cell array. For example substitute the lines 10, 11, 12 and 13 with the following lines:

```
10  case {2,3}
11      disp('You are on the podium, but... not in first position!');
12  otherwise
13      ...
```

If you test the function with $k=2$ or $k=3$, the text displayed at the MATLAB prompt is always the same.

```
>> k=2;
>> ArrOrder
You are on the podium, but... not in first position!
>> k=3;
>> ArrOrder
You are on the podium, but... not in first position!
```

For Loops

Often, there is the need to repeat a block of statements a fixed number of times. For example, let us suppose we want to display the first ten responses to a questionnaire, which are contained within an array of numbers. A possible (but inefficient) solution is to repeatedly write the statement we need to run to see the scores. Another (more elegant and efficient) solution is to use a loop structure. The *for* structure is a loop structure that makes it possible to repeat a block of statements a *fixed* number of times. The *for* format is:

```
for counter = list_of_values;
    statements
end
```

The counter variable consecutively assumes the value of each column of the list from the first value to the last. The counter variable is often used within the loop as an index to address the content of a vector or as a variable for other calculations. Let's see how the for loop works by writing and executing the following M-script.

Listing 4.5

```
1   % First For Loops example
2   % Author: Borgo, Soranzo, Grassi 2012
3
4   ListOfValues=[1,2,3,4];
5   disp('First Test');
6   for counter = ListOfValues
7       disp(counter);
8   end
9
10  disp('Second Test');
11  for counter = 1:4
12      disp(counter);
13  end
```

Once you have saved the file (we named it "FirstForTest") and run it, the result is:

```
First Test
     1
     2
     3
     4
Second Test
     1
     2
     3
     4
```

As you can see, the result of lines from 6 to 8 and from 11 to 13 are identical, i.e., the display of the first four integers. This is because the statement 1:4 at line 11 generates a vector equivalent to the ListOfvalues vector. Note that the disp command is repeated four times, without the necessity of repeatedly writing the statement.

The most common format of the *for* loop is shown below. It may be simpler to understand the *for* loop when it is represented in a flow chart graphical format.

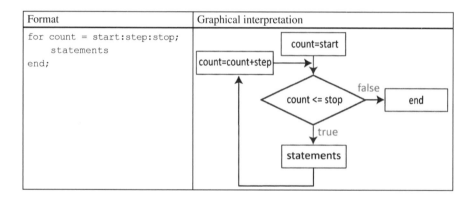

Format	Graphical interpretation

`for count = start:step:stop;`
`    statements`
`end;`	

The variable count is the counter. At the first cycle it is set to the *start* value (the first element of the vector). MATLAB verifies whether the counter count is still less than or equal to the *stop* value, thus that the variable count has not yet reached the last element of the vector. If this is true, MATLAB adds to the counter count the *step* value (count assumes the value of the next element in the vector) and executes the statements. At the next cycle, MATLAB checks whether the counter count is still less than or equal to the *stop* value. If this is false, the next command to be executed is the command after the end command. Please note that the counter should not be changed inside the loop.

Now suppose you need to obtain the average of the values stored in the vector X. You can write an M-script using a *for* loop as follows:

Listing 4.6

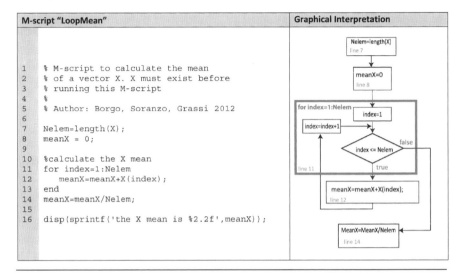

Analysis

Line 7: The number of elements in X is obtained.

Line 8: The vector meanX is *initialized* to zero. This initialization is necessary because the variable is used as an accumulator to store the partial sum of the elements.

Line 11: Here is the for command. First, the variable index is set to 1, then it is compared to Nelem. Next, on line 12, the partial sum is obtained by summing the value of X indexed by index and the previous partial sum value contained in the meanX variable. Line 12 is repeated till index is less than or equal to Nelem. The flow chart represented in the figure illustrates what we have just described. Let's test the M-script (named LoopMean) by typing the following:

```
>> X= [3 4 6 2 7 1 9 11 4 7];
>> LoopMean
the X mean is 5.40
```

The *for* structure can be nested into another *for* structure. For example, here we nest two *for* structures to calculate the mean of a 2-dimensional matrix.

Listing 4.7

```
1   % The M-script to calculate the mean of a 2-dimension X2 matrix.
2   % X2 must exist before running this M-script
3   %
4   % Author: Borgo, Soranzo, Grassi 2012
5
6   [Nrows,Ncols]=size(X2)
7   meanX = 0;
8
9   for indr=1:Nrows
10      for indc=1:Ncols
11          meanX=meanX+X2(indr,indc);
12      end
13  end
14  Nelem=Nrows*Ncols;
15  meanX=meanX/Nelem;
16
17  disp(sprintf('the X mean is %2.2f',meanX));
```

Note here that the counter `indr` is used to address the matrix rows, while `indc` is used to address the matrix columns. The counter `indc` changes in the inner loop, which means that before increasing the `indr` value, all the columns (= `indc` values) have to be considered.

If we save the script (name it NestedFor) and run it, we get:

```
>> X2=[4 5 6; 4 7 8];
>> NestedFor
Nrows =
        2
Ncols =
        3
the X mean is 5.67
```

You can write the *for* loop in a single command line. Here we show the general form:

```
for index = j:m:k, statements, end
```

Remember: do not forget the commas (or semicolons, which are preferable to commas because they prevent the echoing of output in the command window). If you forget, them you will receive an error message. The word *statements* represents one or more statements, separated by commas or semicolons. Remember to "close" the for loop with the `end` statement.

Be careful when you use the counter to address the cells of a matrix. For example, do not set the counter so that it starts from 0. If you do so, you will encounter the following problem:

```
>> for i=0:10; a(i)=i; end;
??? Subscript indices must either be real positive integers or logicals.
```

Clearly, the index of a vector cannot be zero. You can, however, run the loop with no error if you modify it slightly, as follows:

```
>> for i=0:10; a(i+1)=i; end;
>> a
a =
    0   1   2   3   4   5   6   7   8   9   10
```

While

Like the for structure, the *while* structure can be used to repeat a number of statements. The difference between the *while* and the *for* structures is that while allows one to repeat the statements an *indefinite* number of times until a certain condition is true. The while format is as follows:

Format	Graphical interpretation

```while condition```
  ```statements```
```end```
	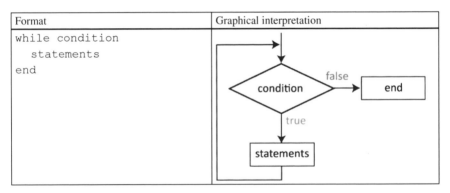

The while construct repeats the statements *while* its condition remains true. The condition is tested each time before the *statements* within the loop are repeated. Note that the condition should refer to the statements within the loop otherwise the loop would never end. While loops are complex to deal with, especially when you start programming, because often MATLAB enters in an infinite loop. If this happens, you can press the buttons CTRL+C and force-quit the loop.

If we use a counter, we can copy the functionality of *for* loop with a *while* loop. Here, for example, we translate the for loop of the LoopMean function example into a while loop.

Listing 4.8

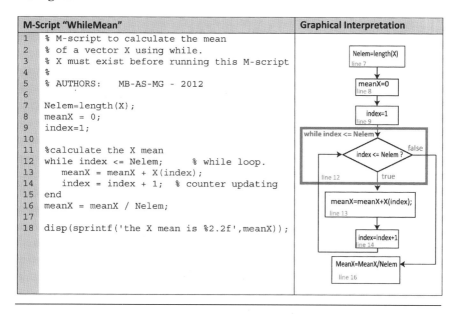

M-Script "WhileMean"	Graphical Interpretation

```
1  % M-script to calculate the mean
2  % of a vector X using while.
3  % X must exist before running this M-script
4  %
5  % AUTHORS:   MB-AS-MG - 2012
6  %
7  Nelem=length(X);
8  meanX = 0;
9  index=1;
10
11 %calculate the X mean
12 while index <= Nelem;      % while loop.
13    meanX = meanX + X(index);
14    index = index + 1;  % counter updating
15 end
16 meanX = meanX / Nelem;
17
18 disp(sprintf('the X mean is %2.2f',meanX));
```

Analysis

Line 9: We define the variable index used as a counter and initialize it to 1.

Line 12: Here is the while command; the condition index < = Nelem is evaluated. If it is true, then (line13) the value of X indexed by index is added to the previous partial sum in the meanX variable.

Line 14: the counter is increased. Note here the difference between the *while* and *for* loops. In the *for* loop, the counter is "automatically" increased and "compared" at each cycle. In contrast, in the while loop, you have to increase the counter inside the loop. Then MATLAB goes to line 13 and evaluates whether index< = Nelem, etc. The flow chart gives you a better picture of what is happening here.

   At first glance, it may seem that the *while* command is not as useful as the *for* structure. For example, the majority of experiments in psychology use a fixed number of trials. In other words, before the subject begins the experiment, we know exactly how many trials the subject is going to run. In the MATLAB language this suggests that one implement a for loop (see also the brick section for an extensive example): *for* the desired number of trials we present the stimulus to the subject and collect the subject's answer. The counter, in this case, is the trial number, which is increased of one unit every time the subject completes one trial. When the current trial number exceeds the total number of trials, we exit the *for* loop.

However, there are experiments in which we do not know in advance how many trials the subject is going to run. The adaptive procedures used in psychophysics are a typical example of experiments that use a variable number of trials (Gescheider 2003). The simplest example is the method of limits (Fechner 1889, but see also Boring 1961). Let's suppose we use this method to estimate the subject's absolute threshold for the intensity of a 1-kHz pure tone. We may proceed as follows. We start the experiment by presenting one tone of a given intensity to the subject. The subject has to respond whether s/he can hear the stimulus (by pressing 1) or not (by pressing any other number, e.g., 2). Every time the subject's answer is positive, we halve the intensity of the tone. At a certain trial n, the subject's answer will be negative because s/he is not able to hear the tone. At this point we have just reached the subject's absolute threshold for the tone's intensity.

We can implement the example just described with a while loop. In detail, while the answer of the subject is 1 (equivalently, until the answer is not 1), we play the tone to the subject and collect the answer. The answer is evaluated in the logical statement that keeps the while loop running. While the answer is TRUE (equivalently, until the answer if FALSE) we repeat the while loop. At the first negative answer we quit the loop.

Listing 4.9

```
1   sf = 44100; % Sampling frequency
2   d = .25;    % Duration in seconds
3   f = 1000;   % frequency in Hertz
4   I = 1;      % starting intensity
5   % tone synthesis
6   t = linspace(0, d, sf*d);
7   tone = sin(2*pi*f*t);
8   % play the sound the first time and get the answer
9   sound(tone, sf);
10  answer = input('Can you hear the tone? ');
11  % repeat the stimulus until the answer changes from "yes" to "no"
12  while answer == 1
13      I = I/2;
14      sound(tone * I, sf);
15      answer = input('Can you hear the tone? ');
16  end
17  % return the threshold
18  fprintf('The threshold is equal to %2.1f dB Fs\n', 20*log10(I));
```

Analysis

The sound functions used in the script are described in detail in the chapter dedicated to sound. Let's see the rest of the script:

Lines 1–4: The variables needed to synthesize the sound are created and set.

Lines 5–7: The tone is synthesized.

Line 9–10: We play the tone for the first time to the subject and store the answer in the variable "answer".

Line 12–16: The while loop. We evaluate the answer of the subject. While the answer of the subject is positive (i.e., equal to 1) we halve the intensity of the tone (line 14) and play the tone at the halved intensity (line 15). Then we repeat the question to the subject.

Lines 17–18: the subject has pressed a button different from "1" and the last intensity value is used to calculate the subject's threshold.

Break

The break command is used to terminate in advance the execution of a while loop or that of a for loop. In nested loops, break terminates the innermost loop only. If you want to program with a good programming style you should avoid the use of the break command. In fact, it is important to know that the break command can be always substituted by for or else statements.

Here we present a variation of the WhileMean M-script without the comments at the beginning.

Listing 4.10

```
1    Nelem=length(X);
2    meanX = 0;
3    index=1;
4
5    %calculate the X mean
6    while 1        % Never ending while loop.
7        meanX = meanX + X(index);
8        index = index + 1;  % counter updating
9        if index <= Nelem
10           break
11       end
12   end
13   meanX = meanX / Nelem;
14
15   disp(sprintf('the X mean is %2.2f',meanX));
```

Note that the condition of the while loop (i.e., 1) is always true, and therefore the loop above is a never-ending loop. This happens because MATLAB interprets every value different from zero as a true logical value. The rows 9, 10, and 11 are there exactly with the aim of terminating the loop. You can try to insert the break command in Listing 4.10 to obtain the same result.

Try–Catch

The try–catch statement is not used to control elements; rather it tries to execute a statement or statements and catch any errors that may occur. The try–catch statement takes the following form:

```
try
      statements
catch
      statements
end
```

The try–catch statement is useful when you are running scripts that can return anomalous responses, such as importing data from a file or using the psychtoolbox commands (see later chapters). When you use the psychtoolbox, it can sometimes happen that your computer seems to crash. In such cases, the CTRL+C command is insufficient to restore the command window. If you want to avoid such behavior, you should write the psychtoolbox commands between `try` and `catch` commands.

Here is an example of how the try–catch statement works. Save the following M-script in the file named trycatchExample and run it:

Listing 4.11

```
1  try
2      for i=0:10; a(i)=i; end;
3  catch
4      disp('Something strange happened!')
5  end
```

```
>> trycatchExample
Something strange happened!
```

This example shows clearly the use of the try/catch statement. The `for` loop generates an error because the i counter is used as index for the vector a. But i starts from 0, and therefore MATLAB cannot read the first datum of a. Because the error is generated within the try portion of the script, the program continues and goes to the catch part, where it returns the sentence "Something strange happened!." If you want to see the error returned by MATLAB, you have to type the command `lasterror` at the prompt.

Loops Versus Matrices and If Versus Logicals

Once people have learned how to use the *for*, the *while* and the *if* structures, they tend to forget the power of using matrices in MATLAB. Let's take a look at the following two statements. These statements do the same thing: they look into a matrix A and return the number of elements whose value is included between 0.2 and 0.3.

Matrices & Logicals	Loops & If
1 `NumEl=length(a(a>0.2 & a<0.3));`	1 `NumEl=0;` 2 `for i=1:size(A,1);` 3 `    for j=1:size(A,2)` 4 `        if A(i,j)>0.2 & A(i,j)<0.3;` 5 `            NumEl = NumEl +1;` 6 `        end` 7 `    end` 8 `end`

As you can see, if you "think in the matrix way," the program you have to write is much shorter. Moreover, the example on the left runs faster than the example on the right: MATLAB is optimized to work with matrices. Therefore, we recommend the use of matrices and logicals whenever possible.

Functions

Scripts work with variables that are defined within the same script or in the command window. However, sometimes we want scripts to receive data as input and return results as output. Such scripts are called *functions*. We have already seen several built-in MATLAB functions, such as sin, sum, and length. However, MATLAB makes it possible to create your own functions.

If we want to write a function, the script must start with the reserved word function, and the M-file name has to match the function name. The difference between M-scripts and function scripts is that **functions communicate with MATLAB through *input* and *output* arguments**. We will stress this concept further throughout the chapter.

Before highlighting the *function* properties, type the following example as a new script. Remember to save the script with the same name you use to call the function. In this case, the name must be "statistic.m"

Listing 4.12

```
1  function [mea, vari] = statistic( x )
2
3  % [mea, vari] = statistic( x )
4  %
5  % The function returns the mean and the standard deviation
6  % of the input vector.
7  %
8  % INPUT:    x vector of numbers. Do not use with matrices.
9  % OUTPUT:   mea = is the mean of the input vector x
10 %          vari = is the variance of vector x
11 % Author:   Borgo, Soranzo, Grassi 2012
12
13 Nelem = length(x);
14 mea=sum(x)/Nelem;
15 vari=sum(x.^2)/Nelem;
```

The aim of our statistic function is to calculate the mean and the variance of a vector passed as argument to the function. Note that we also benefited from the MATLAB built-in function `sum(x)`, which calculates the sum of the elements of vector x, and the MATLAB built-in function `length (x)`, which returns the number of elements of the vector. When we save this script, MATLAB automatically suggests a filename that is identical to the function name; in our case the filename is `statistic`. Let us test the function in the command window by typing the following:

```
>> randnum=rand(100,1);
>> [m,v]= statistic(randnum)
m =
    0.4753
v =
    0.3103
```

Finally, type `help statistic` at the MATLAB prompt. If you do so, you will see the comments we added at the beginning of the script:

```
>> help statistic
  [mea, vari] = statistic( x )

  The function returns the mean and the standard deviation
  of the input vector.

  INPUT:      x vector of numbers. Do not use with matrices.
  OUTPUT:     mea = is the mean of the input vector x
              var = is the variance of vector x
  Author:     Borgo, Soranzo, Grassi 2012
```

Let's see the general form of a function:

When you write a function, the first line must start with the keyword function. The general form of a function is the following:

```
function [ out1, out2, … ] = fun_name( inp1, inp2, … )
% comments to be displayed go here

…

out1 = … ;

…

out2= …;
```

- *Keyword* function: The function must start with the keyword function. As you have seen, the `statistic` function starts with the keyword function.
- *Output argument*: For more than one output argument, the output arguments must be separated by commas and enclosed in square brackets. However, if the function returns only one output variable, this output can be written without square brackets.
- *The function name*: usually the function line name should be identical to the filename (in the previous example function line name `statistic` was saved in

the file named "statistic.m"). If the filename and the function definition line name are different, the latter name is ignored.

• *Input argument*: The input variables are written within parentheses. For more than one input argument, commas must separate the input arguments.

Input and output variables can be of any kind: numerical, logical, text, structures, cells. However, **the input and output variables are "dummies" and serve to define a way for the function to communicate with the workspace**. What happens is that the workspace input arguments are copied into the dummy input arguments within the function when the function is invoked. For example, the variables mea, vari, and x exist only within the function and not outside of it (i.e., in the workspace). This can be seen simply by typing the command who in the command window:

```
>> who
Your variables are:
m          randnum v
```

This does not happen for input and output variables only, but for all the variables that are defined within the function, such as, for example, Nelem. In fact, if we type Nelem at the MATLAB prompt, we get the following error:

```
>> Nelem
??? Undefined function or variable 'Nelem'.
```

In the lines after the first, there are some comments. These lines will be displayed if you type help fun_name at the MATLAB prompt (e.g., help statistic in our case). It is useful to comment your function so that you know exactly what the function does. Consider also writing comments about the input and the output variables, about who wrote the script and when it was made. After the comments, there are some command lines calculating the mean and the variance of the input vector.

All the output variables have to assume a value. If this does not happen, MATLAB informs you that you have not assigned a value to (at least) one variable. Let's test this by commenting the line vari=sum(x.^2)/Nelem; i.e., insert the % symbol at the beginning of the line. Save the function script and call the function from the command window:

```
>> [m,v]= statistic(randnum)
Error in ==> statistic at 13
Nelem = length(x);

??? Output argument "vari" (and maybe others) not assigned during call to
"/Users/Script/statistic.m (statistic)".
```

MATLAB informs you that you have forgotten to assign a value to the output argument. Note that MATLAB returns another error at line 13. However, this error does not exist. It is an artifact of the fact that MATLAB stopped the execution of the function; it gives you the reference of the first useful script line.

Scope of Variables

As we have written above, when a function is called from the workspace or from another function, the variables defined in the function are created and live only within the function. Usually in computer programming, the term *scope* is used (but not limited) to define the visibility or accessibility of variables from different parts of the program. The variables within a function are called *local variables*. The *scope* of Local variables is that they exist only within the function where they are defined. However, there are other types of variables, for example global variables and persistent variables, and these work in a different way from local variables:

1. *Global variables*: They are ubiquitous, or better, they exist everywhere. When you define them in the workspace, they exist not only in the workspace but also inside functions. The *scope* of the variable is to be globally accessible. It is a good practice to use capital letters for global variable names so to identify them easily. Global variables are generated through the `global` command. For example:

   ```
   >> global DEUSVAR
   ```

2. *Persistent variables*: Once they are created, they "live in the space" where they have been created. While local variables normally stop existing when a function returns its value, persistent variables remain in existence between function calls, keeping the value they had after the last manipulation. The following example should clarify this.

Listing 4.13

```
1  function TestPersistent
2  % Function to test persistent variables
3
4  persistent RemCount
5  if isempty(RemCount)
6     RemCount = 0
7  end
8  RemCount = RemCount + 1
```

Analysis

Line 4: we define the variable `RemCount` as a persistent variable

Line 5: The `isempty()` function returns true if the variable within parentheses is empty. For example, test the function with empty text and with text that is not empty:

```
>> txt1 = '';
>> txt2 = 'hallo';
>> isempty(txt1)
```

```
ans =
     1
>> isempty(txt2)
ans =
     0
```

Once you save the function as TestPersistence.m, run it repeatedly from the command window; you should see something like this:

```
>> TestPersistent
RemCount =
     1
>> TestPersistent
RemCount =
     2
>> TestPersistent
RemCount =
     3
```

The first time you run the `TestPersistence` function, the variable `RemCount` does not exist. The command persistence RemCount creates a new empty variable. The result of `isempty` is true, so line 6 is executed, `RemCount=0`. Next line 7 is executed, and `RemCount` becomes 1. By calling again `TestPersistence`, 1 is added to the last value, so `RemCount` becomes 2; and so on. This happens because in contrast to local variables, `RemCount` exists when the function `TestPersistent` is called, and it also remembers its previously assigned values.

Generally, the most-used variables are those with local and global scope.

Change the Number of Inputs and Outputs

Sometimes we need to write functions that can take a different number of input arguments, such as the `plot` function, which we have described in the previous chapter. It is possible to pass as inputs a variable number of arguments. If we need to write a function with such characteristics, we need to use the `varargin` and `nargin` commands, which stand for, respectively, **var**iable **arg**uments **in** and number of **arg**uments **in**. But if necessary, we can also write a function that returns a variable number of outputs. In this case we have to use the `varargout` and `nargout` commands.

Let's see the use of `nargin` and `varargin` and `nargout` and `varargout` by extending the `statistic` function outlined in Listing 4.12. That function returned the mean and the variance of an input vector. Now we want to add the optional possibility to exclude the outliers from the computation and to return the variance as an option. Therefore, we implement the `statTwo` function, which takes an "optional" argument, a logical vector, indicating the values that have to be excluded from the computation because they are outliers. The standard output is the mean of the function. However, the variance can be returned optionally. This function can be written as follows:

Listing 4.14

```
1    function [mea, varargout] = statTwo( x,varargin )
2
3    % The function returns the mean and the standard deviation
4    % on the element of x eventually selected by i.
5    %
6    % INPUT:     x vector of numbers. Do not use with matrices.
7    %            i vector of logicals.
8    % OUTPUT:    mea = is the mean
9    %            if required by the number of outputs, the
10   %            second element is a cell variable containing the
11   %            variance.
12   % Author:    Borgo, Soranzo, Grassi 2012
13
14   disp(sprintf('Number of input: %d',nargin));
15   disp(sprintf('Number of output: %d',nargout));
16   i=logical(ones(size(x)));
17   if nargin == 2
18       i = logical(varargin{1});
19   end
20   Nelem = sum(i);
21   mea=sum(x(i))/Nelem;
22   if nargout == 2
23        varargout{1}=sum(x(i).^2)/Nelem;
24   end
```

Save the function `statTwo` and run it from the command window in this way:

```
>> aa=[2 5 4 7 6];
>> bb=[1 0 0 0 1];
>> cc=[1 2 5 1 1];
>> m = StatTwo(aa)
Number of input: 1
Number of output: 1
m =
    4.8000
```

As you can see, MATLAB returns the number of input arguments (in this case there is only the vector aa) and the number of output arguments (in this case only one). The result of the function is stored in the variable m.

```
>> m = StatTwo(aa,bb)
Number of input: 2
Number of output: 1
m =
    4
```

In this second case, there are two inputs (the vectors aa and bb) and again one output, now the mean is calculated considering only the values 2 and 6. Let's see what happens if we change again the number of inputs and outputs:

```
>> [m,v] = StatTwo(aa,bb)
Number of input: 2
Number of output: 2
m =
    4
v =
   20
>>
>> [m,v] = StatTwo(aa)
Number of input: 1
Number of output: 2
m =
    4.8000
v =
   26
```

Let's see what happens if we pass either multiple inputs or multiple outputs:

```
>> m=StatTwo(aa,bb,cc)
Number of input: 3
Number of output: 1
m =
    4.8000
>>
>> [m,v,boh]=StatTwo(aa,bb)
Number of input: 2
Number of output: 3
??? Error using ==> statTwo
Too many output arguments.

Error in ==> statTwo
```

If we pass multiple inputs, the function works because the vector c is ignored. In contrast, if we pass multiple outputs, the function assigns only two variables at the output. MATLAB does not know what values to store in the vector boh, so it returns an error. We now describe in detail the statTwo function.

Analysis

Line 1: In the first line there are two input arguments; one is the variable x, and the other is varargin. varargin is a cell matrix, which can contain many values, and therefore it can also contain any number of input variables. `varargin` is a **cell matrix variable** that collects all the inputs' indices with the same input order. In the previous example, when we have called the function `m=statTwo(aa,bb,cc)`, a copy of a was put in the variable `x`, a copy of b was put in the cell `varargin{1}`, and a copy of c was put in the cell `varargin{2}`.

`varargin` must appear at the end of the argument lists. In the same way, the outputs are the variable `mea`, and `varargout`. `varargout` is a cell matrix that collects all the outputs.

Lines 13–14: The number of input and output arguments is displayed. Here, we use the commands `nargin` and `nargout`, which return, respectively, the numbers of inputs and outputs of the called function.

Line 15: the `i` vector is initialized in case there is only one input argument. The vector `i` is used as a logical, so that all the values in the vector `x` are considered in evaluating the mean and the variance.

Line 16: Here is used again the command `nargin`. In brief, in this line we evaluate how many input arguments there are. If and only if the number of input arguments is 2, line 17 is executed. In fact, when the number of input arguments differs from 2, line 17 is not executed. If you want always to use the second input argument of the function (when present), you should change line 16 as follows:

```
if nargin >= 2
```

Line 17: Use the second input argument as a logical vector.

If you need for a function to return an indefinite number of output variables, you can use `nargout` and `varargout`. This is the case in the example.

Line 19: verify how many outputs are required. If there are two output values, the variance is computed on line 20 and the result is stored in the first element of the cell matrix `varargout`.

You can use the functions `nargchk` and `nargoutchk` inside an M-file function to check that the desired number of input and output arguments is specified in the call of that function.

For further information, please refer to MATLAB help.

More on Data Import/Export: Script Examples

The current section shows how to write a script (M-script or function) that retrieves data from an unknown file format (e.g., data saved in ASCII form by an old EEG machine, or collections of data, organized in different files that you want to rearrange in a unique dataset). Moreover, the current section teaches you how to save a file in a format that is readable by some other software.

Before we begin to write some examples, we introduce a few new commands especially dedicated to accessing the content of a file. These commands are presented in the following table. Usage examples are given within the next example scripts.

MATLAB function	Description
`fid=fopen(filename)` `fid=fopen(filename,perm)`	`fopen(filename)` open a file specified by the string `filename`. `perm` specifies how the file is opened, according to the following characters: • 'r' read • 'w' write (create the file if necessary) • 'a' append (create the file if necessary) The function returns a value called *file identifier*. Usually the variable `fid` is used to collect it. This variable must be used by other input/output commands If the returned value is equal to −1, the file cannot be opened
`fclose(fid)`	It closes the file associated by the file identifier `fid`. The function `returns 0 if successful or -1 if not`
`feof`	Return 1 when the end-of-file of the file identified by `fid` is reached, and 0 otherwise
`fprintf(fid, format, A,...)`	Write formatted data into a file identified by `fid`. The `format` string is created in the same way as the `sprintf` format. `A` is the variable we write into the file according to the format specified in `format` The function returns the count of the number of bytes written
`fscanf(fid, format)`	This function reads data from the file specified by `fid` and converts it according to the specified `format` string. Moreover, the file content is returned in a matrix. The `format` string has the same property of the format string for functions `fprintf` and `sprintf`
`fgetl(fid)`	This function returns a string with the content of the next line of the file associated to the file identifier `fid` When the function encounters the end-of-file indicator it returns −1
`fgets`	Same as `fgetl`, but it contains the line terminators
`textscan(fid, 'format')`	This function reads data from an open text file identified by the file identifier `fid` and returns the data into a cell. The format input is a string enclosed in single quotes These conversion specifiers determine the type of each cell in the output cell array. The number of specifiers determines the number of cells in the cell array. Some of the specifiers are equal to the `sprintf` formats Note that `testscan` stops when the format is different from the specified one

Here we write an example that displays the content of a file in the command
window.

Listing 4.15

```
1   function DisplayFile(filename)
2
3   % function DisplayFile(filename)
4   %
5   % It reads a text file and displays it on the command window
6   %
7   % INPUT:    filename = a string containing the file name
8   % Author: Borgo, Soranzo, Grassi 2012
9
10  try
11      fid=fopen(filename);        % open file returning the file id.
12      if fid == -1                % file doesn't open correctly
13          disp(sprintf('Unable to open file ''%s'' ',filename));
14      else                        % in this case file opens correctly
15          while ~feof(fid)        % Start loop. End if eof is reached
16              tline = fgetl(fid); % read next line of text from file
17              disp(tline);        % display text line on command window
18          end
19          fclose(fid);            % close the file
20      end
21  catch
22      fclose(fid);
23      disp('Something wrong happened');
24  end
```

Note in the example the use of the try–catch statement: the catch is useful for
closing the file in case something goes wrong. Let's suppose an error occurs before
the script closes the file. In this case, you can have no more access to the file because
the operating system acts as though someone were still using it.

We test the function by reading the file howmany2.m and then by reading a
nonexistent file.

```
>> DisplayFile('howmany2.m')
function[b]= howmany2(A)
b=0;
for i=1:size(A,1);
    for j=1:size(A,2)
        if A(i,j)>0.2 & A(i,j)<0.3;
            b=b+1;
        end
    end
end

>> DisplayFile('LotsOfMoney')
Unable to open file 'LotsOfMoney'
```

The previous function explains how to obtain a string from each line. With such a string it is then possible to do all the processing you need. However, let's suppose you want to obtain the data in a matrix, ready for computation. This can be done, but it is important to know how the content of the file is formatted. For this reason we show here a function that saves the data in a specific format, and then we show a function that reads these data.

Let's suppose you run an experiment that investigates iconic memory (Sperling 1960). In the experiment we present to the subject an n by m matrix on the screen. During the trials, certain cells of the matrix are filled with an arbitrary symbol (e.g., a cross). The matrix stays on the screen for just a short time, and the subject has to tell, by means of a mouse click, the locations of the crosses presented on the screen. At each mouse click we save the mouse position and the time interval (in milliseconds) between the moment the matrix disappeared and the mouse click. Let's suppose we store our data in a structure named STIM, with the following fields: nStim, time, and Mpos. We can save the data in a readable manner using the following function.

Listing 4.16

```
1   function SaveStrangeFormat(filename, STIM)
2
3   % function SaveStrangeFormat(filename, STIM)
4   %
5   % reads text file and display it to the console
6   %
7   % INPUT :    filename = a string containing the file name
8   %        :    STIM = a vector of struct cointaining the following fields
9   %        :      nStim = the stimulus number
10  %        :      MPos = a Matrix 2 x Npos of mouse clicks
11  %        :      time = a vector 1 x Npos of time for each click
12  % Author: Borgo, Soranzo, Grassi 2012
13
14  try
15      if ~exist(filename)       % control if the file doesn't exist
16          fid=fopen(filename,'w');    % open file to write
17          if fid == -1               % it can be not possible
18              disp(sprintf('Unable to write file ''%s'' ',filename));
19          else                       % in this case file opens correctly
20              for i=1:length(STIM)    % write data loop
21                  fprintf(fid,'Stimolous number: %d \n',STIM(i).nStim);
22                  fprintf(fid,'\t Time (ms) \t Mouse Position\n');
23                  for j=1:length(STIM(i).time)
24                      fprintf(fid,'\t %4d \t \t x=%4.0f y=%4.0f \n',...
25                      STIM(i).time(j),STIM(i).MPos(j,1),STIM(i).MPos(j,2));
26                  end
27              end
28              fclose(fid);               % close the file
29              disp('File saved correctly!');
30          end
31      else
32          disp('The file already exists, please change file name');
33      end
34  catch
35      fclose(fid);
36      disp('Something wrong happened');
37  end
```

The function has the same structure of the previous one. The difference is in the use of "open" at line 16, where it is specified that the file is open to write something into it (we added the "w" *perm* character). Pay attention as well to the multiple use of the `fprintf` function to write the data into a file in a formatted way.

We test this function in two steps: we first create the data, then we write the data into a file. We then repeatedly look into the file using the function `DisplayFile` that we created earlier. We use a custom file extension.

```
>> STIM.nStim=1; STIM.time=[123 576 1034];
>> STIM.MPos=[23, 45; 345,15; 256,176];
>> SaveStrangeFormat('TestSave.myf', STIM);
File saved correctly!
>> DisplayFile('TestSave.myf')
Stimolous number: 1
        Time (ms)        Mouse Position
          123            x=  23 y=   45
          576            x= 345 y=   15
         1034            x= 256 y=  176
```

If you copied the example with no errors, everything should work properly. Here, we want to go back to the function and outline the `fprintf` format at line 24. Type:

```
>> STIM
STIM =
    nStim: 1
     time: [123 576 1034]
     MPos: [3x2 double]
```

Note that MPos is a *double* matrix, which is why in the `fprintf` format we uses the `%f` identifier.

Now let's make a further step and import the data from an odd file format, like the previous one. We want to highlight that it is necessary to know exactly how data are formatted and their meaning to import them correctly. Let's take a look at the following function.

Listing 4.17

```
1    function [STIM]=ImportStrangeFormat(filename)
2
3    % function ImportStrangeFormat(filename)
4    %
5    % it reads a text file and displays it on screen
6    %
7    % INPUT :    filename = a string containing the file name
8    % OUTPUT:    STIM = is a vector of struct cointaining the following fields
9    %       :      nStim = stimulus number
10   %       :      MPos = Matrix 2 x Npos of mouse clicks
11   %       :      time = vector 1 x Npos of time for each click
12   % Author: Borgo, Soranzo, Grassi 2012
13
14   try
15       fid=fopen(filename);         % open file
16       if fid == -1                 % it can be not possible
17           disp(sprintf('Unable to write file ''%s'' ',filename));
18       else                         % in this case file opens correctly
19           NStmp=0;
20           while ~feof(fid)         % Start loop. End if eof is reached
21               NStmp=NStmp+1;       % Update the number of NStmp
22               sn=textscan(fid,'Stimulus number: %d'); % read the line
23               STIM(NStmp).nStim=sn{1};     % Save the stimulous number
24               fgetl(fid);          % jump a line
25               STIMtemp=textscan(fid,'\t %4d \t x=%4.0f y=%4.0f');
26               STIM(NStmp).time=STIMtemp{1};       % Create the struct vect
27               STIM(NStmp).MPos=[STIMtemp{2}, STIMtemp{3}];
28           end
29           fclose(fid);             % close the file
30       end
31   catch
32       fclose(fid);
33       disp('Something wrong happened');
34   end
```

Analysis

Line 22: The textscan function is used. textscan skips the string 'Stimulus number:' and reads the number. It converts the number as described by the specifier (%d) and then puts the number in the cell sn. On line 23, the value is stored in the structure.

Line 24: We skip the file line containing the string ' Time (ms) Mouse Position'.

Line 25: We read the following numbers according to the specified format. Note that since textscan finds the same format, it reads multiple lines. The result is put in a cell.

Line 26 and 27: The cell values are put into the structure.

Line 28: The counter NStmp is updated.

Now test the function by typing the following lines:

```
>> STIM1= ImportStrangeFormat('TestSave.myf');
STIM1 =
     nStim: 1
      time: [3x1 int32]
      MPos: [3x2 double]
>> STIM.MPos-STIM1.MPos
ans =
      0         0
      0         0
      0         0
```

As you can see, the data are loaded correctly (remember that STIM was defined to test the SaveStrangeFormat function).

Guidelines for a Good Programming Style

Here we report a few guidelines for a good programming style. When you begin to write a new program, first you have to address the problem and find out a way to solve it, i.e., the algorithm. This means that you have to decide on the basic tools you need to solve the problem. Then you have to follow a design process that decomposes the problem into subordinate problems. This helps you to spot the recursive tasks of your problem and the functions that you need to create. Finally, you have to translate or convert the algorithm into a MATLAB script and test it. This type of approach is called *top-down*. Your ability to use all of MATLAB's potential is limited by your experience. The more you increase your knowledge, the more you will be creative and efficient in solving problems.

In any case, it is important to follow at least some general guidelines that can be learned from expert programmers. Sometimes you can be impatient to get on with your job. However, just a little attention to your programming style can help you later in your work. The goal of these guidelines is to help you in producing code that is clearer and easier to understand and update. If the code can be easily read and understood by yourself and by other users, you can probably quickly modify it and control it to spot where any errors are. These recommendations apply to any programming language. Here, they are simply adapted to the development and writing of MATLAB scripts.

Writing Code

As we wrote previously, the best way to write a long and complex program is to assemble it from well-designed small programs (usually functions). The idea is an IKEA-like programming style: a lot of small parts, each specialized for a specific task, that can be assembled modularly.

So the basic points for modularity are:

- Small and well-designed functions are more likely to be reused by other applications and programs.
- Make the interaction clear: define well the input and output arguments and their format. Structures can be used to avoid a long list of input or output arguments.
- Use a defensive programming approach. This means that the input variables should be controlled. Check whether the input variable is of a type that the function is expecting. For example, if you are writing a function that works with numbers, check whether the input variable is a number, a logical, or a string. This can be done using the conditional structures (i.e., if–else, switch–case) at the beginning of the script. For example:

```
1  function [outvar]=ControlInput(x,filename)
2
3  if ~isnumeric(x)
4      return; % if x is not a number exit from the function
5      disp('No numeric input was given') % communicate the error to the user
6  end
7  if isempty(filename)
8      filename = 'Test' % If the filename is forgotten give a default
9                        % provide with a default name
   end
```

- Insert a default condition if necessary.
- Communicate the errors to the user.

A good visual appearance of your code also helps you to focus on the structure of your script. Therefore:

- Use indentation. Indentation helps you to find where the loops and the conditionals begin and end. MATLAB has a built-in smart indenting tool. Just select the code you are writing, right-click the mouse button, and select *smart indent.*
- Comment your script. Write a comment at the beginning of the script that tells you what the script does. In addition, comment the crucial points of the program. In any case, pay attention to the following:
  - Comment while you are writing your code. Comments that are added later are often confusing. Commenting while you are programming helps you to organize your algorithm/code.
  - Avoid useless or unnecessary comments like:

    ```
    num = 2; % set num equal to 2
    ```

- Variables often have a meaning. Therefore:
  - Use meaningful variable names. For example, use the names in use in your research field.
  - Use long variable names if necessary. The variable names can be as long as you desire. In this book we use the capital letters to separate parts of a compound variable name: responseTime. The same result can be obtained with the underscore (e.g., response_time).

Debug

Errors, like death and taxes, are certain: you will surely produce them. The process of detecting and correcting errors is called *debugging*. MATLAB has an efficient tool for debugging your script. Before explaining this tool, let's have a look at the most frequent errors in MATLAB. They are mainly of three types:

- Typos (e.g., sim(t) rather than sin(t));
- Syntax errors in function calls (e.g., wrong number of parameters)
- Algorithmic errors.

The most difficult errors to spot and fix are the algorithmic ones. Basically, if you make an algorithmic error, you obtain unexpected results when you run your script. Such a type of error is also known as a "run-time error." They are difficult to detect because the function's local workspace is lost when the error forces the return to the MATLAB workspace. However, the MATLAB debugging tool overcomes this problem.

The MATLAB debugger can be activated in the MATLAB editor by putting one (or more) breakpoints in the script. When you run your script, MATLAB stops temporarily at the line where the breakpoint was positioned. Once MATLAB stops, the prompt k>> appears in the workspace. Now you can see the values of all the variables of your program, type commands, etc. Then you can resume the execution of your script until the next breakpoint.

Setting breakpoints is simple. Just go to the left of the target line and click on – (just to the right of the number line). Here we show how the debugger works using the function statTwo.

Action and description	Graphical visualization
Set one breakpoint at line 20 of the script statTwo. A red circle appears to the right of the line in the MATLAB editor	In the editor: ``` 19 - Nelem = sum(i); 20 ● mea=sum(x(i))/Nelem; 21 - vari=sum(x(i).^2)/Nelem; ```
Test the function	In the command window type: `>> statTwo(rand(1,20))`
MATLAB runs the function and stops at line 20 At line 20 a green arrow appears, indicating that MATLAB has temporary stopped at line 20. In the command window appears the number of the line followed by the commands on that line The k>> prompt waits for your (possible) input	In the editor: ``` 19 - Nelem = sum(i); 20 ●⇨ mea=sum(x(i))/Nelem; 21 - vari=sum(x(i).^2)/Nelem; ``` In the command window: ``` >> statTwo(rand(1,20)) 20 mea=sum(x(i))/Nelem; K>> ```

(continued)

(continued)

Action and description	Graphical visualization

You can show the values of the variables used in the function. Line 19 has already been computed by MATLAB, so the variable Nelem exists, while the variable mea does not exist yet	In the command window:
	`K>> Nelem`
	`Nelem =`
	`    20`
	`K>> mea`
	`??? Undefined function or variable 'mea'.`

Now, you can run your function line by line. Just click on the step by step button	In the Editor:

The debugger goes to the next command line. The mea variable is created and calculated	In the Editor:
	`19 -    Nelem = sum(i);`
	`20 ●    mea=sum(x(i))/Nelem;`
	`21 - ➪ vari=sum(x(i).^2)/Nelem;`
	
	In the command window
	`K>> mea`
	`mea =`
	`    0.4972`

You can continue in step-by-step mode, or run the function or script till the next breakpoint. If there are no more breakpoints, the script is executed till the end	In the editor:
To clear the breakpoints click on the red circles or on the clear breakpoints button	In the editor:

MATLAB also provides other tools to help you in writing and managing your M-files. These tools are *M-Lint Code Check* and *Profiler* Reports. They are briefly described in the following paragraphs:

- The M-Lint Code Check Report displays a message for each line of an M-file and determines whether the program can be improved. For example, a frequent M-Lint message is that a variable is defined but never used in the M-file. To activate this tool just select TOOLS and then M-LINT report in the MATLAB toolbar. For further information refer to the MATLAB online help.
- The Profiler helps you to improve the performance of your M-files. When you run a MATLAB statement or an M-file, the Profiler produces a report about the time spent by each function and step of your code. To activate the Profiler just type `profile on` at the prompt. Then you have to type `profile viewer` to stop the Profiler and display the results in the Profiler window. Try to type the following statements:

```
>> A = rand(10);
>> profile on;
>> howmany2(A);
>> profile viewer;
```

A window opens and displays the time used to execute the function howmany2. If the M-script calls more than one function, a list of all these functions also appears. You can look into each function by clicking on the function name. For further information refer to MATLAB help.

Summary

- A script is a list of commands. Use the MATLAB editor to write, edit, and save your scripts. The extension of a MATLAB script is *.m*
- Comments are useful for understanding what a script does. Comments are preceded by the % character.
- An M-script can be run by typing its filename at the MATLAB prompt.
- A script starting with the keyword `function` is a function. A function can have input and output arguments. Input and output arguments are the way the function communicates with the variables in the workspace.
- Comments after the first line of a function are displayed in the command window when the *help* of the function is called for.
- The variables used within a function are *local*: they exist only within the function. In contrast, a global variable can be used everywhere.
- The command `nargin` indicates how many input arguments are used in a particular function call, while `varargin` is a cell matrix variable that collects all the inputs.
- `if-else` executes different groups of statements according to whether a condition is true or false.
- `switch` allows the script to make choices between different cases.
- `try-catch` attempts to execute a block of statements and catch errors.
- The for loop repeats a set of commands a fixed number of times. The for form is:

```
for start:step:stop
     Statements
end
```

- The while loop repeats a set of commands an undefined number of times as long as the specified condition is satisfied. The while form is:

```
while condition
     Statements
end
```

- Loops can be nested. The `break` command can be used to quit the (innermost) loop.
- Use logicals and matrix operations whenever possible.

- It is possible to import/export data in specific formats using commands dedicated to file management: `fopen`, `fclose`, `fprintf`, `textread`.
- Use your own programming style, but remember to write your code as clearly as possible. Clear scripts are more maintainable. Prefer many short functions to a few large ones (i.e., use modular programming).
- Use the MATLAB debugger, profiler, and M-Lint tools to support your programming and to find errors.

Exercises

1. Write an M-script that executes the following for loops:

Question	Solution
| 1.1. Write a loop that generates a column vector A with ten random numbers. Then create a 10×4 matrix having A as its first column, with the remaining columns the product of the first column and the column number | ```
1  for ind = 1:10
2      A(ind)=rand;
3  end
4  for ind2= 1:4
5      B(1:10,ind2) = A*ind2;
6  end
``` |
| 1.2. Write the vector<br><br>color=[2,1,3,0,1,3,1,0,2]<br><br>Write a loop to display in the command window the corresponding color name as follows: 0=yellow; 1=red; 2=green; 3=blue | ```
1  color =[2,1,3,0,1,3,1,0,2];
2  cName ={'yellow','red','green',blue'};
3  for ind=1:length(color)
4      disp(cName{color(ind)+1});
5  end
```<br><br>Note: The values of the color vector are used as index for the cName cell. However, the vector also contains zeros, and for this reason a +1 is used |
| 1.3 Generate a cell with ten element. Each element is a vector of random length (between 1 and 10) containing ones if the length is odd and zeros if the length is even | ```
1  NumOfVector = 10
2  for i = 1:NumOfVector
3      Vlen=floor(rand*10)+1;
4      V{i} = ones(1,Vlen)*rem(Vlen,2);
5  end
```<br><br>Note: To obtain a random number between 1 and 10, we create a random number between 0 and 1 (using rand), then we multiply it by 10, and take the floor to obtain an integer |

2. Repeat Exercise 1.2 using a while loop.
3. Repeat Exercise 1.2 by substituting line 4 with the `switch-case` command.
4. Exit from the for loop of Exercise 1.3 if the vector length is equal to 7 (use `if` and `break`).
5. Rewrite Exercise 4 using `while`.
6. Write a function that displays the bar and the error bar graphics in the same figure having as input the x value, the y value, the color of the bar and the length of the error. Inside your function use the MATLAB function bar and errorbar.
```

A Brick for an Experiment

Now we have sufficient knowledge to write the brick script. As we wrote previously in this chapter, when you plan to program an experiment, there are two choices: you can write a single long program or you can write several subprograms and one main program that calls each of the subprograms. For the brick we use an approach similar to the second.

Let's begin by writing an M-script with only comments in it and save it as SexulerExp.m:

Listing 4.18

```
1  % M-script to realize a experiment based on the crossmodal perception
2  % The experiment first performed by Sekuler, Sekuler and Lau (1997)
3  % Author: Borgo, Soranzo, Grassi 2012
4  % EXPERIMENT'S SETTINGS
5  % STIMULI (SELECTION)
6  % STIMULI (CREATION)
7  % STIMULI (PRESENTATION)
8  % COLLECT SUBJECT'S ANSWER
9  % STORE RESULTS
```

Remember that comments are important. It is important to comment your program so that you know, when you read your code after a certain time, what the various parts of the code were there for. Here, the comments highlight the crucial points of the program.

Now we can write one of the corollary functions and program a function that writes an event table. As we have written in this chapter, the majority of experiments in psychology are fixed-stimuli experiments, i.e., we know in advance the stimuli we are going to present, how many times we are going to present them, and even the random sequence of trials that we will present to the subject. This is an event table: the storyline of the sequence of events that occur during the experiment, in other words, a place where the particular stimulus we have to present in each successive trial is written. In MATLAB, the event table is a matrix organized in rows and columns, where each row represents one trial and each column represents one variable. The event table we design here has the trial number in the leftmost column and in the right columns, one variable that represents the kind of disc motion (continuous or with the stop) and one variable that represents the presence/absence of the sound. Once we have set and written the event table, when we are running the experiment, at the moment we have to present a stimulus to the subject, we read the content of the event table for that specific trial so that we know which stimulus is to be presented.

Let's write the function `GenerateEventTable`. This function will receive as input the conditions of the experiment, the number of repetitions for each condition, and a logical value that informs the function whether the trials are to be written in a random or fixed order.[2] The conditions have to be passed to the function in matrix form. We define a matrix in which each row represents one combination of factors and each column represents one factor. In brief, for the experiment that we implement in the brick, the variable "conditions" could be written as follows:

```
>> cond = [1, 1; 1, 2; 2, 1; 2, 2]
```

Here the 1, 1 content of the first row represents the continuous motion (1, left column) without sound (1, right column), the 1, 2 content of the second row represents the continuous motion (1, left column) with sound (2, right column), and so on.

Listing 4.19

```
1    function EventTable = GenerateEventTable(conds, repetitions, isfixed)
2
3    % function GenerateEventTable(conds, repetitions, isfixed)
4    %
5    % reads text file and displays it to the console
6    %
7    % INPUT :    conds = vector containing factors/number
8    %       :    repetitions = number of repetitions
9    %       :    isfixed = 0: random order  1: fixed order
10   % OUTPUT:    EventTable = is a vector of struct
11   %
12   % Author: Borgo, Soranzo, Grassi 2012
13
14   EventTable = [];
15   for i=1:repetitions
16       EventTable = [EventTable; conds];
17   end
18
19   TotalNumberOfTrials = length(EventTable(:, 1));
20
21   if isfixed == 1
22       FixedTrialSequence = (1:TotalNumberOfTrials)';
23       EventTable = [FixedTrialSequence, EventTable];
24   else
25       RandomTrialSequence = randperm(TotalNumberOfTrials)';
26       EventTable = [RandomTrialSequence, EventTable];
27       EventTable = sortrows(EventTable, 1);
28   end
29
```

---

[2] It is often useful to run an experiment in fixed order, in particular when you are debugging the experiment.

Analysis

Let's analyze the function. As you can see, at lines 14–17, the function
GenerateEventTable repeatedly copies the condition variable to itself. This is
done for the number of times the stimuli will be repeated during the experiment.
This copying process returns a variable that is very similar to the final event table
(although without the trial number). At line 19 we calculate the number of trials.
The number of trials is equal to the number of rows of the EventTable variable
created at line 16. Lines 21–28 control the isfixed variable, and according to its
value, write the final event table. If isfixed is equal to 1, the function appends to the
left of the event table a successive number (i.e., the trial number) but leaves the rest
of the EventTable variable unchanged. In contrast, if isfixed is equal to 0 (i.e., the
event table has to be sorted in random order), the function first generates a random
sequence of TotalNumberOfTrials by means of the function randperm (see row
n. 26). Successively, the function appends to the left of the EventTable matrix the
vector just created (row 26). Finally, the content of the EventTable matrix is sorted
according its leftmost column (column number 1), i.e., the column that contains the
trial number written in random order. This sorting randomizes the rows of the event
table, i.e., randomizes the trial sequence of our experiment.

Now let's return to the main script (i.e., SekulerExp) and modify it as follows:

Listing 4.20

```
1    % M-script to realize a experiment based on the crossmodal perception
2    % The experiment first performed by Sekuler, Sekuler and Lau (1997)
3    % Author: Borgo, Soranzo, Grassi 2012
4    % EXPERIMENT'S SETTINGS
5
6    % set the experiment details
7    conditions = [1, 1; 1, 2; 2, 1; 2, 2];
8    repetitions = 20;
9    EventTable = GenerateEventTable(conditions, repetitions, isfixed);
10   TotalNumberOfTrials = length(EventTable(:, 1));
11
12   % STIMULI (SELECTION)
13   % STIMULI (CREATION)
14   % STIMULI (PRESENTATION)
15   % COLLECT SUBJECT'S ANSWER
16   % STORE RESULTS
```

We add the settings (rows 7–8), we call for the GenerateEventTable function
(row 9), and calculate the number of trials by reading the event table (row 10).

Let's take the script a step further. As we have written in this chapter, fixed-
stimuli experiments can be programmed with a for loop. We can now write the
main for loop driving the experiment. In the for loop, each time we make one cycle,
the subject performs one trial. Therefore, each time we make one cycle we generate

the appropriate audio/video stimulus that we have to present by reading the content of the `EventTable` matrix:

Listing 4.21

```
1    % M-script to realize an experiment based on the crossmodal perception
2    % The experiment first performed by Sekuler, Sekuler and Lau (1997)
3    % Author: Borgo, Soranzo, Grassi 2012
4    % EXPERIMENT'S SETTINGS
5
6    % set the experiment details
7    conditions = [1, 1; 1, 2; 2, 1; 2, 2];
8    repetitions = 20;
9    if nsub == 0
10       repetitions = 1;
11   end
12   EventTable = GenerateEventTable(conditions, repetitions, isfixed);
13   TotalNumberOfTrials = length(EventTable(:, 1));
14   for trial = 1:TotalNumberOfTrials
15
16       % STIMULI (SELECTION)
17       VideoStimulusToPlay = EventTable(trial, 2);
18       SoundStimulusToPlay = EventTable(trial, 3);
19
20       % STIMULI (CREATION)
21       % STIMULI (PRESENTATION)
22       % COLLECT SUBJECT'S ANSWER
23   end
24   % STORE RESULTS
```

At rows 14–23 there is a for loop that keeps the experiment running trial after trial. At rows 17–18, within the for loop, we read the event table to know the stimulus that we have to generate and present to the subject. Note that we use the step variable "trial" as index to read the content of the event table matrix. Moreover, in the script we introduced a feature that may help the experimenter (see rows 9–11). Often, when we run an experiment, it may be useful to have the possibility to run a short version of it. Let's insert this option in our program (lines 9–11). Here we use a rule that is similar to that used in the E-Prime and MEL software (Schneider 1990; Schneider et al. 2002). If the subject number is equal to zero, the subject runs the complete experiment (i.e., s/he observes all stimuli) but each stimulus is repeated only once and no data will be written in the data file (see later bricks).

Note that for the moment, there is no way to tell the program the subject number as well as the `isfixed` value. These will be given later through the graphical interface. Note also that we wrote the conditional if after the number of repetitions has been declared and before the `GenerateEventTable` function. Otherwise, the operation would have no effect.

References

Boring EG (1961) Fechner: inadvertent founder of psychophysics. Psychometrika 26:3–8

Fechner GT (1889) Elemente der Psychophysik, 2nd edn. Breitkopf & Härtel, Leipzig

Gescheider GA (2003) Psychophysics: the fundamentals, 3rd edn. Lawrence Erlbaum Associates, Hillsdale

Schneider W (1990) MEL user's guide: computer techniques for real time psychological experimentation. Psychology Software Tools, Pittsburgh

Schneider W, Eschman A, Zuccolotto A (2002) E-prime user's guide. Psychology Software Tools, Pittsburgh

Sperling G (1960) The information available in brief visual presentations. Psychol Monogr 74:1–29

Suggested Readings

Hahn BD, Valentine DT (2009) Essential MATLAB for engineers and scientists, 4th edn. Elsevier/ Academic Press, Amsterdam

Sayood K (2007) Learning programming using MATLAB. Morgan & Claypool, San Rafael, CA

Singh YK, Chaudhuri BB (2008) MATLAB programming. Prentice-Hall of India, New Delhi

Chapter 5
A Better Sound

MATLAB is an extremely powerful tool for dealing with sounds. You can use MATLAB for sound synthesis as well as for sound analysis. It is possible to create your own custom sound from scratch, and it is also possible to edit at will an existing sound. Furthermore, MATLAB can be used to understand several acoustical characteristics of digital sounds. This chapter shows how to do all of these.

Generate a Sound

First, let's generate a white noise (i.e., a random succession of amplitude values) having a duration of 1 s and a sample rate of 44,100 Hz and then play it.[1]

Listing 5.1

```
1  sr = 44100;    % the sample rate in Hz
2  d = 1;    % the duration of the noise (in sec)
3  noise = rand(1, round(sr*d));
4  noise = noise*2; % expansion
5  noise = noise-1; % translation
6  sound(noise, sr)
```

Lines 1 and 2 set the sample rate and the sound duration. Line 3 implements the vector noise; to the `rand()` function we have passed the product of the sample rate and the duration of the sound in seconds. This operation will be repeated several times in this chapter; it returns the array length of the digital sound, at the desired sample rate. To prevent MATLAB warnings such as "`Warning: Size vector`

---

[1] Although MATLAB enables the generation of sounds at several sample rates, 44,100 Hz is the most used. This is, for example, the sample rate of an audio CD.

M. Borgo et al., *MATLAB for Psychologists*,
DOI 10.1007/978-1-4614-2197-9_5, © Springer Science+Business Media, LLC 2012

should be a row vector with integer elements", it may be convenient to round the result of this multiplication. Lines 4 and 5 expand and translate the amplitude values of the white noise within the −1/+1 range. We need to do this because MATLAB wants sounds to range within the −1/+1 limits.

The next thing we may wish to do is to synthesize a pure tone, i.e., a sinusoidal tone. We now synthesize a pure tone of 1,000 Hz and 1 sec duration (a *must* in psychoacoustics).

Listing 5.2

```
1  sr = 44100; % the sample rate in Hz
2  f = 1000;   % the tone's frequency (in Hz)
3  d = 1; % the tone's duration
4  t = linspace(0, d, sr*d); % a time vector
5  tone = sin(2*pi*f*t); % the actual, final tone
6  sound(tone, sr);
```

In Listing 5.2, we calculate the sine of an argument that completes f cycles (i.e., 2*pi) in time t. The time t has been represented digitally, with an array starting at 0 and arriving at the specific sample rate (44,100 Hz) at the overall sound's duration. With these few command lines, we can create different pure tones by changing f and d.

Now let's play the tone twice using the command sound twice in rapid succession.

```
>> sound(tone, sr)
>> sound(tone, sr)
```

If your fingers were fast enough you could hear a single unpleasant tone rather than two tones in succession. This is because the sound function works asynchronically; in other words, the second tone would be played while the first tone is still playing.

There are two ways to avoid this. The first is to use (wavplay)[2] which lets you decide whether you want to work synchronically ('sync' parameter) or asynchronically ('async' parameter). Use the function in the following way to play the tones synchronically (i.e., the second tone is played only after the first tone has ended).

```
wavplay(tone, sr, 'sync');
wavplay(tone, sr);
```

If you pass the parameter 'async' instead of 'sync', you will get the same unpleasant output resulting from the use of sound(). Another way to avoid the asynchrony problem is to use the sound functions included in PsychToolbox. These functions will be described in the chapters dedicated to this toolbox.

The tone we have created can be saved in your computer as a wav file by means of the wavwrite() function. wavwrite() transforms the array into a wav sound file.

---

[2] Note that wavplay is only for use with windows machines.

Note that if you do not want a clipped sound, the array's values should range between -1 and $+1$. wavwrite() quantizes the values of the given vector according to the number of bits you are using (16 by default). This means that if you are working at 16 bits, the lower value without clipping is $-1 + 1/(2^{nbit-1})$. In the pure tone example, the sin() function returns values in the range -1 to $+1$, and therefore all -1s are clipped when playing the file. If you multiply the sound array by the minimum possible quantized value, i.e., $-1 + 1/(2^{nbit-1})$, then the sound amplitude will be compressed into a sound file without clipping.

```
>> wavwrite(tone, sr, 'my_first_tone')
Warning: Data clipped during write to file:my_first_tone
> In wavwrite>PCM_Quantize at 247
  In wavwrite>write_wavedat at 267
  In wavwrite at 112
```
Matlab clips the lower values and gives a warning message. For common usage, the error is insignificant (a quantization step). If you wish not to obtain a warning message, you can rescale the signal using the following formula:

```
>> nbits=16; tone=tone*(1-1/(2^nbits-1));
>> wavwrite(tone, sr, 'my_first_tone')
```

We are now ready for something more complex: let's build a harmonic tone that is the sum of two or more pure tones having a harmonic relation. Let's create a complex tone with three harmonics and with a fundamental frequency of 250 Hz:

Listing 5.3

```
1   sr = 44100; % the sample rate in Hz
2   f0 = 250;   % the frequency of the tone in Hz
3   d = 1;      % the tone's duration in sec
4   t = linspace(0, d, sr*d);   % a time vector
5   first_component = sin(2*pi*f0*t);
6   second_component = sin(2*pi*(f0*2)*t);
7   third_component = sin(2*pi*(f0*3)*t);
8   harmonic = first_component + second_component + third_component;
9   harmonic = harmonic/max(abs(harmonic));
10  sound(harmonic, sr);
```

In Listing 5.3 we have generated three sine waves (lines 5, 6, and 7) and then added the simple tones together to create a complex tone. Line 9 needs a bit of clarification. Since the complex variable implemented in line 7 results from the sum of three components, its amplitude exceeds the $-1/+1$ range. Therefore, if we play the tone as it is, it will result in a distorted sound (and MATLAB does not warn you about this distortion!). To avoid any distortions, we need to normalize the sound, which is what line 8 does. The normalization is done by dividing the harmonic variable by its maximum absolute value.

Another solution to the distortion problem is to use the `soundsc()` function, which automatically scales the sound's amplitude within the −1/+1 range no matter how "large" the sound's amplitude is. So lines 8 and 9 could have been replaced by the following code:

```
soundsc(harmonic, sr);
```

We are now able to produce pure and complex tones of any desired frequency and duration. By the same token, we can now produce an inharmonic tone, i.e., a tone whose frequency components are not in a harmonic relation.

Listing 5.4 generates an inharmonic tone:

Listing 5.4

```
1   sr = 44100; % the sample rate in Hz
2   f1 = 200;   % the frequency of the tone in Hz
3   f2 = 250;
4   f3 = 380;
5   d = 1;      % the tone's duration in sec
6   t = linspace(0, d, sr*d);   % a time vector
7   first_component = sin(2*pi*f1*t);
8   second_component = sin(2*pi*f2*t);
9   third_component = sin(2*pi*f3*t);
10  inharmonic = first_component + second_component + third_component;
11  soundsc(inharmonic, sr);
```

In this example, we have solved the distortion problem by using `soundsc()` instead of normalizing the sound. Let's now change the timbre of the complex tone by changing its waveform so that the sound is, for example, a sawtooth wave. In sawtooth waves, the amplitude of each successive harmonic is half of the amplitude of the previous harmonic. Therefore, we have to multiply the amplitude of each successive harmonic by a factor ½, ¼, 1/8 and so on. Let us start with the following code:

Listing 5.5

```
1   sr = 44100; % the sample rate in Hz
2   f0 = 250;   % the frequency of the tone in Hz
3   d = 1;      % the tone's duration in sec
4   t = linspace(0, d, sr*d);   % a time vector
5   first_component = sin(2*pi*f0*t); % full amplitude
6   second_component = 1/2 * sin(2*pi*(f0*2)*t); % 1/2 amplitude
7   third_component = 1/4* sin(2*pi*(f0*3)*t); % 1/4 amplitude
8   complex = first_component + second_component + third_component;
```

If we plot the first 10 ms of the sound (i.e., the first 441 samples, since we are working at a sample rate of 44,100 Hz), we see that the waveform does not look like a sawtooth wave (Fig. 5.1):

```
plot(complex(1:441))
```

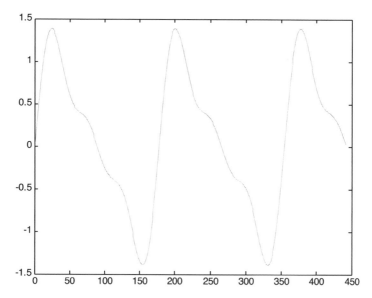

Fig. 5.1 A sawtooth wave with a limited number of harmonics

This is because of the limited number of harmonics we have used to generate the wave. However, if we make the complex tone with, let's say, 20 harmonics, then the waveform's shape will be more sawtooth-like. The following code listing shows how to do it by means of a `for` cycle:

Listing 5.6

```
1  f0=250; amplitude = 1;
2  for i = 1:20
3       component(i, :) = amplitude * sin(2*pi*(f0*i)*t);
4       amplitude = amplitude/2;
5  end
6  complex = sum(component);
7  complex = complex/max(abs(complex));
```

In each `for` cycle, the amplitude of successive components is halved. If you now plot the first 441 samples, you can check that the waveform is much smoother than the previous one. Moreover, if we plot some of the single components (the first three, for example), we can get an idea of the summation process we have implemented. Listing 5.7 does the job.

Listing 5.7

M-script	Graphical Result
| ```
1   figure;
2   for i= 1:4
3     subplot(2, 2, i);
4     if i ~= 4
5       plot(component(i, 1:441));
6     else
7       plot(complex(1:441));
8     end
9     axis([1, 441, -1, 1])
10  end
``` | 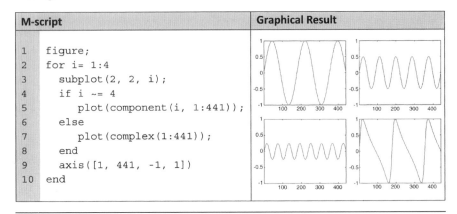 |

Multiple Sounds

Sometimes it can be useful to create short melodies, i.e., sequences of tones. In order to do this, we have to concatenate the various arrays of the tones (and silences) we want to put in our little tune. Listing 5.8 plays the notes middle C, D, and E, followed by a pause of 1 s and then the note C again.

Listing 5.8

```
1   sr = 44100;  % the sample rate in Hz
2   d = .5;
3   f_do = 261.6;
4   f_re = 293.6;
5   f_mi = 329.6;
6   t = linspace(0, d, sr*d); % a time vector
7   do = sin(2*pi*f_do*t);
8   re = sin(2*pi*f_re*t);
9   mi = sin(2*pi*f_mi*t);
10  silence = zeros(1, sr*d);
11  soundsc([do, re, mi, silence, do], sr);
```

Let's run a more "psychological" example: let us play the pulsation threshold example. The pulsation threshold (Houtgast 1972) is a case of auditory continuity. The stimulus we need to synthesize is a succession of brief noises and tones, for example a noise followed by a tone, followed by a noise, and so on. If the intensity of the tone is low in comparison with that of the noise, the tone is heard as continuous, i.e., the tone is heard even within the noise (even though there is no tone within the noise).
```

Let's synthesize the tone and the noise:

```
>> sr = 44100;
>> f = 1000;
>> d = .2;
>> t = linspace(0, d, d*sr);
>> tone = sin(2*pi*f*t);
>> noise = (rand(1, sr*d)*2)-1;
```

We have now to reduce the amplitude level of the tone. Here, we first reduce the tone's amplitude 1/100 (i.e., 40 dB) from its original amplitude and successively create the noise–tone sequence:

```
>> tone = tone * .01;
>> sequence = [noise, tone];
>> sequence = [sequence, sequence]; % sequence of 4 sounds
>> sequence = [sequence, sequence]; % sequence of 8 sounds
>> sequence = [sequence, sequence]; % sequence of 16 sounds
>> sequence = [sequence, sequence]; % sequence of 32 sounds
>> sound(sequence, sr)
```

You should be able to hear the tone as continuous within the noise bands (although you should be well aware that there is no tone within the noise bands!).

Let's suppose you need to synthesize a number of tones sounding together in time, but one (or more) of the tones needs to have just a little onset asynchrony so that it can be heard as popping out from the other tones sounding together (Darwin and Ciocca 1992). Here we implement this example with three tones and add a little onset asynchrony to the second and third tones. First, we add three tones together so that they begin simultaneously in time.

```
>> sr = 44100;
>> f1 = 300;
>> f2 = 550;
>> f3 = 640;
>> d = 5;
>> t = linspace(0, d, d*sr);
>> tone1 = sin(2*pi*f1*t);
>> tone2 = sin(2*pi*f2*t);
>> tone3 = sin(2*pi*f3*t);
>> complex = tone1+tone2+tone3;
>> soundsc(tone1+tone2+tone3, sr)
```

Now we add the temporal offset to the second and third tones:

```
>> offset_dur = .5;
>> offset = zeros(1, sr*offset_dur);
>> tone1 = [tone1, offset, offset];
>> tone2 = [offset, tone2, offset];
>> tone3 = [offset, offset, tone3];
>> soundsc(tone1+tone2+tone3, sr)
```

If you listen to the sound, you may note that the individual components are indistinguishable in the first example. However, in the second example they can be easily distinguished. This is because of the onset asynchrony of the tones.

Manipulating a Sound's Level

With MATLAB, it is possible to manipulate precisely the relative levels of sounds. In fact, the absolute level of a sound depends on several factors such as the sound card of your computer, the headphones, the loudspeakers, the amplifiers, and so on. The digital synthesis moves within a dynamic range of 2^{bits} (2^{16}, i.e., 96 dB, is a very common dynamic range for most PCs). In digital audio, 0 is arbitrarily set as the maximum level, and all softer levels are represented with negative numbers. In practice, a sound whose level is 0 dB is louder than a sound whose level is −10 dB. For example, let us play a tone twice but the second time 10 dB softer:

Listing 5.9

```
1   sr = 44100;   % the sample rate in Hz
2   f = 500;      % the frequency of the tone in Hz
3   d = 1;        % Sound duration in sec
4   t = linspace(0, d, sr*d); % a time vector
5   tone = sin(2*pi*f*t);
6   softer_tone = tone * 10^(-10/20);
7   wavplay(tone, sr, 'sync');
8   wavplay(softer_tone, sr);
```

When you are working with a sound's amplitude, you should use the sound() function rather than the soundsc() function, because soundsc() normalizes the sound's amplitude before playing the sound. Therefore, any manipulation you have done on the sound's amplitude is ineffective if you use soundsc.

The same amplitude attenuation can be done with a noise:

Listing 5.10

```
1   sr = 44100;   % the sample rate in Hz
2   d = 1;        % Sound duration in sec
3   noise = (rand(1, sr*d)*2)-1;
4   wavplay(noise, sr, 'sync')
5   wavplay(noise*10^(-20/20), sr)
```

In Listing 5.10, the level of the second noise is 20 dB lower than that of the first one.

Match the Level of Sound with Different Waveforms

In this section we show how to match the levels of sounds of differing waveforms. Let's suppose that we need to play several environmental sounds during an experiment. Let's also suppose that we want these (very different) sounds to be perceived as similarly loud. These sounds have different waveforms. Therefore, the sound pressure of each sound will be different. There are two options for matching the levels of sounds having different waveforms. The first option is to normalize the amplitude of the sounds. For example, let's suppose that we have two sounds stored in two arrays (s1 and s2) in our workspace. To normalize the amplitude of the two sounds, we need to increase their amplitudes so that the peak for both sounds is equal to one. This can be done in this way:

```
>> s1 = s1/max(abs(s1));
>> s2 = s2/max(abs(s2));
```

A simpler alternative could be, once again, that of using the sounsc() function, which normalizes the sounds' amplitudes before playing them.

The second option is to match the two sounds using the root mean square (RMS) amplitude. This process is often more efficient than normalization, in particular when the sounds are very different. Listing 5.11 shows how to do this.

Listing 5.11

```
1   rms_s1 = sqrt(mean(s1.^2));   % rms mean of sound 1
2   rms_s2 = sqrt(mean(s2.^2));   % rms mean of sound 2
3   rms_ratio = rms_s1/rms_s2
4   if rms_ratio > 1
5       fprintf('The first was the loudest\n');
6       s2 = s2 * rms_ratio;
7   else
8       fprintf('The second was the loudest\n');
9       s1 = s1 * rms_ratio;
10  end
```

Analysis

The root mean square of each sound can be calculated as in lines 1 and 2. If the first sound is on average greater in amplitude than the second, we need to attenuate its amplitude (lines 4–6). In contrast, we may need to amplify the amplitude of the second (lines 7–9).

The two sounds now have identical mean amplitudes. In fact, if we recalculate the RMS amplitude, we will find out that the second sound has the same mean amplitude as the first.

Stereophonic Sounds for ITD and ILD[3]

We can use MATLAB to create sounds with simulated interaural time difference (ITD) or interaural level difference (ILD). First, let's create a pure tone of 3,000 Hz and 500 ms duration (recall that ILD cues are relevant at relatively high frequencies in particular, Moore 2003).

```
>> sr = 44100;
>> f = 3000;                          % the tone's frequency (in Hz)
>> d = .5;
>> t = linspace(0, d, sr*d);          % a time vector
>> tone = sin(2*pi*f*t);
```

All the sounds we have created so far are monophonic, and monophonic sounds are useful in the majority of psychological applications. If the monophonic sound is coded within a single array, the corresponding stereophonic sound will be coded within two arrays, the first containing the sound for the left channel and the second containing the sound for the right channel. Therefore:

```
>> stereo_tone = [tone', tone'];
>> sound(stereo_tone, sr);
```

Note that both arrays need to be rotated. This is because the sound() function wants as input a stereophonic matrix having two columns, one for the left channel and one for the right channel. This can be tested by playing one channel at time. In the following example, we play the sound, but we multiply the amplitude of the left channel by zero:

```
>> sound([tone'*0, tone'], sr)
```

Because the left channel consists entirely of 0s, it is silent. You can make the right channel silent by passing 0s to the right column of the matrix in this way:

```
>> sound([tone', tone'*0], sr)
```

Let's suppose we want an ILD of 10 dB that simulates a sound source at your left side. What we need to do is to attenuate the right channel by 10 dB, as follows:

```
>> stereo_tone = [tone', tone'*10^(-10/20)];
>> sound(stereo_tone, sr)
```

You can hear that the tone is louder in the left channel than in the right channel. Mutatis mutandis, the same operations (inverting the matrix columns) can be used to create a sound that is perceived as coming from the right.

It is only somewhat more complex to add interaural phase difference (ITD) to our sounds. To get ITD into our sounds we need to control the sound's phase. Theoretically, the ITD is a temporal difference, usually expressed in microseconds, in

---

[3] We recommend to use headphones for better appreciating the sounds described in this section.

the arrival of the sound at the two ears. However, because of this temporal difference, the sound arrives at each ear with a different phase. This phase difference is called interaural phase difference (IPD). In digital synthesis, it is easier to create a phase difference than a temporal difference. The IPD cue is important for sound localization along the azimuth for frequencies up to 1,500 Hz (Moore 2003). Let's first write a command for controlling a tone's phase. It can be done as follows:

```
>> sr = 44100;
>> f = 250;
>> d = .5;
>> t = linspace(0, d, sr*d);
>> phase = 0; % starting phase of the tone in radians
>> tone = sin(2*pi*f*t+phase);
```

Now let's suppose we want to create a sound that seems to originate from the right channel. This channel leads, and it is followed after a certain ITD by the sound that arrives at the left ear. Suppose that we want to simulate an ITD of 0.4 ms, i.e., $4*10^{-4}$:

```
>> ITD = 4*10^-4;
>> IPD = 2*pi*f*ITD;
>> phase_left = 0;
>> phase_right = IPD;
>> tone_left = sin(2*pi*f*t+phase_left);
>> tone_right = sin(2*pi*f*t+phase_right);
>> sound([tone_left', tone_right'], sr)
```

As you can hear, the tone seems to be originating from your right.

We are now ready to do something more complex. Let's say that we want to play 13 sounds starting from the left channel and slowly moving to the right one. Listing 5.12 does this:

Listing 5.12

```
1    sr = 44100;
2    f = 250;
3    d = .25;
4    t = linspace(0, d, sr*d);
5    for i = -6:6
6        ITD = i*10^-4;
7        IPD = 2*pi*f*ITD;
8        phase_left = 0;
9        phase_right = IPD;
10       tone_left = sin(2*pi*f*t+phase_left);
11       tone_right = sin(2*pi*f*t+phase_right);
12       wavplay([tone_left', tone_right'], sr, 'sync')
13   end
```

At every iteration of the for loop, we synthesize a stereo tone and play it. The ITD variable content is changed at every iteration by multiplication of the variable i, and this results in a different ITD value every time i changes its value.

A Sound's Envelope

You may have noticed that in all the sounds we have played so far, there were audible clicks both at the beginning and at the end of the sounds. This is because the amplitude of the sound at onset and offset started abruptly. To remove these disturbing clicks, we need to modulate the amplitude of the very first and very last portions of the sound with an onset and offset ramp, whereas we need to leave unmodulated the middle portion of the sound. In other words, we need to smooth the onset and offset a bit so that the clicks will be inaudible. This smoothing is a very common operation, and usually ramps of 10 ms are sufficient to smooth the sound. In the majority of cases, onset and offset are modulated with raised cosine ramps, i.e., half of a cosine cycle, and precisely the half ranging from π to 2π:

```
>> sr = 44100
>> gatedur = .01; % the duration of the gate in seconds (i.e., 10 ms)
>> gate = cos(linspace(pi, 2*pi, sr*gatedur));
```

Let's now generate a tone:

```
>> f = 250; % frequency of the tone in Hz
>> d = .5; % duration of the tone in seconds
>> time = linspace(0, d, sr*d); % a time vector
>> tone = sin(2*pi*f*time);
```

If we play it, we can hear the onset and offset clicks:

```
>> sound(tone, sr)
```

If we want to modulate the amplitude of the tone's onset and offset, we need to multiply the tone by an envelope. The envelope of a sound is an imaginary line connecting all the positive (or negative) peaks of the sound. In digital synthesis, the envelope's values must lie within the 0/+1 range. Therefore, we now need to adjust our modulator (the gate variable created previously) so that its range is within the 0/+1 limits:

```
>> gate = gate+1; % this operation translates all the values
of the modulator to the 0/+2 range
>> gate = gate/2; % this operation compresses the values within
the 0/+1 range
```

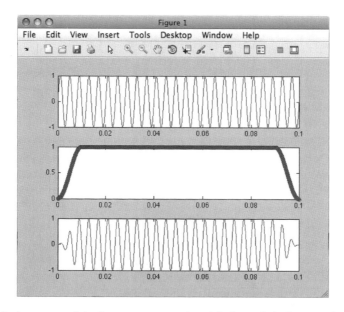

Fig. 5.2 At the *top* part of the figure you can see the original sound. At the *center* is shown the envelope that was used to modulate the sound's onset and offset. At the *bottom* of the figure is displayed the resulting modulated sound. Note that the onset and offset are not abrupt as in the *top left* graph

Now the gate is within the correct range. We can now easily create the offset gate by flipping the array containing our onset gate as follows:

```
>> offsetgate = fliplr(gate);
```

The last thing we need to do is to create the "sustain" portion of our envelope, in other words, the portion that will not modulate the sound's amplitude. Because we are going to perform a multiplication, if we want the tone's central part unchanged after the multiplication, we need to create an array of ones, the neutral factor for the multiplication. The length of the sustain portion will be equal to the tone's length minus the lengths of the onset and offset gates. In this way, the length of our envelope (i.e., onset gate, sustain, and offset gate) will be identical to that of the tone:

```
>> sustain = ones(1, (length(tone)-2*length(gate)));
>> envelope = [gate, sustain, offsetgate];
>> smoothed_tone = envelope .* tone;
```

If we now play the tone, we no longer hear any clicks. Moreover, a graph showing the original tone, the envelope, and resulting smoothed tone may explain visually what we have done so far (Fig. 5.2).

```
>> sound(smoothed_tone, sr)
>> subplot(3, 1, 1); plot(t, tone)
>> subplot(3, 1, 2); plot(time, envelope, 'o')
>> subplot(3, 1, 3); plot(time, smoothed_tone)
```

Sound Filtering

In this section we describe how to filter sounds. One of the purposes of filtering is to generate noises of various kinds (e.g., lowpass, highpass, bandpass). In this section we will see how to filter a noise and how to generate any kind of filtered noise. The first thing we have to do is to create a white noise[4]:

```
>> sr = 44100;
>> d = 1; % the duration of the noise (in sec)
>> noise = (rand(1, sr*d)*2)-1;
>> sound(noise, sr);
```

In order to filter our noise, we need to look at our sound in the frequency domain, i.e., we need to apply a fast Fourier transform (FFT):

```
>> fnoise = fft(noise);
```

The magnitude spectrum of our noise looks almost flat along the frequency axis, as it should for white noises.

Command	Graphical result
`>> plot(20*log10(abs(fnoise(1:22050))))`	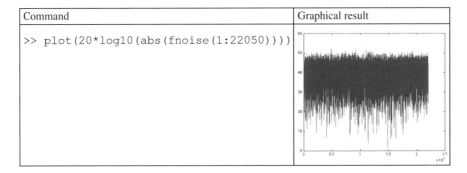

As you can see, the FFT command returns an array as long as the original noise array. However, the new array contains complex numbers. This array is our original noise. However, now we are looking at it from the frequency domain rather than from the time domain. Therefore, if in the original array each element represented a given amplitude value in time, in the new array, each element represents a frequency with its relative amplitude and phase (note that we are dealing with complex numbers, i.e., numbers having a real and an imaginary part). In the array returned by the FFT, all frequencies up to the half of the sampling rate (i.e., the Nyquist frequency) will be represented twice and symmetrically (see below).

---

[4] Note that it is possible to generate white noises according to various distributions. For example, the rand function returns random and uniformly distributed numbers. Therefore, our white noise would be a "uniform white noise." If we use randn, a function that generates random numbers according to the normal distribution, we would have a Gaussian white noise instead. See, for instance, Wikipedia for further details.

If we want to filter the noise, we need to create a filter array as long as our noise array. The filter array will contain elements ranging from 0 to 1. Later, we will convolve this filter array on the noise array. The frequencies convoluted with elements smaller than 1 will be filtered, and the filtering will be greater, the closer the value of the filter is to 0. The frequencies convoluted with 1 will, however, be untouched. Now let's suppose we want to create a low-pass filter with a cutoff frequency of 5 kHz. We have to proceed as at lines 3–7 of the following script:

Listing 5.13

M-script	Graphical Result
1 `sr = 44100;` 2 `d = 1; % the duration of the noise (in sec)` 3 `noise = (rand(1, sr*d)*2)-1;` 4 `cutoff = 5000;` 5 `cutoffinsamples = cutoff * d;` 6 `filter = zeros(1, length(noise));` 7 `filter (1:cutoffinsamples)=1;` 8 `filter (end-cutoffinsamples:end)=1;` 9 `figure; subplot(2,1,1);` 10 `plot (filter);` 11 `axis([1 length(filter) -0.1 1.1]);` 12 `fnoise = noise .* filter;` 13 `subplot(2,1,2);` 14 `plot(20*log10(abs(fnoise)))`	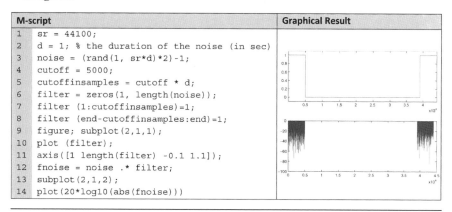

Listing 5.13 creates the filter. Note that the filter is symmetric because frequencies are represented twice and symmetrically within the noise array. Specifically, we have convolved[5] our filter to the noise (line 10) and plotted the spectrum of the filtering (line 11) process. As you can see, a large band of frequency components is now missing (what was removed by the filter). Moreover, you can see the symmetric representation of frequency. If we want to listen to our filtered noise, there are a couple of more things to do. The filtered noise is represented in the *frequency* domain, but we need to represent it in the *time* domain. To do this, we first apply the inverse of the FFT, and then we extract the real part of the complex number array:

```
>> fnoise = ifft(fnoise);
>> fnoise = real(fnoise);
>> fnoise = fnoise/max(abs(fnoise));
>> sound(fnoise, sr)
```

Note that we have normalized the noise's amplitude before playing it. This is because the filtering can return a sound whose amplitude exceeds the −1/+1 range.

---

[5]Convolution is an operation done in time. Thanks to Fourier transform properties, the convolution operation in time become a simple product in frequency between the Fourier transform of the noise and the filter frequency response.

In Listing 5.14 we include a plot to represent the filtering, step by step. In the example, we band-pass filter a Gaussian white noise and keep the frequency components from 2,000 to 6,000 Hz:

Listing 5.14

```
1    % in the following example we generate
2    % a band-pass filtered noise
3    sr = 44100; % sample rate in Hz
4    d = 1; % duration of the noise in seconds
5
6    % generate a uniformly distributed white noise
7    % and normalize its amplitude
8
9    whitenoise = randn(sr*d, 1);
10   whitenoise = whitenoise/max(abs(whitenoise));
11   wnoise_in_freq = fft(whitenoise);
12
13   % Calculate the band-pass filter
14   lf = 2000; % lowest freq. of the cutoff freq.
15   hf = 6000; % highwest freq. of the cutoff freq.
16   lf_insamples = lf * d;
17   hf_insamples = hf * d;
18   filter = zeros(length(wnoise_in_freq), 1);
19   filter(lf_insamples:hf_insamples) = 1;
20   filter(end-hf_insamples:end-lf_insamples) = 1;
21
22   % Filter the noise
23   filtnoise_in_freq = filter .* wnoise_in_freq;
24
25   % Obtain the filtered noise in time
26   filterednoise = ifft(filtnoise_in_freq);
27   filterednoise = real(filterednoise);
28
29   %Plot results
30   figure;
31   subplot(3, 2, 1);
32   plot(whitenoise);
33   xlabel('time (sec)'), ylabel('amplitude');
34   subplot(3, 2, 2);
35   plot(20*log10(abs(wnoise_in_freq(1:22050))));
36   xlabel('frequency Hz'), ylabel('dB');
37   subplot(3, 2, 3:4);
38   plot(1:22050,filter(1:22050));
39   xlabel('frequency (Hz)'), ylabel('dB')
40   subplot(3, 2, 5);
41   plot(20*log10(abs(filtnoise_in_freq(1:22050))));
42   xlabel('frequency (Hz)'), ylabel('dB')
43   subplot(3, 2, 6);
44   plot(filterednoise)
45   xlabel('time (sec)'), ylabel('amplitude');
```

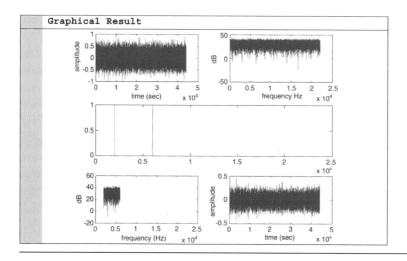

Sound Analysis

The analysis of the sound's acoustical characteristics can range from very simple to very complex (see Giordano and McAdams 2006 for a list of possible sophisticated analyses). In this section we show only some simple analyses because these are the most common in psychology. The first things we may want to know are the digital characteristics of the sound. These characteristics are returned by the wavread() function, which takes as argument the wav filename. Let's see how this function works, assuming that we have saved a sound in mywavefile.wav:

```
>> [s, sr, bits] = wavread('mywavefile');
```

Here s is a vector variable containing the sound. The sr and bits variables are the sound's sample rate in hertz and the sound's resolution in bits, respectively. The sound's duration can be obtained by dividing the length of the sound vector by the sample frequency:

```
>> duration = length(s)/sr;
```

The root mean square power of a sound can be obtained by squaring sound's array and then calculating the average of the resulting values. Finally, we calculate the square root. Because the returned value is linear, we may want to transform it into decibel units.

```
>> s2 = s^2;
>> ms2 = mean (s2);
>> rms = sqrt(ms2);
>> dB_rms = 20*log10(rms);
```

If we want to know the peak amplitude of the file, we just need to calculate the maximum absolute value of the sound vector as follows:

```
>> peak = max(abs(s));
>> peak_dB = 20*log10(peak);
```

We may want to look at the sound's magnitude spectrum in order to obtain its frequency content. We first calculate the fast Fourier transform (FFT) of the sound, and then obtain the absolute value to plot the magnitude spectrum. The magnitude spectrum repeats itself. Therefore, we have to plot only the first half of the data:

```
>> s_fft = fft(s);
>> s_fft = abs(s);
>> s_fft = s_fft(1:length(s_fft)/2);
>> plot(s_fft)
```

We now may want to see the amplitude of the various frequency components on a decibel scale rather than on a linear scale. Moreover, we may want to have a more meaningful x-axis as well as to add labels to the plot (Fig. 5.3):

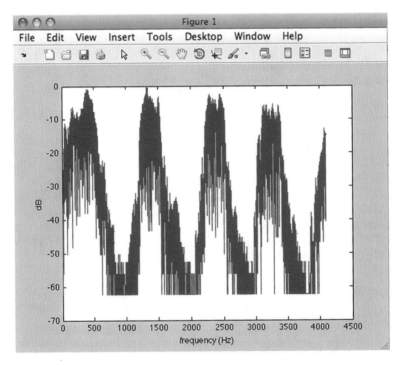

Fig. 5.3 Magnitude spectrum of "chirp." The following spectrum was plotted by loading the variable "chirp" and then by performing the operations written in the text. Note that when you load chirp, the sound array automatically gets the variable name y, whereas the sample rate gets the variable name Fs. Therefore, the following lines must be written at the beginning of the script: load chirp; s = y; sr = Fs; Note that the spectrum of the chirp shows peaks at 500 Hz, 1,500 Hz, 2,500 Hz, showing an evident harmonic structure of the spectrum

```
>> f = linspace(0, sr/2, length(s_fft));
>> plot(f, 20*log10(s_fft))
>> xlabel('frequency (Hz)')
>> ylabel('dB')
```

Summary

- Sounds are represented by arrays and should lie within the −1/+1 range.
- White noises (and noises in general) are generated by means of the rand (or randn) function.
- Pure tones are generated by means of the sin function.
- Complex tones are generated by adding two or more simple tone arrays.
- Silences can be generated with arrays of zeros.
- Sounds can be played with the sound, soundsc, and wavplay functions. soundsc scales normalize the sound's amplitude automatically. Wavplay is the only MATLAB command that makes it possible to work synchronically.
- A sound's sequences are generated by concatenating the sound's arrays.
- A sound's level can be manipulated by multiplying the sound's array by the desired factor of attenuation/amplification.
- Stereophonic sounds use matrices containing two columns (i.e., two sound arrays).
- A sound's envelope can be manipulated by multiplying the sound's array by an envelope array. The envelope array must contain values within the 0–1 range.
- Sounds can be filtered by means of the fft function.

Exercises

1. Synthesize a 2-kHz, 2-s duration pure tone.
2. Synthesize a white noise of 0.5 s duration.
3. Synthesize a white noise of 0.5 s duration followed by 0.1 s of silence and then the noise again.
4. Synthesize a 200-Hz four-harmonic complex tone (0.5 s duration), followed by the same tone attenuated by 30 dB.
5. Write the previous tone to a wav file.
6. Open the file just created and calculate the root mean square of the first half of the sound and of the second half of the sound and calculate the level difference between the two tones in dB.
7. Synthesize the following stimulus for a forward masking experiment: a band-pass noise of 200 ms followed by a sinusoidal signal of 1,000 Hz. The noise frequency content must range within the 500–2,000 Hz limits.
8. Synthesize a pure tone (300 Hz, 0.2 s duration) with 600 µs of ITD.
9. Synthesize a 500-ms low-pass filtered noise (cutoff frequency 5,000 Hz) and smooth the onset and the offset of the noise with 50-ms raised cosine ramps.

A Brick for an Experiment

In the experiment developed by Sekuler et al. (1997), the visual display of a disc's
motion is accompanied by a sound. The authors actually used more than one sound
in the various conditions of the experiment. The sound, described in greater detail,
is a tone of 440 Hz and 100 ms duration. No other details are provided. For our brick
experiment we can use a sine wave of 440 Hz and of 50 ms duration (the effect
observed by Sekuler et al. is more compelling if the sound has a short duration),
gated on and off with two 5-ms raised cosine ramps, just to prevent clicks at the
onset and offset of the sound. Let's create this sound:

```
% stimuli (creation)
sr = 44100;
d = .05;
f = 440;
% tone synthesis
t = linspace(0, 0.1, sr*d);
tone = sin(2*pi*f*t);
% ONSET AND OFFSET GATING
gatedur = .005; % the duration of the gate in seconds (i.e., 5-ms)
ongate = cos(linspace(pi, 2*pi, sr*gatedur));
ongate = ongate+1;
ongate = ongate/2;
offgate = fliplr(ongate);
sustain = ones(1, (length(tone)-2*length(ongate)));
envelope = [ongate, sustain, offgate];
tone = tone .* envelope;
```

   This code needs to be extended for our purposes. In our experiment the sound
needs to be switched on while the discs are in motion, and in particular, when the
discs overlap. In later chapters, we will see that this is going to happen at frame 70
(i.e., at the x coordinate of 140). We have to append, at the beginning of the sound,
a silence for the duration we have to wait before switching on the sound. To do that,
we need to anticipate the use of the screen function. This function will be extensively described later. The screen is the most important function of the psychtoolbox
functions and can do several things. One of the things that this function does is to
interrogate the video card to know the refresh rate that is currently set in your computer. Here we use screen to get the refresh rate of your monitor.

```
refreshrate = FrameRate(screennumber); % get the frame rate of
the monitor
silencepre_dur = (1/refreshrate) * 70;
silencepre = zeros(1, round(sr * silencepre_dur));
SoundToPlay = [silencepre, tone];
```

Now write everything within a single `GenerateSound()` function. This function receives as argument a digit representing the sound we want to play (1 for no sound, 2 for the sound) that is stored in the EventTable and a screen number (see later chapters). The function's output will be a sound array. Note that the input number is used at the end of the function to decide whether to return silence or the tone.

Listing 5.15

M-script

```
1   function SoundToPlay = GenerateSound(whichsound, screennumber)
2
3   % stimuli (creation)
4   sr = 44100;
5   d = .05;
6   f = 440;
7   % tone synthesis
8   t = linspace(0, 0.1, sr*d);
9   tone = sin(2*pi*f*t);
10  % ONSET AND OFFSET GATING
11  gatedur = .005; % the duration of the gate in seconds
12  (i.e., 5-ms)
13  ongate = cos(linspace(pi, 2*pi, sr*gatedur));
14  ongate = ongate+1;
15  ongate = ongate/2;
16  offgate = fliplr(ongate);
17  sustain = ones(1, (length(tone)-2*length(ongate)));
18  envelope = [ongate, sustain, offgate];
19  tone = tone .* envelope;
20  refreshrate = Screen(0, 'FrameRate'); % get the frame
21  rate of the monitor
22  silencepre_dur = (1/refreshrate) * 70;
23  silencepre = zeros(1, round(sr * silencepre_dur));
24  SoundToPlay = [silencepre, tone];
25  if whichsound == 1
26      SoundToPlay = SoundToPlay * 0;
27  end
```

References

Darwin CJ, Ciocca V (1992) Grouping in pitch perception: effects of onset asynchrony and ear of presentation of a mistuned component. J Acoust Soc Am 91:3381–3390

Giordano BL, McAdams S (2006) Material identification of real impact sounds: effects of size variation in steel, glass, wood, and plexiglas plates. J Acoust Soc Am 119:1171–1181

Houtgast T (1972) Psychophysical evidence for lateral inhibition in hearing. J Acoust Soc Am 51:1885–1894

Moore BCJ (2003) An introduction to the psychology of hearing, 5th edn. Academic, San Diego

Sekuler R, Sekuler AB, Lau R (1997) Sound alters visual motion perception. Nature 385: 308

Suggested Readings

There are a number of MATLAB tools developed by researchers that can be used in audition. Here is a certainly incomplete list of the available tools:

Grassi M, Soranzo A (2009) MLP: a MATLAB toolbox for rapid and reliable auditory threshold estimations. Behav Res Methods 41:20–28 (This paper implements several psychoacoustic experiment together with sound generators and modifiers.)

Peeters G, Giordano BL, Susini P, Misdariis N, McAdams S (2011) The Timbre Toolbox: Extracting audio descriptors from musical signals. J Acoust Soc Am 130:2902–2916 (This paper shows a toolbox for the analysis of musical signals.)

Malcom Stanley has released a toolbox that implements several popular auditory models:

http://cobweb.ecn.purdue.edu/~malcolm/interval/1998-010/

Pérez E, Rodriguez-Esteban R (2006) Oreja: a MATLAB environment for the design of psychoacoustic stimuli. Behav Res Methods 38:574–578 (The Oreja software package was designed to study speech intelligibility. It is a tool that allows manipulation of speech signals to facilitate study of human speech perception.)

Readers interested in MATLAB tools for audition should take a look at the following journals: *Behavior Research Methods* and the *Journal of Neuroscience Methods*. Both journals often publish MATLAB tools for audition.

Readers Interested in more technical and advanced audio processing should read the following book:

McLoughlin I (2009) Applied speech and audio processing: With Matlab examples. Cambridge: Cambridge University Press

Chapter 6
Create and Proccess Images[1]

MATLAB is a powerful tool for image processing. You can use MATLAB to create visual stimuli either by importing/exporting images or by drawing them from scratch in a quite simple manner. In this chapter, we give an introduction to image drawing and image manipulation.

Images Basics

A digital image may be defined as a two-dimensional function $f(x,y)$. Here x and y are spatial coordinates and f(x,y) is the intensity of the image at the particular coordinates. For example, in a grayscale image, f(x,y) is the intensity of the gray at the particular x and y position.

Digital images differ from analog images (e.g., analog photos) because x, y coordinates and the $f(x,y)$ intensity values are discrete instead of continuous. In digital images, a single (x,y) point is called a *pixel*. The intensity $f(x,y)$ depends on the number of bits used to represent it. Usually the intensity is represented with 8 bits, yielding 2^8 values. As an example, a gray-scale image has intensity values within the 0–255 range, or in other words, the gray can assume 256 different levels from black (0) to white (255). Often, the range is normalized within the 0–1 range (i.e., the intensity values are divided by 255) (Fig. 6.1).

To get a color image, we need to superpose different colors, for example *Red*, *Green*, and *Blue* in the *RGB* system. In color images, each coordinate has n intensity values, one for each of color of the system in use. For example, each pixel of an RGB image is a triplet of intensity values, one for red, one for green, and one for blue. By default, MATLAB represents these triplets with 8 bits, for a total of 24 bits, yielding 2^{24} colors. This type of image is usually called *TrueColor*.

---

[1] Note that, although the book figures are black and white, the commands reported in the current chapter generate color figures.

M. Borgo et al., *MATLAB for Psychologists*,
DOI 10.1007/978-1-4614-2197-9_6, © Springer Science+Business Media, LLC 2012

Fig. 6.1 An example of a
5×5 gray-scale image. The
first pixel in position (1, 1)
has intensity equal to 32

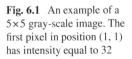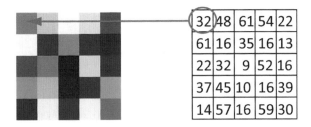

32	48	61	54	22
61	16	35	16	13
22	32	9	52	16
37	45	10	16	39
14	57	16	59	30

There is also another method of treating color images: *indexing images*. Each pixel has a value that represents not a color but the index in a *color map* matrix. The *color map* (or *color palette*) is a list of all the colors used in that image. Such indexing images occupy less memory than RGB images, so they are a good option for saving space. The indexing concept is graphically illustrated in Fig. 6.2.[2] Each image has a zoomed area of 17×17 pixels. Each zoomed area shows the intensity for the gray-scale image and the RGB values for the color image. The indexed image is obtained from the RGB image using a palette with the 60 colors included in the RGB image.

MATLAB uses indexing images by default, and has a default color map from which it gets the colors for plotting figures such as histograms, pies charts, and 3-D graphs. Let's see the first five rows of the default color map by typing the following statement:

```
>> colormap('default');
DefColMap = colormap;
>> whos DefColMap
        Name           Size              Bytes   Class       Attributes
        DefColMap      64x3               1536   double
>> DefColMap(1:5,:)
ans =
        0              0         0.5625
        0              0         0.6250
        0              0         0.6875
        0              0         0.7500
        0              0         0.8125
```

The `colormap(cmap)` function can be used to set the color map to the matrix cmap. In our case, `colormap` sets the matrix color map to the default one. If we write the statement `colormap` as is, MATLAB returns the current color-map matrix. Here we saved the current color map into the `DefColMap` variable. As can be seen, the default color map has 64 colors (number of rows) and three columns: the first column corresponds to the color red, the second to green, and the third to blue. For example, in the first row of `DefColMap` there is 0% red, 0% green, and 56.25% blue (the values of the default color map are normalized), so the first five rows correspond to a variation of the blue color only.

---

[2] The image is copyrighted by the artist Mirta Caccaro.

Image Type	Image
Gray Scale	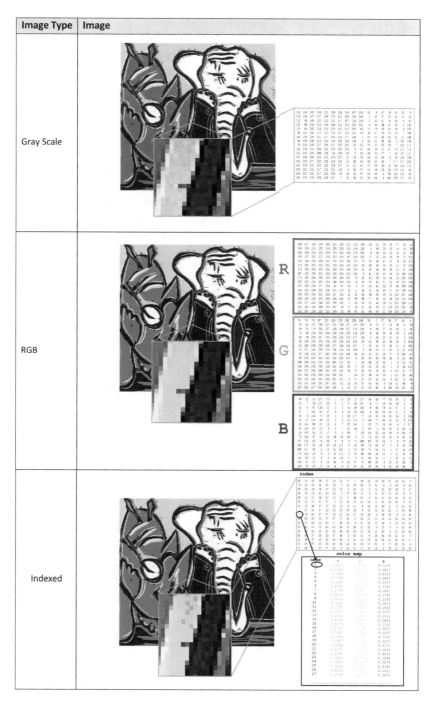
RGB	
Indexed	

Fig. 6.2 Three different digital representations of the same image

Let's acquire a better understanding of the color map by creating a custom color map. Let's suppose we want to create a color map whose first color is red, the second is green, the third is blue, the fourth corresponds to a light azure, and the fifth corresponds to orange. Then we create a 3×5 indexed image with $3 \times 5 = 15$ pixels using the colors of the color map. In the following example we write code that does the job:

Example	Graphical result
```>> Mycolormap = [1 0 0; 0 1 0; 0 0 1;… 0 1 1; 1 0.5 0]; >> im = [5 4 3 2 1; 3 2 1 5 4; 1 3 5 4 2] >> image(im) >> colormap(Mycolormap)```	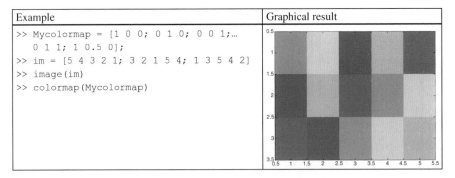

As you can see, the top leftmost pixel is orange, which corresponds to the index (row) 5 in the color map, or equivalently to the combination of 100% red, 50% green, and 0% blue.

You can change the color map just created using the command `colormapeditor`; it displays the current figure's color map as a strip of rectangular cells in the color-map editor. Node pointers are colored cells below the color-map strip that indicate points in the color map where the rate of the variation of R, G, and B values changes. Please refer to MATLAB help for detailed information.

Example	Graphical result
```>> colormap('default') >> colormapeditor;```	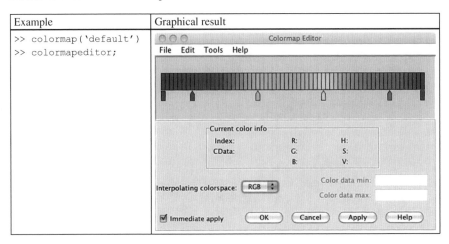

Importing and Exporting Images

The function that enables one to load images into the MATLAB workspace is `imread`. A=imread(filename, fmt) reads a gray-scale or color image from the file specified by the string *filename* and stores the result in the matrix A. The text string fmt specifies the format of the file by its standard file extension. However, it is not necessary to write the extension if the filename already has the standard extension. If the image is an RGB image, the matrix A is a cube, i.e., an *Nrows × Ncolumns × 3* matrix. For indexed images, the function imread returns the specific color map of the image.

If you need to write an image to a file, the function imwrite. imwrite(A,filename,fmt) writes the image A into a file with the specified filename and in the format specified by the string fmt. For indexed images, such as *gif* figures, for example, the function is imwrite(X,map,filename,fmt). The function accepts other input parameters as well, such as the quality of *jpeg* images or the transparency matrix for *png* images. For further information, refer to the online MATLAB help.

An additional way to export your images is through the print function. The print function can be used as described in Chapter 3, once the image is displayed (see next section). Alternatively, select Copy Figure from the figure window's Edit menu. This action copies the image to the clipboard. Then you can paste the figure wherever you like.

MATLAB handles different image formats, the most common of which are presented in the following table:

File format	Extention	Description	Function use

TIFF	TIFF image	Color, gray-scale, or indexed image(s). The tiff format was originally created in the 1980s to support data output from scanners. This format can contain information about colorimetry calibration, etc.; examples occur with remote sensing	`Tim=imread(filename, 'tiff');`
			`[Tim, TColMap]=imread(filename,'tiff');`
			`imwrite(Tim,filename,'tiff');`

PNG	PNG image	True color, gray-scale, and indexed image(s). Very efficient lossless compression, supporting variable transparencies	`Pim=imread(filename,'png');`
			`[Pim, PColMap]=imread(filename,'png');`
			`imwrite(Pim,filename,'png');`

BMP	BMP image	True color or indexed image native format for Microsoft Windows. Can support up to 24-bit color. Originally uncompressed	`Bim=imread(filename,'bmp');`
			`[Bim, BColMap]=imread(filename,'bmp');`
			`imwrite(Bim,filename,'bpm');`

(continued)

(continued)

File format	Extention	Description	Function use
JPEG	JPEG image	True color or gray-scale image. 24-bit (true color) support. Created to support the photographic industry with various levels of compression. Compression can result in noticeable loss of image quality in some images	`Jim=imread(filename,'jpg');` `imwrite(Bim,filename,'jpg');`
GIF	GIF image	Indexed image, Very common and used extensively in the Internet. It works well for illustrations or clip-art that have large areas of flat colors. Limited to 256 colors	`[Gim, GColMap]=imread(filename,'gif');` `imwrite(Gim,filename,'jpg','Quality',75);`

Display Images

If you need to display an image, use the function `image`. Now let's try to load an image and display it as in the following example:

Example	Graphical result

`>> [Trees,mapTrees] = imread`
`('trees.tif');`
`>> image(Trees);`
`>> axis off;`
`>> size(mapTrees)`
`ans =`
`    256     3`
	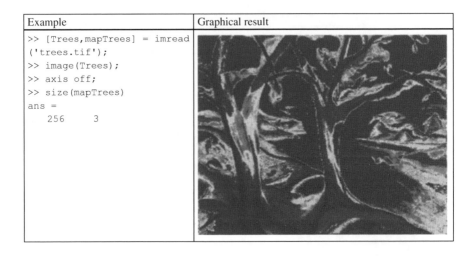

The image you see seems to have the wrong colors. The reason is the following. The image was indexed with its own custom color map. However, MATLAB does not load the image color map but uses the default color map instead. To show the correct image, you need to change the color map as follows:

```
>> colormap(mapTrees)
```

Note that `mapTrees` is the color-map matrix obtained using the command `imread`.

If you have the MATLAB image-processing toolbox, there is another function for displaying images: `imshow(X,map)`, where X is the image and `map` is the color map. Use only one argument in case of true-color or gray-scale images.

If you need to obtain the gray-scale version of the previous image, you need to change the color map. You can do it in either of two ways, by editing a new custom color map or by using the function `gray(M)`. The function `gray(M)` returns an M-by-3 matrix containing a linear gray-scale color map. Use `gray` as in the following example:

Example 1	Example 2	Example 3
`colormap(gray(100));`	`colormap(gray(450));`	`>> colormap(gray(256));`

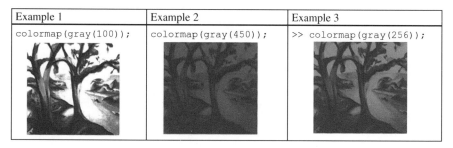

The effect of using a color map with fewer (or more) colors than those we are starting with (= 256 in this case) can give unexpected results. The color map can have up to a maximum of 256 entries (= rows). If we create a color map with only 100 rows, all the indices with values greater than 100 will not know which color refer to. MATLAB automatically sets all the indexes greater than 100 to point at the last row, i.e., the 100th row. This is why the image in Example 1 appears lighter. In contrast, Example 2 shows a darker image. This is because only the first 256 colors are used (which correspond to darker grays).

Note that for true color images, the image data will be read as a three-dimensional array. In such a case, `image` will ignore the current color map, and assign colors to the display based on the values in the array.

Basic Manipulation of Images

In MATLAB, images are treated as numbers embedded in matrices; therefore, they can be manipulated like any other array. Each intensity value is related to a pixel of the images and can be changed with a simple transformation. Such single-pixel transformations are generally called *point operations*. A different approach is to consider not only a single pixel but also a set of neighboring pixels. There is usually a strong correlation between the intensity values of a set of pixels that are close to each other. For example, we can change the gray level of a given pixel according to the values of the gray levels in a small neighborhood of pixels surrounding the given pixel. These transformations are called *neighborhood processing*. The current section shows some simple processing functions.

Point Operations

Intensity Transformation

Within the point operations, the intensity transformation is the simplest form of processing. Let's suppose we have an indexed gray-scale image. If the gray scale is linear, the index of a pixel is equivalent to its intensity. Such a value (the intensity) can be added/subtracted or multiplied/divided by a constant value. If we refer to indices, it is important to round the result (to obtain an integer where necessary) of the operation and to "clip" the values when they are greater than the maximum or lower than the minimum.

Let's load an image (The file mandrill contains the image X variable and the color-map map variable) and add a constant equal to 128 to each pixel's intensity value:

```
>> load mandrill
>> Y = X +128;
>> Y(9,1)
ans =
   270
```

as you can see, the pixel intensity value in position (9,1) is greater than 255 (= 2^8). In this case we need to "clip" the value and set it to 255. The operation can be done efficiently by selecting the minimum between the actual value and 255.

```
>> Y(9,1)=min( Y(9,1) , 255);
>> Y(9,1)
ans =
   255
```

We now use the function floor to round the result (if necessary) to obtain an integer. The floor function returns the greatest integer less than or equal to the input argument.

In the same way, if we need to be sure the values of an intensity matrix are greater than 0, we should type:

```
>> Y=floor(max(Y,0));
```

We show here the code to obtain the aforementioned intensity transformation with the MATLAB image called mandrill (Fig. 6.3).

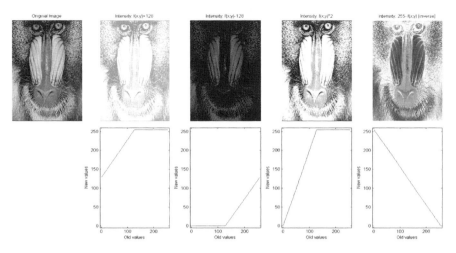

Fig. 6.3 Intensity variations applied to the same image

Listing 6.1

```
1   % Test the intensity transformation
2   % AUTHOR:   Borgo-Soranzo-Grassi   2012
3
4   load mandrill            % load a MATLAB image. X is the image.
5                            % map is the colormap
6   ColMap=gray(255);        % Calculate a colormap of 255 values.
7   X1=floor(min(X+128,255));  % Increase the intensity and clip
8   X2=floor(max(X-128,0));    % Decrease the intensity and clip
9   X3=floor(min(X*2,255));    % Multiply the intensity by 2 and clip
10  X4=256-X;                % invert the intensity
11
12  figure;
13  subplot(2,5,1); image(X); axis off;
14  subplot(2,5,2); image(X1); axis off;
15  subplot(2,5,3); image(X2); axis off;
16  subplot(2,5,4); image(X3); axis off;
17  subplot(2,5,5); image(X4); axis off;
18  colormap(ColMap);
19
20  Oldval=[1:255];
21  subplot(2,5,7)
22  plot(Oldval,floor(min(Oldval+128,255))); % Show the new Intensity value
23  axis([-5 260 -5 260]);                    % vs. the old ones
24  xlabel('Old values'); ylabel('New values');
25
26  Oldval=[1:255];
27  subplot(2,5,8)
28  plot(Oldval,floor(max(Oldval-128,0))); % Show the new Intensity value
29  axis([-5 260 -5 260]);                    % vs. the old ones
30  xlabel('Old values'); ylabel('New values');
31
32  Oldval=[1:255];
33  subplot(2,5,9)
34  plot(Oldval,floor(min(Oldval*2,255)));   % Show the new Intensity value
35  axis([-5 260 -5 260]);                    % vs. the old ones
36  xlabel('Old values'); ylabel('New values');
37
38  Oldval=[1:255];
39  subplot(2,5,10)
40  plot(Oldval,256-Oldval);                 % Show the new Intensity value
41  axis([-5 260 -5 260]);                    % vs. the old ones
42  xlabel('Old values'); ylabel('New values');
```

Note that we are providing an example with a gray-scale image. For color images, all the intensity matrices (e.g., the red, green, and blue matrix for RGB images) should be changed with the same function, or equivalently, by changing the color map. In any case, the most useful intensity transformations are brightening and contrasting. There are two built-in functions that operate within the color map and do these jobs: the `brighten` and the `contrast` functions. They are present in the following table.

Function	Description
`Brighten(beta)`	Brighten increases or decreases the color intensities in the current color map. The modified color map is: - brighter if 0 < beta < 1 - darker if −1 < beta < 0.
`cmap=contrast(X)`	The contrast function enhances the contrast of an image. It creates a new gray color map, cmap, that has an approximately an equal intensity distribution. All three elements in each row are identical

The MATLAB Image Toolbox gives a simple graphical interface to explore, display, and perform common image-processing tasks. The Image Tool provides access to several other tools. For example, you can get information about single pixels and distances, and you can adjust the contrast of an image or crop a portion of it. Type `imtool(filename)` at the MATLAB prompt to use these tools. You can try out these tools with the image of the trees by typing `imtool('trees.tif')`.

Windowing

The concept of windowing is the multiplication of an image matrix by a matrix of the same size having values within the range from 0 to 1. The "window" can be thought of as another image. It is often used to smooth edges or to highlight certain parts of the image. Here we show an example:

Listing 6.2

```
1    % M-Script to test the windowing concept
2    %
3    % Authors: Borgo, Soranzo, Grassi
4    % Date: 2009
5
6    load mandrill
7    WCentx=size(X,1)/2;        % calculate the center of image, x axis
8    WCenty=size(X,2)/2;        % calculate the center of image, y axis
9    WSize=100;                 % WSize is HALF the length of the square window
10
11   % Create the Window
12   SqWindow=zeros(size(X));
13   SqWindow([-WSize:WSize]+WCentx,[-WSize:WSize]+WCentx)=1;
14
15   [Xax,Yax]=meshgrid([1:size(X,2)],[1:size(X,1)]);
16   StanDev = 100;                          % Standard deviation
17   GaWindow=(1/sqrt(2*pi*StanDev)).*exp(-0.5*(((Xax-WCentx)/StanDev).^2+...
18           ((Yax-WCenty)/StanDev).^2));
19   GaWindow=GaWindow./max(max(GaWindow));   % Normalization
20
21   SqWindowedImage=X.*(SqWindow);   % Windowing of the original image;
22   GaWindowedImage=X.*(GaWindow);   % Windowing of the original image;
23
24   figure;                    % Display the window
25   colormap(gray(255));
26   subplot(1,2,1);
27   imagesc(SqWindow);         % imagesc is the same as image
28                              % but scale the data to the full
29                              % range of the current colormap
30   axis off;title('Square Window');
31   subplot(1,2,2); imagesc(GaWindow*254+1);
32   axis off;title('Gaussian Window');
33
34   figure;                    % Display the windowed image
35   colormap(gray(255));
36   subplot(1,2,1);imagesc(SqWindowedImage);
37   axis off; title('Squared Windowed Image');
38   subplot(1,2,2);imagesc(GaWindowedImage);
39   axis off;title('Gaussian Windowed Image');
```

The matrix SqWindow is a matrix of ones and zeros. If you multiply it by the original image, the resulting image in unchanged only where the window is equal to one. However, the resulting image will change in those pixels where the value of the window is less than one (i.e., zero in this case). The result of this windowing is shown in Fig. 6.4. This type of windowing works best with gray-scale images. Keep in mind that in the case of or RGB images, the windowing has to be applied to each color. Such a windowing type is useful for creating gabor patches.

Square Window   Gaussian Window   Square Windowed Image   Gaussian Windowed Image

Windows   Windowed images

Fig. 6.4 Windowing concept. Two different windows are applied to the same figure

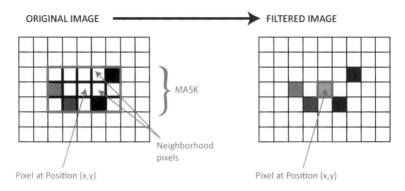

ORIGINAL IMAGE ⟶ FILTERED IMAGE

MASK

Neighborhood pixels

Pixel at Position (x,y)   Pixel at Position (x,y)

Fig. 6.5 Neighborhood processing concept

Neighborhood Processing

In the previous section we have seen how to modify images by applying a transformation of the intensity to each pixel. In this section we extend such an approach by including as well a neighborhood of each pixel. Overall, the neighboring pixels belong to a mask centered on the pixel where we want to obtain the new intensity value. The new intensity is calculated by combining all the intensities of the mask. Such an operation is called space *filtering*. In Fig. 6.5, the concept is illustrated graphically.

Spatial filtering requires two steps:

1. Place the mask over the current pixel,
2. Calculate the intensity combination of all the pixel intensities within the mask.

Here we give a simple example: a filter that gives the average of the nearest pixel. The mask is a matrix of 3×3 pixels. The operation to obtain the new pixel intensity is simple: multiply each intensity in the mask by 1/9 (9 is the total number of pixels in a mask) and sum them. The operation is performed for each image pixel using the function filter2.

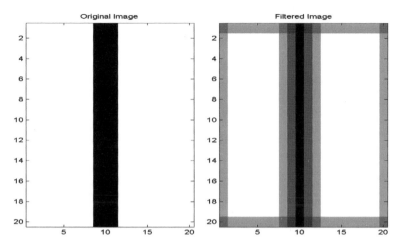

Fig. 6.6 Image filtering example

Listing 6.3

```
1   % M-Script to test the filtering concept
2   %
3   % Authors: Borgo, Soranzo, Grassi
4   % Date: 2009
5
6   Filter = ones(3,3)*1/9;      % generate the filter
7   ImageTest=ones(20,20)*255;   % generate a white image
8   ImageTest(:,9:11)=1;       % Plot a three pixel width vertical line
9
10  Filtered=filter2(Filter, ImageTest, 'same'); % do the filtering
11
12  figure;                    % show the original and filtered image
13  subplot(1,2,1)
14  image(ImageTest);
15  title('Original Image');
16  subplot(1,2,2)
17  image(Filtered);
18  title('Filtered Image');
19  colormap(gray(255));
```

The result is shown in Fig. 6.6.

At line 10 we used the function `filter2`, which is a function that filters the data in the second argument with the FIR filter (the mask and the values of such a mask) in the first argument. The third argument of the function controls how the edges are treated. You may have noticed that the filtered image has artifacts on the edges. These artifacts are explained in the following section.

If you have the MATLAB image toolbox, use `imfilter()` instead of `filter2()`.

There are many types of filters, e.g. low-pass, high-pass. The filtering action is always the same, but the difference lies in the filter's design. Here we do not want to explore the world of filter design. However, we would like to give you just another example: the Gaussian filter.

Listing 6.4

```
1   % M-Script to test the Gaussian Filter
2   %
3   % Authors: Borgo, Soranzo, Grassi
4   % Date: 2009
5
6   [MoonPic,Moonmap] = imread('moon.tif');
7   [Xax,Yax]=meshgrid([1:21],[1:21]);
8   StanDev=4;
9   FilterG = (1/sqrt(2*pi*StanDev)).*exp(-0.5*(((Xax-11)/StanDev).^2+...
10  ((Yax-11)/StanDev).^2));
11  FilterG = FilterG/sum(sum(FilterG));
12
13  Filtered1=filter2(FilterG, MoonPic, 'same');
14
15  figure;
16  subplot(1,2,1)
17  image(MoonPic);
18  title('Original Image');
19  axis image;
20  subplot(1,2,2)
21  image(Filtered1);
22  title('Filtered Image');
23  axis image;
24  colormap(gray(255));
25  figure;
26  mesh(Xax,Yax,FilterG);
27  title('Filter Values');
```

The result of Listing 6.4 is shown in Fig. 6.7. On the right we show the filter values.

As we mentioned before, filter design is not simple. However, the MATLAB image toolbox has a function called fspecial that helps you to create 2-D filters. The function h = fspecial(type) creates a two-dimensional filter h of the specified type, which is the appropriate form to use with imfilter. Here type is a string having one of the following values: 'average', 'disk', 'gaussian', 'laplacian', 'log', 'motion', 'prewitt', 'sobel' and 'unsharp'. Each type needs some other specific values (i.e., mask dimension and other parameters). For example, in order to create a Gaussian filter similar to the one we have used in the previous example, type the following:

```
>> FilterGSpecial = fspecial('gaussian', 21, 4);
```

FilterGSpecial is a rotationally symmetric Gaussian filter of size 21 pixels with standard deviation of 4 pixels. For further information please refer to the MATLAB help.

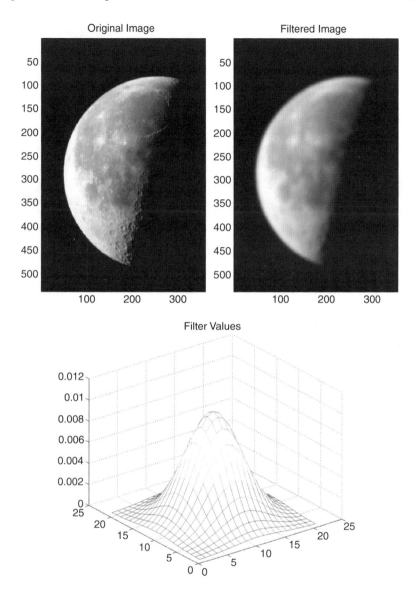

Fig. 6.7 A lunar image filtered with a Gaussian filter. The Gaussian (spatial) filter values are given on the *right*

We conclude this section by reminding you that the resizing procedure is also a form of neighborhood processing. The `imresize` function does image resizing. When you resize an image, you specify the image you want to resize and the magnification factor. To enlarge an image, specify a magnification factor greater than 1.

To reduce an image, specify a magnification factor between 0 and 1. Here there is an example to reduce the image by 50%:

```
>> TreesRes = imresize(Trees,0.5);
>> image(TreeRes);
```

The Edges of the Image

When we filter an image, there is a problem at the edges, where the mask partly falls outside them. There is a number of different approaches to solve this problem:

* *Ignore the edges.* The mask is applied only to those pixels of the image where the mask fully lies within the image. This results in an output image that is smaller than the original. To obtain this result, you should specify `'valid'` as the third argument of the `filter2` function.
* *Pad with zeros.* The missing values in the neighborhood of edge pixels are set to zero. This gives us a complete set of values to work with, and the result will be an output image of the same size as the original, but it may have the effect of introducing unwanted artifacts around the image. To obtain this result, you should specify `'same'` as the third argument of the `filter2` function.

Advanced Image Processing

The aforementioned methods are not straightforward. However, these methods are useful if you need to create and modify images. If you need more complex images processing, perhaps it is simpler to use the MATLAB image toolbox.

There are also devoted software packages for working with images, such as Adobe Photoshop. However, MATLAB can be useful when you need to modify repeatedly a certain number of images in the same way: writing a MATLAB script could be less time-consuming than repeatedly performing the same operation with Photoshop. Moreover, starting from version CS3, MATLAB and Photoshop (using Photoshop Extended) are connected: MATLAB can use Photoshop functions (and vice versa). For further information please read the Photoshop Manual.

Creating Images by Computation

In this section we see how to design and plot simple images. There is a partial over-lap between the way to plot images in the current section and the way to plot images using the PsychToolbox as explained in the following chapters. However, it is useful to know both, so that you can use the best method according to your specific needs.

It is quite simple to plot images using the `plot` command. However, MATLAB has other simple functions to plot in 2-D (lines and polygons) and 3-D (spheres, cylinders, etc.). In the following table the main plotting commands are presented:

Function	Description
`line(x,y)` `line(x,y,z)`	Plot a multiline to the current figure. x and y are vectors of the same size specifying the endpoints of the line. `line(X,Y,Z)` creates lines in 3-D coordinates
`fill(x,y,c)`	Fills the 2-D polygon defined by vectors x and y with the color specified by c. c can be a string (such as a plot color specification) or an RGB vector. If c is a vector of numbers of the same length as x and y, its elements are used as indices into the current color map to specify colors at the vertices; the color within the polygon is obtained by bilinear interpolation of the vertex colors
`fill3(x,y,z,c)`	This is equivalent to `fill` but in 3-D space
`cylinder(r,n)` `[x,y,z]=cylinder(r,n)`	Forms a 3-D unit "cylinder" with n equally spaced vertices around the circumference of radius r. If r is a vector, the resulting figure is the connection between successive vertices at different radii, expressed by the vector r. It returns three matrices to be used with the function `surf`
`ellipsoid(xc,yc,zc,xr,yr,zr,n)` `[X,Y,Z]=ellipsoid(xc,yc,zc,xr,yr,zr,n)`	Plot an ellipsoid with center at xc, yc, and zc and radii xr, yr, zr. It returns three matrices to be used with the function `surf`. n is the number of surfaces used to form the ellipsoid

Here we provide a simple script to show the simultaneous lightness contrast effect [which is the condition whereby a gray patch on a dark background appears lighter than an identical patch on a light background; see Kingdom (1997) for a historical review of this perceptual phenomenon] and the successive color contrast effect, which is the condition whereby the perception of currently viewed colors is affected by previously viewed ones (see, for example, Helmholtz (1866/1964)), using some of the commands presented previously.

Fig. 6.8 Example of contrast and successive contrast effect images

Listing 6.5

```
 1  % M-Script to test the function to
 2  % generate simple graphics.
 3  % This show a figure with simultaneous
 4  % Contrast and successive contrast
 5  % effect
 6  %
 7  % Authors: Borgo, Soranzo, Grassi
 8  % Date: 2009
 9
10  figure; hold on;
11  colormap(gray(255));            % Set Colormap
12  fill([0,4,4,0],[0,0,3,3],30);   % plot
13  fill([1,3,3,1],[1,1,2,2],170);  % different
14  fill([0,4,4,0],[3,3,6,6],200);  % color
15  H=fill([1,3,3,1],[4,4,5,5],170);% rectangles
16  set(H,'EdgeAlpha',0);           % Clean last rectangle edge
17
18  Npoint=30;                      % Number of points
19  x=[1:Npoint]./Npoint*2*pi;       % to plot a circumference.
20
21  figure;
22  subplot(2,1,1); hold on;
23  fill([0,4,4,0],[0,0,2,2],[0 0 0]);   % Plot a black rectangle
24  fill(sin(x)+1,cos(x)+1,'r');         % plot a red circle centered in
25                                       % x=1,y=1
26  fill(sin(x)*0.1+1,cos(x)*0.1+1,'k'); % plot a little black circle
27  fill(sin(x)+3,cos(x)+1,'g');         % plot a green circle
28  fill(sin(x)*0.1+3,cos(x)*0.1+1,'k');
29  axis off;
30  subplot(2,1,2); hold on;
31  fill([0,4,4,0],[0,0,2,2],[0 0 0]);
32  fill(sin(x)+1,cos(x)+1,'y');
33  fill(sin(x)*0.1+1,cos(x)*0.1+1,'k');
34  fill(sin(x)+3,cos(x)+1,'y');
35  fill(sin(x)*0.1+3,cos(x)*0.1+1,'k');
36  axis off;
```

If you run the above script, you should see the images in Fig. 6.8.

Not all images can be designed using lines or polygons. Let's suppose that you want a two-dimensional sinusoidal image with a frequency of eight cycles per image, rotated by a certain angle. The following function does the job.

Listing 6.6

```
1   function [ImOut]=Sinusoid2D(xysize,SAngle,Fcxi,PhGrad)
2
3   % function [ImOut]= Sinusoid2D(xysize,SAngle,Fcxi,PhGrad))
4   %
5   % the function return a 2-D Spatial Sinusoid
6   %
7   % INPUT:     xysize  is the vector containing the x per y dimension
8   %                    if it is a scalar a square image is created
9   %            SAngle  is the spatial angle in degree of the sinusoid
10  %                    0 = vertical, 90 = horizontal
11  %            Fcxi    is the sinusoid frequency in cycles per image
12  %            PhGrad  is the phase of the sinusoid (in degree).
13  % OUTPUT     ImOut   the image of dimension express by xysize.
14  %
15  % Authors: Borgo, Soranzo, Grassi
16  % Date: 2012
17
18  % Calculate the image grid.
19  Boundx=xysize(1);
20  if length(xysize) == 2
21      Boundy=xysize(2);
22  else
23      Boundy=Boundx;
24  end
25  [x,y]=meshgrid(1:Boundx, 1:Boundy);
26
27  % define the costant for the cosine
28  wo=SAngle/180*pi;    % conversion from deg to rad
29  PhRad=PhGrad/180*pi;% conversion from deg to rad
30  f=Fcxi/xysize(1);    % frequency conversion
31
32  ax = f*cos(wo);      % convert the spatial frequency along y
33  by = f*sin(wo);      % convert the spatial frequency along x
34
35  % Calculate the Sinusoid
36  %(+1 is to obtatin all values being more than 1)
37  ImOut=sin(2*pi*(ax*x+by*y)+PhRad)+1;
```

Now save it with the name Sinusoid2D and test it with the following parameters.

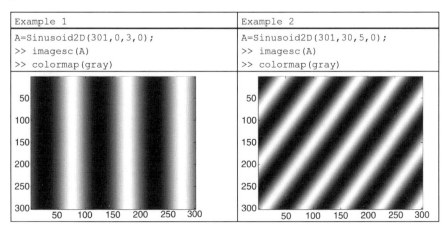

Example 1	Example 2
A=Sinusoid2D(301,0,3,0); >> imagesc(A) >> colormap(gray)	A=Sinusoid2D(301,30,5,0); >> imagesc(A) >> colormap(gray)

If we want to obtain a Gabor patch (i.e., a sine-wave grating in a gaussian window) we need to apply a gaussian window to the sinusoidal images we generated previously. The following function does it for you:

Listing 6.7

```
1   function [ImOut]=Gabor2D(xysize,SAngle,Fcxi,PhGrad,sigx,sigy)
2
3   % function [ImOut] = Gabor2D(xysize,SAngle,Fcxi,PhGrad,sigx,sigy)
4   %
5   % The function return a Spatial (2-D) Gabor image(Filter)
6   % defined in space domain as follow
7   % g(x,y) = s(x,y) * wr(x,y)
8   % where s(x,y) is the sinusoid (called also the carrier)
9   %        wr(x,y) is the gaussian window (called also envelope)
10  %
11  % the function return a 2-D Spatial Sinusoid
12  %
13  % INPUT:     xysize  is the number of pixel of the image
14  %            SAngle  is the spatial angle in degree of the sinusoid
15  %                    0 = vertical, 90 = horizontal
16  %            Fcxi    is the sinusoid frequency in cycles per image
17  %            PhGrad  is the phase of the sinusoid (in degree).
18  %            sigx    is the variance in pixels for the gaussian
19  %                    window on x axis.
20  %            sigy    is the variance in pixels for the gaussian
21  %                    window in y axis.
22  %                    if not specify, sigy=sigx;
23  % OUTPUT     ImOut   the image of dimension xysize X xysize.
24  %
25  % Authors: Borgo, Soranzo, Grassi
26  % Date: 2009
27
28  if nargin==5
29      sigy=sigx;
30  end
31
32  % Calculate the grid of point where calculate the image.
33  Bound=floor(xysize/2);
34  [x,y]=meshgrid(-Bound:Bound,-Bound:Bound);
35
36  % Calculate the gabor
37  S=Sinusoid2D(xysize,SAngle,Fcxi, PhGrad);
38  gaussEnv = exp(-((x/sigx).^2)-((y/sigy).^2));
39  ImOut=S.*gaussEnv;
```

You can rearrange the scripts and put all the operations in a single code listing. Here we show some examples, using the function Gabor2D:

Example 1	Example 2
>> A=Gabor2D(301,0,4,0,70); >> imagesc(A) >> colormap(gray) >> axis square	>> A=Gabor2D(301,45,5,90,70,30); >> imagesc(A) >> colormap(gray) >> axis square
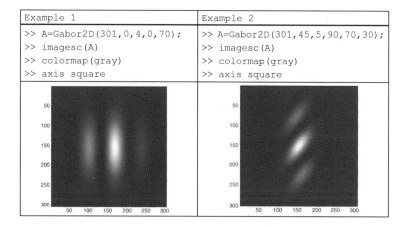	

Now that we have drawn a Gabor Patch, it should be quite simple to realize Gabor patches randomly distributed on the screen. Simply use the Gabor2D function as filter! Let's have a look:

Example	Graphical result
``` >> F=zeros(500); >> GaborFilter=Gabor2D(51,0,3,90,10); >> for i=1:20; >> F(floor(rand*500),floor(rand*500))=1; >> end; >> RandIm=filter2(GaborFilter,F,'valid'); >> imagesc(RandIm); >> colormap(gray); ```	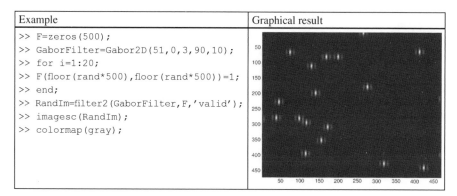

Here, each single point is set to 1 at a random position, and it is filtered with a Gabor patch created using Gabor2D function. The result is simply the displacement of the gabor patches of the screen. As you can see, you have a complete tool to work with Gabor patches.

Summary

- Digital pictures consist of a discrete number of *pixels.*
- Each pixel is associated with a value:
  - In gray-scale images the value corresponds to a gray level.
  - For color images, the color in the pixel is represented by n values, one for each basic color (i.e., for **RGB** images, one intensity for red, one intensity for green, and one intensity for blue).
  - For indexed images, the value corresponds to the index of a color-map table.

- The function `colormap` sets and retrieves the current color map used for indexed images.
- The function `imread` reads an image from a file, while the function `imwrite` writes an image file.
- The *point operation* changes each pixel value by modifying its intensity value using direct transformations. The `brighten` and the `contrast` functions are two useful point operations.
- *Windowing* is a point operation whereby there is a multiplication between two matrices: the image matrix and the window matrix. It is often used to create smooth edges, or to highlight certain parts of the image.
- The *neighborhood operation* changes each pixel's intensity value by considering the intensity of a certain number of pixels, generally in a mask around the pixel to be changed. Such an operation is called *space filtering*.
- Space filtering is done using the function `filter2`. Alternatively, you can use the function `imfilter`.
- Using specific commands like `line`, `cylinder`, `fill`, `fill3`, `ellipsoid`, it is possible to create simple 2-D and 3-D images.
- Gabor patches are created using windowing and filtering techniques.

Exercises

1. Write an M-script to create a color map of seven colors. Create a picture of seven circles. Each circle should be filled with a different color taken from the color map. Display another figure having seven circles but in gray scale (i.e., change the color map)

Solution	Graphical result
``Ncirc = 7;

% create a random colormap
Mycolormap = rand(Ncirc,3)

Npoint=30;
x=[1:Npoint]./Npoint*2*pi;

figure;
hold on;
for i = 1:7
    fill(sin(x),cos(x)+(i-1)*2,i);
end
axis equal
% Apply the colormap
colormap(Mycolormap);

figure;
hold on;
for i = 1:7
    fill(sin(x),cos(x)+(i-1)*2,i);
end
axis equal
 % Apply the grayscale
colormap(gray(7));``` | 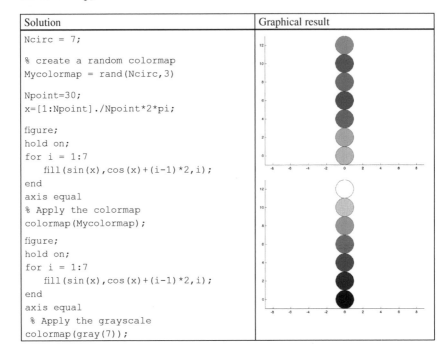 |

2. Read the image 'forest.tif', display it, and increase its brightness using a beta of 0.2. Resize it to 75% of its original size. Then save it with the new name 'MyForest.tif'.

Solution	Graphical result
``` >> [X1,map1]=imread('forest.tif'); >> image(X1); >> colormap(map1); >> brighten(0.2); >> X1res = imresize(X1,0.75); >> image(X1res); >> print -dtiff myforest; ```	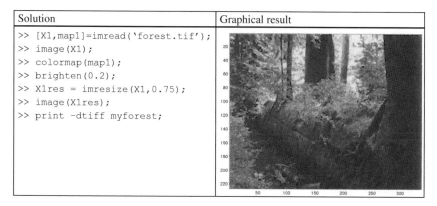

3. Load the file clown (i.e., type `load clown`) and use a gray-scale color map. Apply a sinusoidal window with a frequency of three cycles per image. You can create the window using the function `Sinusoid2D` in Listing 6.6. Apply to the original image a filter created with `fspecial` of type 'motion', with length 25 and an angle of 45°. Use the MATLAB help to see how to apply fspecial. Display the three (gray) images.

Solution	Graphical result
``` >> load clown; >> SinWin=Sinusoid2D(size(X),0,3,0); >> h = fspecial('motion', 25, 45); >> Xfiltered=filter2(h,X); >> figure; >> subplot(3,1,1); >> image(X); >> subplot(3,1,2); >> image(X.*SinWin); >> subplot(3,1,3); >> image(Xfiltered); >> colormap(gray(length(map))); ```	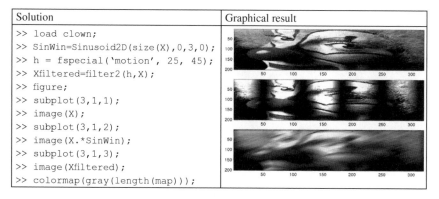

References

Helmholtz HV (1866/1964) Helmholtz's treatise on physiological optics. Optical Society of America, New York

Kingdom F (1997) Simultaneous contrast: the legacies of Hering and Helmholtz. Perception 26(6):673–677

Suggested Readings

Some of the concepts illustrated in this chapter can be found, in an extended way, in the following books:

Gonzalez RC, Woods RE, Eddins SL (2009) Digital image processing using MATLAB. Gatesmark Publishing

Poon T-C, Banerjee PP (2001) Contemporary optical image processing with MATLAB. New York: Elsevier Science Ltd

Chapter 7
Data Analysis

This chapter outlines the main statistics used by psychologists. Some of the functions described here are included in the Statistics toolbox, a toolbox specifically devoted to statistical analysis. Moreover, the chapter presents how to get some of the signal detection theory indexes.

The purpose of this chapter is to help the reader to build upon existing statistical knowledge in order to support its application in MATLAB. Most of the functions detailed here are included in the Statistics toolbox, a devoted MATLAB toolbox for statistics. In addition, a number of files and functions running statistical analysis can be found in file exchange section of the Mathworks website at the following link (see the brick for an example): http://www.mathworks.com/matlab-central/fileexchange/

The first part of the chapter outlines statistics, first descriptive statistics and then the inferential statistics. The last part outlines the signal detection theory indexes.

Descriptive Statistics

Measures of Central Tendency

The most-used measures of central tendency, such as the mean, the mode, and the median, are provided by built-in MATLAB functions. Specifically, `mean()`, `mode()`, and `median()` return the measures of the central tendency of a data vector. When the argument is a matrix, the functions return the measure of central tendency for each *column*. Table 7.1 shows these functions.

Additional descriptive measures can be acquired through the Statistics toolbox. For example, the toolbox includes functions for calculating the geometric mean, the harmonic mean, and the trimmed mean. Table 7.2 lists these functions. Note that with these functions, too, when the argument is a matrix, the function outputs the measure of central tendency for each *column*.

Table 7.1 Principal measures of central tendency

MATLAB function	Description
mean()	For vectors, mean(v) returns the arithmetic mean of the elements in v. For matrices, mean(X) returns the arithmetic mean of each *column*
mode()	For vectors, mode(v) returns the most frequent of the elements in v. For matrices, mode(X) returns the most repeated of the elements in each *column*
median()	For vectors, median(v) returns the median value of the elements in v. For matrices, median(X) returns a the median of the elements in each column

Table 7.2 Additional measures of central tendency provided by the Statistics toolbox

Statistical toolbox function	Description
Goemean()	Geometric mean of the input variable
harmmean()	Harmonic mean of the input variable
trimmean(v,percent)	m=trimmean(v,percent) calculates the mean of the variable v excluding the highest and lowest (percent/2%) of the observations

Table 7.3 Principal measures of dispersion

MATLAB function	Description	Output considering the vector v=1:10;
max(v)-min(v)	Range	>> max(v)-min(v) ans = 9
std(v)	Standard deviation	>> std(v) ans = 3.0600
var(v)	Variance	>> var(v) ans = 9.3636
std(v)/sqrt(length(v))	Standard error	>> std(v)/sqrt(length(v)) ans = 0.9226
median(v(find(v>median(v))))-median(v(find(v<median(v))))	Inter-quartile range	>> median(v(find(v>median(v))))-median(v(find(v<median(v)))) ans = 6

Measures of Dispersion

Range, standard deviation, variance, and standard error are the most-used measures of dispersion. Range, standard error, and interquartile difference, are built-in MATLAB functions. Additional dispersion measures are included in the Statistics toolbox [for example, range() and iqr()]. Table 7.3 shows the main dispersion measures assuming that the vector v=1:10 is the input argument.

By default, these functions adopt the unbiased estimator of dispersion (i.e., N–1). If you need the second moment of the function, pass the optional argument 1. For example, std(v,1) returns the second moment of the standard deviation (i.e., uses N instead of N–1).

Bivariate and Multivariate Descriptive Statistics

Correlation and covariance are the most used-statistics to measure the strength of the relationships among variables. `corrcoef()` returns the correlation between two input vectors. If a matrix is passed instead, then `corrcoef()` calculates the correlation among all the columns of the matrix. By default, `corrcoef()` returns only a matrix of correlation coefficients. However, additional outputs can be requested such as:

1. A matrix of p-values indicating the correlation's significance;
2. Two matrices of the lower and the upper bounds of the 95% confidence interval for each regression coefficient.

The following MATLAB code returns the correlation matrix R, the correlation p-values P, matrices RLO and RUP for the lower and upper bound confidence intervals for each coefficient in R:

```
>>[R,P,RLO,RUP] = corrcoef(X);
```

Let us suppose that a psychologist wants to find out whether there is a correlation between listening span (e.g., the number of remembered sentences of a story) and the number of errors in an arithmetic test in 7-year-old children. Twenty children participate in the study and the data are as presented in Table 7.4.

Listing 7.1 runs the correlation analysis on the data.

Listing 7.1

```
1  % Runs the correlation analysis on hypothetical data
2  % AUTHOR:   Borgo-Soranzo-Grassi
3  span = [2 4 4 4 5 5 3 3 2 1 2 6 6 6 5 4 4 4 3 3];
4  errors = [4 2 2 4 3 4 3 2 2 6 5 1 2 1 1 2 2 1 2 3];
5  [R,P,RLO,RUP] = corrcoef(span, errors);
```

Listing 7.1 outputs the following arguments:

1. The correlation matrix R, showing that there is a negative correlation between the two variables: the higher the listening span, the lower the number of errors in the arithmetic test.

```
R =
    1.0000   -0.6214
   -0.6214    1.0000
```

Table 7.4 Hypothetical data of a correlation study. The table reports the listening span (measured as the number of remembered sentences of a story) and number of errors in an arithmetic test of 20 seven years old children

Child id	1	2	3	4	5	6	7	8	9	10	11	12	13	14	15	16	17	18	19	20
Span	2	4	4	4	5	5	3	3	2	1	2	6	6	6	5	4	4	4	3	3
Errors	4	2	2	4	3	4	3	2	2	6	5	1	2	1	1	2	2	1	2	3

2. The probability matrix P, showing that the probability is only 0.0035 of getting a correlation of −0.6214 by random chance when the true correlation is zero.

```
P =
   0.0035
```

3. The interval bounds matrices RLO and RUP showing that the lower and the upper bounds for a 95% confidence interval of the correlation coefficient are −0.8344 and −0.2467, respectively.

```
RLO =
    1.0000    -0.8344
   -0.8344     1.0000
RUP =
    1.0000    -0.2467
   -0.2467     1.0000
```

Covariance

The covariance matrix of a set of data X can be obtained by typing `cov(X)` at the MATLAB prompt. The diagonal of the output matrix contains the variance of each variable. The variances of a number of variables can be obtained using the `diag()` function in combination with the `cov()` function, in the following way: `diag(cov(X))`. With this function, too, we can pass the optional argument 1 to get the second moment of the function.

Simple and Multiple Linear Regression

There are different ways to run a linear regression analysis in MATLAB. Perhaps the easiest one is to use `regstats()`, which is included in the Statistics toolbox. The function takes the dependent variable as first argument and a matrix of predictors as second argument. It is also possible to pass an optional third argument for nonlinear regressions. If you type

```
regstats(y,X);
```

MATLAB displays a GUI listing the diagnostic statistics that can be saved into the workspace (Fig. 7.1).

The diagnostic statistics can be saved in a structure in this way:

```
s=regstats(y,X); saves the diagnostic statistics in structure s.
```

Imagine that a psychologist wants to discover a regression model for a class of 13 students by knowing their IQs and the number of hours they study per week. Table 7.5 lists the data:

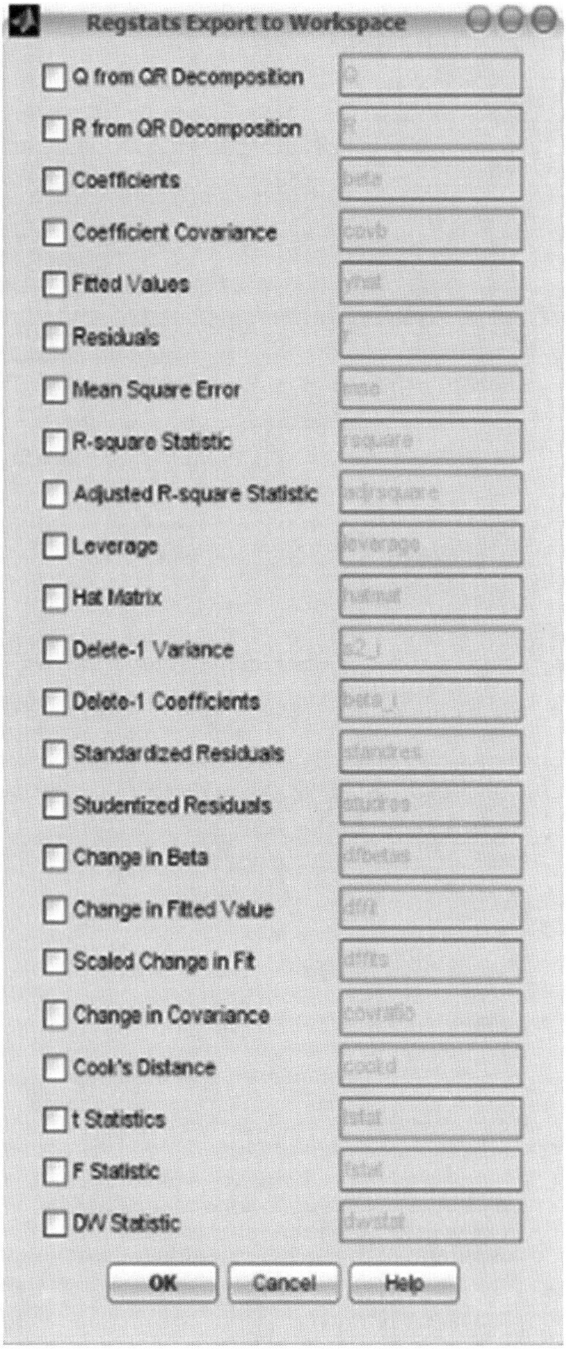

Fig. 7.1 GUI output by the `regstats()` function

Table 7.5 Hypothetical data for a regression analysis. The table lists the grade, the IQ, and the number of hours studied per week by 13 students

Student id	1	2	3	4	5	6	7	8	9	10	11	12	13
Grade	1	1.6	1.2	2.1	2.6	1.8	2.6	2	3.2	2.6	3	3.6	1.9
IQ	110	112	118	119	122	125	127	130	132	134	136	138	125
StudyTime	8	10	6	13	14	6	13	12	13	11	12	18	7

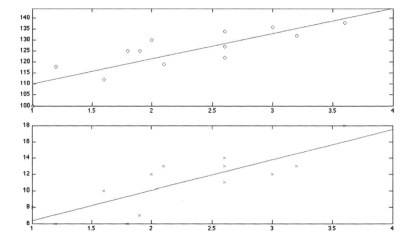

Fig. 7.2 Linear regression plot resulting from code listing 7.2

Listing 7.2 runs the regression analysis on these data.

Listing 7.2

```
1    grade = [1 1.6 1.2 2.1 2.6 1.8 2.6 2 3.2 2.6 3 3.6 1.9];
2    iq = [100 112 118 119 122 125 127 130 132 134 136 138 125];
3    studytime=[8 10 6 13 14 6 13 12 13 11 12 18 7];
4    s=regstats(grade', [iq' studytime']);
5    subplot(2,1,2)
6    plot(grade, studytime,'x')
7    lsline
8    subplot(2,1,1)
9    plot(grade, iq,'o')
10   lsline
```

By inspecting the structure s, we can see that the regression coefficients are −5.3178 and 0.0505 0.1125 (s.beta), that they are all significant at an alpha level of 0.05 (s.tstat) and that the amount of variance explained by the predictors is 90.8% (s.rsquare). Figure 7.2 shows the scatterplots for both the predictors with the regression lines.

The regression line can also be obtained through the built-in fitting feature: after plotting the data, select Tools > Basic Fitting from the Figure menu bar. This will show the GUI presented in Fig. 7.3.

As can be seen from Fig. 7.3, different polynomials can be fitted.

The next table shows the main functions fitting different polynomials.

Fig. 7.3 The built-in MATLAB feature for Basic fitting. Plot the data and select Tools > Basic Fitting from the menu bar to fit different polynomials to the data

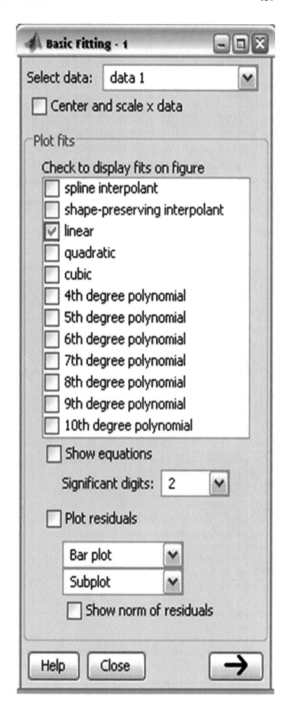

MATLAB function	Description
p, S]=polyfit(X,y,n)	Finds the coefficients of a polynomial *p(x)* of degree *n* that fits the data in a least squares sense. p is a vector of length n; each value is the polynomial coefficient. S is for use with polyconf to obtain error estimates or predictions
y=polyval(p,x)	Returns the value of a polynomial of degree n (having coefficient p) evaluated at x
y,delta]=polyconf(p,X,S)	Returns the value of a polynomial p evaluated at x. Use the optional output S created by polyfit to generate 95% prediction intervals. If the coefficients in P are least squares estimates computed by polyfit and the errors in the data input to polyfit were independent, normal, with constant variance, then there is a 95% probability that y±delta will contain a future observation at x

The next example (Listing 7.3) shows how to use each of these functions.

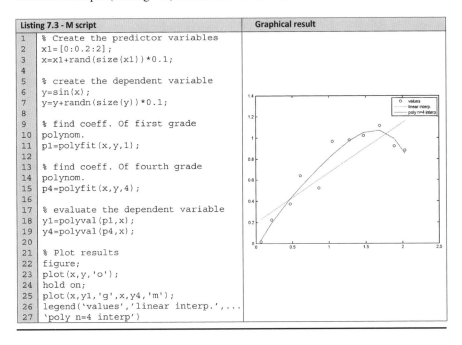

Listing 7.3 - M script	Graphical result
1 % Create the predictor variables 2 x1=[0:0.2:2]; 3 x=x1+rand(size(x1))*0.1; 4 5 % create the dependent variable 6 y=sin(x); 7 y=y+randn(size(y))*0.1; 8 9 % find coeff. Of first grade 10 polynom. 11 p1=polyfit(x,y,1); 12 13 % find coeff. Of fourth grade 14 polynom. 15 p4=polyfit(x,y,4); 16 17 % evaluate the dependent variable 18 y1=polyval(p1,x); 19 y4=polyval(p4,x); 20 21 % Plot results 22 figure; 23 plot(x,y,'o'); 24 hold on; 25 plot(x,y1,'g',x,y4,'m'); 26 legend('values','linear interp.',... 27 'poly n=4 interp')	

Generalized Linear Model

The Statistics toolbox includes the glmfit() function, which computes the generalized linear model regression of different distributions; that is, in addition to the default normal distribution, it is possible to use the binomial, the gamma, the inverse Gaussian, and the Poisson distributions.

Besides the regression coefficients, glmfit() returns the deviance of the fit at the solution vector and a structure with several pieces of information about the analysis, such as a *t*-test for each coefficient (t), the significance of each coefficient (*p*), and different types of residuals.

Table 7.6 Hypothetical data for a logistic regression analysis on a change blindness experiment. Detection is the binomial Dependent Variable (DV) indicating whether participants have detected the change within 5 s or not. Contrast is the Independent Variable (IV) of the scene contrast with three levels: low, medium, and high

Participant id	1	2	3	4	5	6	7	8	9	10	11	12	13	14	15	16	17	18	19	20
Detection	0	1	1	1	0	1	1	1	0	0	0	0	1	0	0	0	1	1	1	0
Contrast	1	2	2	3	3	1	3	2	2	1	1	1	2	1	1	2	2	1	2	3

Let's see an example of the use of `glmfit()`. In a hypothetical change blindness experiment,[1] a psychologist wants to arrive at the regression function for predicting the probability of detecting a change within 5 s of the stimulus presentation (detected = 1; not-detected = 0) as a function of the contrast of the whole scene (low-contrast = 1; medium-contrast = 2; high-contrast = 3). Twenty participants took part in the study, and the data presented in Table 7.6 have been collected.

The following code runs the logistic regression analysis on the data of Table 7.6.

```
>> contr = [1 2 2 3 3 1 3 2 2 1 1 1 2 1 1 2 2 1 2 3];%levels
of the contrast IV
>> detection = [0 1 1 1 0 1 1 1 0 0 0 0 1 0 0 0 1 1 1 0];%DV
>> [b dev stats]=glmfit(contr', detection', 'binomial')
b =
    -1.3421
     0.7483
dev =
    26.2642
stats =
              beta: [2x1 double]
               dfe: 18
              sfit: 1.0581
                 s: 1
           estdisp: 0
              covb: [2x2 double]
                se: [2x1 double]
         coeffcorr: [2x2 double]
                 t: [2x1 double]
                 p: [2x1 double]
             resid: [20x1 double]
            residp: [20x1 double]
            residd: [20x1 double]
            resida: [20x1 double]
>> stats.p
ans =
     0.2763
     0.2431
```

---

[1] See Simons and Chabris (1999) for a funny example of change blindness.

This code outputs:

- Vector b= [-1.3421; 0.7483] indicates that the regression coefficient is 0.7483 and the value of a regression constant is −1.3421;
- Scalar dev= [26.2642] indicates the deviance of the fit;
- Structure stat; shows, among others things, that our regression coefficients are not statistically significant (stats.p= [0.2763; 0.2431]).

Inferential Statistics

Once we have described the data, we are interested in making inferences on these data, that is, to test our hypothesis. The Statistics toolbox includes several statistical tests for this purpose. The main parametric and nonparametric tests are outlined in the following sections.

Parametric Statistics

This section outlines the main MATLAB functions for parametric statistical analysis. However, in order to run a parametric analysis, parametric assumptions (e.g., a normality test on the data) have to be ascertained.

Assessing the Parametric Assumptions

To check for normality, we can look at the histograms and we can inspect their shape using the hist() function. The kurtosis() function returns the kurtosis of the distribution of the input vector. The function takes the optional argument zero (0), whether you want to correct for bias; by default there is no correction. The skewness() function returns a measure of the asymmetry. To test whether the data are normally distributed, the kstest() function performs a Kolmogorov–Smirnov test that compares the data to a standard normal distribution. It outputs 1 when the null hypothesis can be rejected. The probability of the test can be obtained as an additional output. For small sample sizes it might be preferable to use the lillietest() function, which performs a *Lillilifors* test of the default null hypothesis that the sample in the vector argument comes from a normal distribution, against the alternative hypothesis that it does not. Alternatively, the jbtest() function performs a Jarque–Bera test. The null hypothesis is that the sample comes from a normal distribution with unknown mean and variance.

z-Test

The Statistics toolbox includes the ztest(v,m,sigma) function for performing the *z*-test. The function takes as first argument a data vector v whose mean is equal to m (the second argument), and whose standard deviation is equal to sigma (the third argument). In practice, this function is rarely used in psychology, since we normally do not know in advance the actual mean and standard deviation of the population. Much more common is, instead, the *t*-test.

t-Test

The Statistics toolbox includes two functions that perform the *t*-test: `ttest()` and `ttest2()`. The former is used to run both the one-sample *t*-test and the related *t*-test, while the latter is used to run a two-sample unrelated *t*-test. The significance level of the test and the direction of the hypotheses can be specified in both functions as optional parameters. The next section shows how to perform a one-sample *t*-test by means of the `ttest()` function; the following section details how to perform a two-sample *t*-test either through `ttest()` or through `ttest2()` depending on whether the data are related or unrelated, respectively.

One-Sample *t*-Test

The `ttest()` function tests the hypothesis that a vector's mean is different from zero. If the experimental hypothesis is against a different value, an additional argument has to be passed to the function specifying the desired value. The hypothesis that the mean is different from zero is performed against the default significance level of 0.05. A different value can be passed as third argument. In addition, the "tail" parameter, specifying the direction of the test, can be passed when you have a directional hypothesis. Pass 'left' when you are expecting that the mean is less than 0 (or the desired value); pass 'right' otherwise. By default, this optional argument is set to 'both' indicating that the test is bidirectional.

The function returns the test result in binary form: 1 means that the null hypothesis *can be* rejected; 0 means that it *cannot* be rejected. Additional outputs can be requested: (1) the probability of the test; (2) the confidence interval; and (3) a structure whose fields are the t value, the degrees of freedom, and the sample standard deviation.

To show how to use the *t*-test, we test whether the mean of 20 randomly generated numbers (ranging from 0 to 1) is actually different from 0.

```
>> [H, p, CI, stats]=ttest(rand(20, 1)) ;
H =
    1
p =
    2.6460e-06
CI =
    0.3360
    0.6491
stats =
    tstat: 6.5860
       df: 19
       sd: 0.3345
```

Table 7.7 Hypothetical data of ten participants where RTs are measured with both a red and a yellow probe

Participant id	1	2	3	4	5	6	7	8	9	10
Yellow	300	287	301	400	211	399	412	312	390	412
Red	240	259	302	311	210	402	390	298	347	380

`H = 1` indicates that the null hypothesis can be rejected; `p = 2.6460e-06`: the probability of finding these results by random chance is extremely low; `CI = 0.3360 0.6491`: the confidence intervals of the mean are within these values. Finally, the function returns a structure with the details of the analysis.

Two-Sample *t*-Test

The Statistics toolbox includes two functions performing the two-sample *t*-test: (1) `ttest()` for the paired, or repeated measure, *t*-test, and (2) `ttest2()` for the unrelated, or independent measure, *t*-test.

The first two arguments to be passed to both functions are data vectors. Each vector represents either a condition, in the `ttest()` case, or a group, in the `ttest2()` case. Hence, the same `ttest()` function performing the one-sample *t*-test also performs the paired *t*-test. When this function receives as argument one vector only, or one vector and one scalar, it performs the one-sample *t*-test. When instead two vectors are passed, it performs the paired *t*-test. In this latter case, the participants' scores have to be in the same position in the two vectors, and the vectors should be of the same length. This constraint does not apply to the `ttest2()` function, where the two vectors might have different lengths.

`ttest2()` has the same default arguments as those of `ttest()`. Hence, the significance level is set to 0.05; again, a different value can be passed as third argument. In addition, the "tail" parameter, specifying the direction of the test, can be set. Pass `'left'` when you are expecting that the mean difference between the first and second samples is less than 0; pass `'right'` otherwise (`'both'` is the default).

`ttest2()` shares the same outputs as `ttest()`. That is, both functions return the test result in binary form: 1 to signify that the null hypothesis *can be* rejected; 0 to signify that the null hypothesis *cannot be* rejected. Additional outputs can be requested: (1) the probability of the test; (2) the confidence interval; and (3) a structure whose fields are the t value, the degree of freedom, and the sample standard deviation.

Let us suppose that a psychologist wants to run an experiment to test the effects of a probe color on Reaction Times (RTs). Specifically, the psychologist is interested in finding out whether RTs *decrease* when the color of a probe is red instead of yellow at an alpha level of 0.01. Ten participants are tested, and RTs, in milliseconds, are collected as shown in Table 7.7.

Listing 7.4 runs the related *t*-test analysis on these data.

Listing 7.4

```
1   % M-script to verify how ttest function works
2   % Authors: M.Borgo - A.Soranzo - M. Grassi
3   yellow = [300 287 301 400 211 399 412 312 390 412];
4   red = [240 259 302 311 210 402 390 298 347 380];
5   [h p ci stats]=ttest(yellow,red, 0.01,'right')
```

Since the alpha level is 0.01, we pass this number as a third argument. In addition, there is an expected direction of the test: we are expecting that RTs in the "red" condition should be faster than in the "yellow" condition. If we pass the vector "yellow" as a first argument, then we are expecting that the difference between the means should be larger than 0. Hence, the right argument has to be passed to the function.

Let's inspect the code's output.

```
h =
   1
p =
   0.0067
ci =
   2.3241 Inf
stats =
   tstat: 3.0719
     df: 9
     sd: 29.3381
```

$h = 1$ indicates that the null hypothesis can be rejected at the alpha level of 0.01; indeed, the probability of finding these results by random chance is equal to 0.0067 (*p*). ci = 2.3241 – Inf is the confidence interval (since the hypothesis is directional, one bound is Infinite); finally, stats is the structure with the *t*-test results.

If there were two different groups of participants, that is, one group was tested with the yellow probe only and the other group with the red probe only, then we would need ttest2() as follows:

```
>> [h p ci stats]=ttest2(yellow,red, 0.01,'right')
h =
   0
p =
   0.1787
ci =
  -48.5131 Inf
stats =
   tstat: 0.9446
     df: 18
     sd: 67.4690
```

In contrast to the within-subjects case, the null hypothesis cannot be rejected at the alpha level of 0.01. By looking at the p value, we find out that the probability of obtaining these results by chance with independent samples is 17.87%.

ANOVA

The Statistics toolbox includes three different functions for runing Analysis of Variance (ANOVA) analysis: `anova()`; `anova1()`, and `anova2()`. `anova1()` is used when there is one independent variable in between-subjects experiments; `anova2()` performs a balanced two-ways ANOVA in between-subjects experiments; `anovan()` performs both balanced and unbalanced ANOVA in between-subjects experiments with two or more factors; in addition, it performs ANOVAs in within-subjects experiments. Hence, both `anova2()` and `anovan()` can be used to run balanced two-ways ANOVAs . However, since `anovan()` has a broader application, its use is more common than `anova2()`.

One-Way ANOVA

The Statistics toolbox includes the `anova1()` function to run a one-way, independent-samples ANOVA. The function can take as argument a matrix: the matrix's cells are scores, and the matrix's columns are the groups [`anova1(X)`]. Alternatively, you can pass two arguments: the dependent variable and the group [`anova1(dv, group)`]. The latter way is useful when groups do not have the same size.

When groups have the same size, the group vector can be implemented directly in the function call to increase readability in the following way:

```
anova1([group1' group2' group3' ...])
```

Unless otherwise specified, `anova1()` displays two figures: the ANOVA table and a box plot. In addition, it returns the following arguments: (1) the *p*-value; (2) a text version of the ANOVA table; (3) a structure with values that can be used for a multicomparison analysis (see below).

To show how the function works, consider the experiment on the effects of the probe color on RTs (see the independent *t*-test section). Imagine that in that experiment, a third group is tested in which participants' RTs are measured when presented with a black probe.

The experiment's results are listed in Table 7.8.

Table 7.8 Hypothetical data of three groups made by ten participants each. RTs are measured as a function of probe color (three levels: yellow, red, and black)

Yellow	300	287	301	400	211	399	412	312	390	412
Red	240	259	302	311	210	402	390	298	347	380
Black	210	230	213	210	220	208	290	300	201	201

The following vectors are therefore implemented:

```
>> yellow = [300 287 301 400 211 399 412 312 390 412];
>> red = [240 259 302 311 210 402 390 298 347 380];
>> black = [ 210 230 213 210 220 208 290 300 201 201];
```

Since the number of participants per group is the same, anoval() can be used in both its ways. Let's see both of them. The first is to pass as first argument a matrix whose columns are the results of the groups (as observed above, this matrix can be implemented directly in calling the function). We also pass to the function an optional argument 'names' to improve output readability.

```
>> names = [{'yellow'} ; {'red'}; {'black'}];
>> [p table stats]=anoval([yellow' red' black'], names);
```

Figures 7.4 and 7.5 show the ANOVA table and the box plot outputted by the above code.

ANOVA Table

Source	SS	df	MS	F	Prob>F
Columns	70528.1	2	35264.03	10.15	0.0005
Error	93763.4	27	3472.72		
Total	164291.5	29			

Fig. 7.4 ANOVA table resulting from the hypothetical probe color example

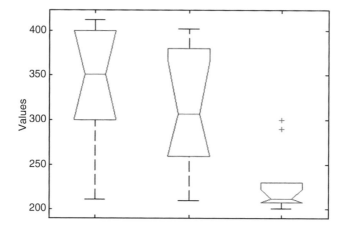

Fig. 7.5 Box plot resulting from the hypothetical probe color example

An alternative way of using `anova1()` is to pass as arguments a single vector with all RTs (i.e., of length 30) and a second vector having the same size as the first one, specifying the group type. Keep in mind that this is the only possible way of using the function when group sizes differ.

First, we merge the three groups' RTs into a single vector:

```
X=[yellow red black]';
```

Second, the vector with the groups' names has to be implemented in such a way that each group type is repeated for the number of participants belonging to the group (in this case the number of participants is the same for the three groups).

```
n_yellow=repmat({'yellow'},10,1);
n_red=repmat({'red'},10,1);
n_black=repmat({'black'},10,1);
group= [n_yellow' n_red' n_black']';
```

We added "n_" in front of the cell array's name to specify that these are names. Note the use of the apostrophe to transpose the vectors when the group vector is implemented.

Finally, we run the ANOVA test, whose results should be the same as in the previous case.

```
[p table stats]=anova1(X,group);
```

By looking at the function outputs, the null hypothesis can be rejected: there is a significant effect of the probe color on RTs.

The next step is to run a multicomparison analysis to find out the differences among groups. `multcompare()` is the function we want. It works together with the `anova1()` function and takes as argument the third argument returned by `anova1()`. The multicomparison test is returned by `multcompare(stats)` in the form of a five-column matrix. The first two columns indicate the group pair being compared, the third column is the estimated difference in means, and the last two columns are the interval for the difference.

In addition, the function returns an interactive figure. By clicking on the group symbol at the bottom, in part of the figure is displayed the group(s) from which the selected one statistically differs. In addition to the structure argument, some other arguments may be passed. The second one is the desired alpha level; the third is whether to display a plot, which can be set on or off. The fourth, which is more interesting, indicates the comparison type we need. There are several options: `'hsd'` for Tukey's honestly significant difference criterion (default); `'lsd'` for Tukey's least significant difference procedure; `'bonferroni'` for the Bonferroni adjustment to compensate for multiple comparisons; `'dunn-sidak'` for the Dunn and Sidák adjustment for multiple comparisons; and `sheffe()` for critical values from Scheffé's procedure.

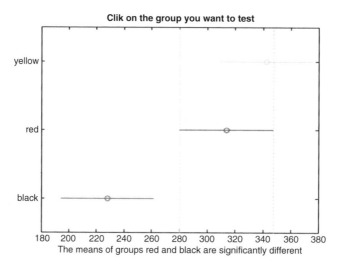

Fig. 7.6 Interactive plot resulting from multicomparison with Bonferroni correction

Let's suppose that we want to run a multicomparison test on the stats structure resulting from the previous ANOVA, using Bonferroni correction and that we are happy with the other defaults. The following code will do the job:

```
multcompare(stats,[],[],'bonferroni');
```

The interactive figure outputted by this code is shown in Fig. 7.6.

Two- and n-Way ANOVA

The anova2() function performs a balanced two-way ANOVA in a between-subjects experiment. It takes as first argument a matrix in which data of different columns represent changes in the first factor, while data in the rows represent changes in the second factor. If there is more than one observation for each combination of factors, an optional second argument can be passed to the function indicating the number of replicates in each position, which must be the same and a multiple of the number of rows.

Let's see how to use anova2() with an example. Imagine again the experiment on the effects of the probe color on RTs, but now we consider an additional factor that is probe size with two levels: small and large.

The data that have been collected for the six experimental groups are displayed in Table 7.9.

Table 7.9 Hypothetical data of six groups made by ten participants each. RTs are measured as a function of probe color (three levels: Yellow, Red, and Black); and as a function of probe size (two levels: Small and Big)

Small	Yellow	300	287	301	400	211	399	412	312	390	412
Small	Red	240	259	302	311	210	402	390	298	347	380
Small	Black	210	230	213	210	220	208	290	300	201	201
Big	Yellow	289	289	300	402	251	389	422	332	360	422
Big	Red	210	229	300	301	200	340	350	290	317	320
Big	Black	226	220	253	218	260	228	380	300	221	211

```
                          ANOVA Table

   Source        SS        df     MS        F      Prob>F
   ----------------------------------------------------------
   Columns     108971.2    2    54485.6   16.42   0
   Rows             4.3    1        4.3    0       0.9715
   Interaction   6760.9    2     3380.5    1.02    0.3678
   Error       179142     54     3317.4
   Total       294878.4   59
```

Fig. 7.7 Two-way ANOVA table output

Listing 7.5 performs a two-way ANOVA on the above data. Note that since we have ten participants per group, reps = 10. When implementing the matrix to be passed to anova2(), we need to be careful. Specifically, each column of the matrix has to be made in such a way that the corresponding rows indicate a score of the same level of the second variable, which is organized in rows. Since in this case the second variable has two levels, the first 10 scores belong to its first level, while the last 10 scores belong to the second one (Fig. 7.7).

Listing 7.5

```
1   % M-script to test the anova2 function
2   % Authors: M. Borgo - A. Soranzo - M. Grassi
3   small_yellow = [300 287 301 400 211 399 412 312 390 412];
4   small_red = [240 259 302 311 210 402 390 298 347 380];
5   small_black = [210 230 213 210 220 208 290 300 201 201];
6   big_yellow = [289 289 300 402 251 389 422 332 360 422];
7   big_red = [210 229 300 301 200 340 350 290 317 320];
8   big_black = [226 220 253 218 260 228 380 300 221 211];
9   yellow = [small_yellow big_yellow];
10  red = [small_red big_red];
11  black = [small_black big_black];
12  [p,table,stats]= anova2([yellow' red' black'],10);
13  multcompare (stats)
```

Table 7.10 Hypothetical data of one group of ten participants. In a repeated-measure design, RTs are measured as a function of probe color (three levels: Yellow, Red, and Black)

Participant id	1	2	3	4	5	6	7	8	9	10
Yellow	300	287	301	400	211	399	412	312	390	412
Red	240	259	302	311	210	402	390	298	347	380
Black	210	230	213	210	220	208	290	300	201	201

As can be seen from the table, the results show a significant effect of the Color variable (organized in columns) and no significant effect of the Size variable (organized in rows). The interaction between the two variables is not significant. However, the use of `anova2()` is uncommon; generally, `anovan()` is used when there is more than one Independent variable, because it can be used with both balanced and unbalanced data.

anovan()

`anovan()` performs both balanced and unbalanced multiple-way ANOVA for comparing the means of the observations in X (the first argument vector) with respect to different groups (the second argument). Hence, it works in a similar way to the `anova1()` function when group sizes are different. The first vector argument has to be carefully implemented. In detail, the position of the factors' levels has to correspond to the group name in the second vector argument. For example, if the first factor has three levels, the numbers in the vector should be organized in triplets. The second argument is a cell array containing the name of the conditions. Hence, with two factors, the code is as follows:

```
anovan(X,{IV1 IV2})
```

Note that the second argument is a cell array passed to the function by means of the curly braces.

`anovan()` receives many further optional arguments, including the 'alpha' level, the 'model' type (the interaction type is very often used in psychology because we are interested not only in the main effects of the factors but also in their interactions), and the 'names' cell array containing the names of the factors.

`anovan()` outputs the same arguments as `anova1()`, as well an additional vector with the main and interaction terms. The following example illustrates `anovan()` use.

Example

To show the use of `anovan()`, let's return to the experiment on the effects of the probe color on RTs that we have used to study `anova1()`. Listing 7.6 rearranges the data of Table 7.10 to be used with `anova1()`.

Listing 7.6

```
1   % M-script to test the anovan and multicompare functions
2   % Authors: M. Borgo - A. Soranzo - M. Grassi
3   small_yellow = [300 287 301 400 211 399 412 312 390 412];
4   small_red = [240 259 302 311 210 402 390 298 347 380];
5   small_black = [210 230 213 210 220 208 290 300 201 201];
6   big_yellow = [289 289 300 402 251 389 422 332 360 422];
7   big_red = [210 229 300 301 200 340 350 290 317 320];
8   big_black = [226 220 253 218 260 228 380 300 221 211];
9   nsubjsy=10;
10  nsubjsr=10;
11  nsubjsb=10;
12  nsubjby=10;
13  nsubjbr=10;
14  nsubjbb=10;
15  sizesmall=repmat({'small'},nsubjsy+nsubjsr+nsubjsb,1);
16  sizebig=repmat({'big'},nsubjsy+nsubjbr+nsubjbb,1);
17  Size=[sizesmall; sizebig];
18  yellowsmall=repmat({'yellow'},nsubjsy,1);
19  redsmall=repmat({'red'},nsubjsr,1);
20  blacksmall=repmat({'black'},nsubjsb,1);
21  yellowbig=repmat({'yellow'},nsubjby,1);
22  redbig=repmat({'red'},nsubjbr,1);
23  blackbig=repmat({'black'},nsubjbb,1);
24  Color=[yellowsmall; redsmall; blacksmall; yellowbig; redbig; blackbig];
25  X=[small_yellow small_red small_black big_yellow big_red big_black]';
26  [p table stats terms]=anovan(X,{Size Color}, 'model','interaction',
    'varnames',{'Size' 'Color'});
27  multcompare(stats,'dimension', [1 2])
```

Code listing 7.6 has been implemented for general purposes. Indeed, in this hypothetical experiment all groups have the same size, and there was no need to implement different variables for each group size (rows 9–14). This code could have been written in many different ways. For example, it is possible, and quicker, to assign a number to each group rather than a label. However, these changes would have reduced the output's legibility. Figure 7.8 shows the results of the ANOVA analysis.

Analysis of Variance

Source	Sum Sq.	d.f.	Mean Sq.	F	Prob>F
Size	4.3	1	4.3	0	0.9715
Color	108971.2	2	54485.6	16.42	0
Size*Color	6760.9	2	3380.5	1.02	0.3678
Error	179142	54	3317.4		
Total	294878.4	59			

Constrained (Type III) sums of squares.

Fig. 7.8 ANOVA table output from listing 7.6

By looking at the ANOVA table we can conclude that there is a significant effect of the color variable, while there is no effect of the probe dimension on RTs (results are exactly the same as those obtained with `anova1()`).

One-Way Repeated-Measure ANOVA Analysis with `anova1()`

Let's reconsider the experiment on the effects of the probe color on RTs. However, imagine that the data come from a repeated-measure design in which the same participants have been tested with probes of different colors. Hence, the hypothetical data are the same as before, as displayed in Table 7.10.

To run a one-way repeated-measure ANOVA, we use the `anovan()` function by passing the variable Subject as a second factor having random effects, whose levels are the participants. To do this, we add the optional argument `'random'` specifying that the second variable has random effects. Since there are two variables only, it would be not necessary to specify that the variable Subject has random effects. However, for the sake of clarity, it is better to specify that these variables' effects are not fixed. In addition, we familiarize ourselves with the use of the optional argument 'random', whose use becomes necessary in ANOVAs designs with more than one factor. Hence, we have to implement two factors: the first, Color, with three levels (yellow, red, and black) and the second, Subject, with ten levels (the ten participants).

Listing 7.7 will do the job:

Listing 7.7

```
1    yellow = [300 287 301 400 211 399 412 312 390 412];
2    red = [240 259 302 311 210 402 390 298 347 380];
3    black = [ 210 230 213 210 220 208 290 300 201 201];
4    nsubj=10;
5    ncond=3;
6    s=repmat(1:nsubj,ncond,1);
7    col=repmat(1:ncond,nsubj,1);
8    X=[yellow; red; black];
9    X=reshape(X,nsubj*ncond,1);
10   Subj=reshape(s,nsubj*ncond,1);
11   Color=reshape(col',nsubj*ncond,1);
12   [p table stats]=anovan(X,{Color Subj},'random',2);
13   multcompare(stats)
```

Two-Way Repeated-Measure ANOVA

Listing 7.8 shows how to run a two-way repeated-measure ANOVA using `anovan()`. For this purpose, we will use again the experiment on the effects of probe size and color on RTs, but now we hypothesize that the experimental design was within subjects (i.e. that the same participants run all the conditions).

Listing 7.8

```
1   yellow = [300 287 301 400 211 399 412 312 390 412];
2   red = [240 259 302 311 210 402 390 298 347 380];
3   black = [ 210 230 213 210 220 208 290 300 201 201];
4   big_yellow = [289 289 300 402 251 389 422 332 360 422];
5   big_red = [210 229 300 301 200 340 350 290 317 320];
6   big_black = [226 220 253 218 260 228 380 300 221 211];
7   X=[small_yellow small_red small_black big_yellow big_red big_black]';
8   nsubj=10;
9   nlevelsSize=2;
10  nlevelColor=3;
11  Subj=repmat(1:nsubj,1,nlevelsSize*nlevelColor)';
12  sizesmall=repmat({'small'},1,nlevelColor*nsubj)';
13  sizebig=repmat({'big'}, 1,nlevelColor*nsubj)';
14  Size= [sizesmall' sizebig']';
15  Colyellow=repmat({'yellow'},nsubj,1);
16  Colred=repmat({'red'},nsubj,1);
17  Colblack=repmat({'black'},nsubj,1);
18  Color= [Colyellow' Colred' Colblack' Colyellow' Colred' Colblack']';
19  [p table stats terms]=anovan(X,{Size Color Subj}, 'random', 3, 'model', 2,
    'varnames', {'Size' 'Color' 'Subj'});
20  multcompare(stats,'dimension', [1 2])
```

Note the use of the "'random', 3" argument in anovan() to specify that the third factor has random effects. Note also the use of the argument "'dimension', [1 2]" in multcompare() to specify that we want to run a multiple comparisons test between the first two variables.

Three-Way Mixed-Measures ANOVA

To conclude the anovan() overview, let's see how to run an ANOVA with mixed models, when some factors are within subjects, and others are between subjects. To do this, we have to pass to anovan() an additional optional argument, "nesting". Indeed, if one factor is between subjects in an otherwise repeated-measure design, then it can be said that the variable "subjects" is "nested" within the between-subjects variable. For example, let's consider again the experiment on the effects of color and size of a probe on RTs. The experimenter wants to test also whether there is a difference in RTs between males and females. In this case, we say that the variable 'Subjects' is "nested" within the sex variable. We have to pass to anvoan() an additional argument specifying which is the nested variable. To do this, we need to implement a square matrix whose dimensions are equal to the number of factors, and each row and column represents a factor in the same order in which they are passed to the function. So row 1 and column 1 represent factor 1; row 2 and column 2 represent factor 2; and so on. Each matrix cell represents the nesting relationship between each pair of variables. The cell value will be 0 when there is no nesting relationship and 1 otherwise. Specifically, it will be 1 when the factor represented by the row is nested within the IV represented by the column. If the third factor is nested within the fourth, then cell 3,4 will be 1. The implementation of this matrix may be slightly laborious; at the end of the chapter we will see a way to make it simpler.

In addition, since a three-way mixed-measures design is quite a complex one, modeling the interactions might be laborious as well. We will see a shortcut for the implementation of this argument. But first, let's analyse code Listing 7.9 to see how to implement both the "nesting" and "modeling" variables and how to pass them to anovan(). Data are the same as in the two-way repeated-measures example above, but now we also take into account the Gender of the participants as an independent variable: the first five subjects were males, and the remaining five were females, and we are interested in testing whether there is any difference in the RTs between these two groups.

Listing 7.9

```
1   yellow = [300 287 301 400 211 399 412 312 390 412];
2   red = [240 259 302 311 210 402 390 298 347 380];
3   black = [ 210 230 213 210 220 208 290 201 201];
4   big_yellow = [289 289 300 402 251 389 422 332 360 422];
5   big_red = [210 229 300 301 200 340 350 290 317 320];
6   big_black = [226 220 253 218 260 228 380 300 221 211];
7   X=[small_yellow small_red small_black big_yellow big_red big_black]';
8   nsubj=10;
9   nlevelsSize=2;
10  nlevelColor=3;
11  nmales=5;
12  nfemales=5;
13  Subj=repmat(1:nsubj,1,nlevelsSize*nlevelColor)';
14  sizesmall=repmat({'small'},1,nlevelColor*nsubj)';
15  sizebig=repmat({'big'}, 1,nlevelColor*nsubj)';
16  Size= [sizesmall' sizebig']';
17  Colyellow=repmat({'yellow'},nsubj,1);
18  Colred=repmat({'red'},nsubj,1);
19  Colblack=repmat({'black'},nsubj,1);
20  Color= [Colyellow' Colred' Colblack' Colyellow' Colred' Colblack']';
21  male= repmat({'m'},1,nmales)';
22  female= repmat({'f'},1,nfemales)';
23  Gender=repmat([male; female]',1,nlevelsSize*nlevelsColor)';
24  nesting=[0 0 0 0; 0 0 0 0; 0 0 0 0; 0 0 1 0 ];
25  modeling=[1 0 0 0; 0 1 0 0; 0 0 1 0; 0 0 0 1; ... %main effects
26     1 1 0 0; 1 0 1 0; 1 0 0 1 ; ... %first IV interactions
27     0 1 1 0; 0 1 0 1;... %second IV interactions
28     1 1 1 0];      % all interactions among IVs apart the nested one
29  [p table stats terms]=anovan(X,{Size Color Gender Subj }, 'random',4,
    'model',modeling,'nested',nesting,'varnames',{'Size' 'Color' 'Gender'
    'Subj'});
```

Figure 7.9 shows that there was a significant effect of Gender on RTs, while the interactions with both the Size and Color factors were not statistically significant.

Let's return to Listing 7.9 and see how we can implement the two matrices for modeling and nesting in a simpler way. Regarding the modeling matrix, we could have passed the "interaction" label to the "model" argument [i.e.: anovan(.... 'model', 'interaction',...)]. However, when used in this way, anovan() computes all the first-term interactions without computing the interactions among more than two variables. Hence, the remaining error is larger, since it is not explained by the interactions among more than two factors. Hence, unless you do not have good theoretical reasons to assume that some interactions have to be omitted, this is

Analysis of Variance

Source	Sum Sq.	d.f.	Mean Sq.	F	Prob>F
Size	4.3	1	4.3	0.01	0.915
Color	108971.2	2	54485.6	16.23	0.0001
Gender	64813.1	1	64813.1	12.15	0.0082
Subj(Gender)	42667	8	5333.4	1.53	0.2197
Size*Color	6760.9	2	3380.5	15.24	0.0002
Size*Gender	180.3	1	180.3	0.51	0.4944
Size*Subj(Gender)	2813.1	8	351.6	1.59	0.2059
Color*Gender	10746.1	2	5373.1	1.6	0.2324
Color*Subj(Gender)	53700	16	3356.2	15.13	0
Size*Color*Gender	672.9	2	336.5	1.52	0.2494
Error	3549.5	16	221.8		
Total	294878.4	59			

Constrained (Type III) sums of squares.

Fig. 7.9 ANOVA table output from listing 7.9

not always a good option. A handy shortcut to model the interactions, however, might be to pass to the "model" argument a scalar corresponding to the number of the not-nested factors [in this way: anovan(.... 'model', 3)]. The drawback of doing this is negligible: the error is wrongly attributed to the interaction among all the variables, and therefore the "real" error of the statistic will be set to 0. Figure 7.10 shows the output of the same listing as above, but the anovan() call is the following:

```
[p table stats terms]=anovan(X,{Size Color Gender Subj }, 'random',4,
'model',3,'nested',nesting,'varnames',{'Size' 'Color' 'Gender'
'Subj'});
```

As can be seen from Fig. 7.10, the last interaction term is actually the error shown in Fig. 7.9.

The shortcut that we can suggest to implement the matrix specifying the nesting relationship among the variables is the following. Remember to pass to anovan() the variable "Subjects" and the nesting variable as the last one and the second from the last, respectively. Implement the "nesting" matrix with all zeros and then replace with 1 the cell whose coordinates are [number of variables, number of variables−1]. Hence, in Listing 7.9, line 24 could have been replaced by:

```
Ivnumber=4;
nesting=zeros(IVnumber,IVnumber);
nesting(IVnumber,IVnumber-1)=1;
```

Analysis of Variance

Source	Sum Sq.	d.f.	Mean Sq.	F	Prob>F
Size	4.3	1	4.3	0.01	0.915
Color	108971.2	2	54485.6	16.23	0.0001
Gender	64813.1	1	64813.1	12.15	0.0082
Subj(Gender)	42667	8	5333.4	1.53	0.2197
Size*Color	6760.9	2	3380.5	15.24	0.0002
Size*Gender	180.3	1	180.3	0.51	0.4944
Size*Subj(Gender)	2813.1	8	351.6	1.59	0.2059
Color*Gender	10746.1	2	5373.1	1.6	0.2324
Color*Subj(Gender)	53700	16	3356.2	15.13	0
Size*Color*Gender	672.9	2	336.5	1.52	0.2494
Size*Color*Subj(Gender)	3549.5	16	221.8	Inf	NaN
Error	0	0	0		
Total	294878.4	59			

Constrained (Type III) sums of squares.

Fig. 7.10 The last interaction term is actually the error term in Fig. 7.9 (see text for details)

Obviously, this shortcut can be applied only if you have only one between (nested) subjects variable in an otherwise repeated-measure design. If your design includes more than one nested Independent variable, a more general shortcut to the full implementation of the matrix might be the following:

```
nesting=zeros(factornumber,factornumber);
for i = 1: NestedNumber
    nesting(factornumber,factornumber-i)=1;
end
```

where factornumber and NestedNumber are the number of factors and the number of between-subjects factors, respectively. It has to be remembered that this solution can be applied only when the variable Subjects is passed to anovan() as the last argument and the nested variables are passed just before it.

Nonparametric Statistics

Categorical Data

Binomial Distribution

The first categorical statistic we see in this section is the binomial distribution, which is used when each independent trial results in one of two mutually exclusive outcomes (Bernoulli trial). The probability of getting x (usually called "success") out of n trials given the probability p of a success on any one trial is given by the number of combinations of n objects taken x at a time. We use the MATLAB built-in function nchosek(n,x), which computes the combinations of n things taken x at a time. The following code returns the probability of x successes out of n trials:

```
nchoosek(n,x)*p^x*(1-p)^(n-x)
```

The same result can be obtained using the binopdf(x,n,p) function (which is included in the Statistics toolbox).

Chi2

The chi-square statistic is often used to understand whether the distribution of the results is consistent with a theoretical distribution. In this case, we use the chi2gof() function, which tests the goodness of fit between a theoretical distribution and empirical data. By default, chi2gof() returns 1 when the null hypothesis can be rejected and 0 otherwise. We can ask for further outputs such as the probability of the test and for a structure, whose fields are:

- chi2stat, is the value of the chi square statistic;
- dof, degrees of freedom;
- edges, vector of categories' edges that have been used to calculate the frequencies;
- O, observed frequency for each category;
- E, expected frequencies for each category according to our theoretical distribution.

(Expected values can be taken from any function. The default function used by chi2gof() is the normal distribution, but we can ask for a different function by passing it as optional argument).

Let's see an example of the chi2gof() function in action. A psychologist is interested in finding out whether there is any systematic preference for a specific display position to pick an object at will (for example, for an object that is at eye level). Each stimulus display consists of five identical objects placed in five different positions. Let us assume that both participants' choices and frequencies of position are uniformly distributed (i.e., we do not expect there is any specific preference for any of the positions of the display). Listing 7.10 runs the test.

Listing 7.10

```
1  x = round(rand(100,1)*4)+1;   % generate 100 random numbers
2                                 % within the 1-5 range
3  ctrs = [1, 2, 3, 4, 5];        % an array that keeps the coding
4                                 % of the values we expect
5  expectedCounts = [20, 20, 20, 20, 20]; % the expected freq. for each value
6  [h,p,st] = chi2gof(x,'ctrs',ctrs,'expected',expectedCounts)
```

This code returns the following variables:

```
h = 1
p = 0.0197
st =
  chi2stat: 11.7000
        df: 4
     edges: [0.5000 1.5000 2.5000 3.5000 4.5000 5.5000]
         O: [14 28 25 23 10]
         E: [20 20 20 20 20]
```

h informs that the null hypothesis can be rejected. p shows that the probability if finding these results by chance is equal to 0.0197. Then the structure st shows the chi2 value, the degrees of freedom, the vector of categories' edges that have been used to calculate the frequencies, and the observed and expected frequencies.

The chi2gof() function has several options; each one is written in string form (e.g., "expected" in the previous example) that is followed by the function's optional values (in the above example, an array with the expected frequencies).

Ordinal Data

Rank data are used with ordinal data or when the parametric assumptions to run parametric tests are not met.

Wilcoxon Signed Rank Test

The signrank() function performs the Wilcoxon signed rank test and tests the hypothesis that the median of the vector argument is significantly different from zero. Similarly to the ttest() function, it is possible to pass an additional second argument specifying a different median value of the experimental hypothesis. When the second optional argument is a vector, the function tests the hypothesis that the median for the two vectors is different. Use this option with paired samples. If your samples are independent, use ranksum() instead.

To show an example of the Wilcoxon signed rank test, let us consider a boundary extension (BE) experiment, where BE is the tendency to remember scenes as if they included information beyond the boundaries (Intraub and Richardson 1989). A psychologist wants to test the hypothesis that alcohol consumption favors this phenomenon. In a repeated-measures design, participants were presented with ten pictures on two different days (with and without alcohol consumption). In a recognition task, participants were presented with ten pictures, and after 1 min they were asked to select from two pictures which one had been presented before. One of these two pictures was the original one, while in the other the boundary was extended. The number of BE occurrences has been recorded in the two vectors shown in Table 7.11.

Table 7.11 Hypothetical data of ten participants, where BE occurrences (out of ten pictures) are measured after alcohol consumption or without alcohol consumption

Part id	1	2	3	4	5	6	7	8	9	10
Alcohol	6/10	4/10	5/10	6/10	3/10	3/10	6/10	7/10	8/10	2/10
No alcohol	1/10	3/10	3/10	6/10	3/10	2/10	5/10	6/10	6/10	3/10

Listing 7.11 runs the nonparametric test on the hypothetical data presented in Table 7.1.

Listing 7.11

```
1  NoAlcohol =[1/10 3/10   3/10  6/10   3/10  2/10  5/10  6/10  6/10  3/10];
2  Alcohol =   [6/10        4/10 5/10  6/10  3/10  3/10  6/10  7/10  8/10
          2/10];
3  [p,h,stats]= signrank(Alcohol , NoAlcohol);
```

Listing 7.11 outputs $h = 1$ and $p = 0.0391$. Hence, the Wilcoxon signed rank test indicates that we can reject the null hypothesis at level 0.05 of significance: alcohol consumption affects BE occurrences.

Mann–Whitney U Test (or Wilcoxon Rank Sum Test)

The ranksum() function performs the Mann–Whitney U test. It is the equivalent of the ttest2() function for parametric data. It tests the hypothesis that the median of the two independent groups is equal. It takes the same optional arguments as ttest2().

Again, we use the same data we used for the Wilcoxon signed rank test (see Listing 7.11), but now let us say that the data come from two independent groups. The following line of code runs the analysis:

```
>> [p,h,stats]= ranksum(Alcohol , NoAlcohol)
```

This code outputs $h = 0$ and $p = 0.1864$. Hence, the Mann–Whitney U indicates that we cannot reject the null hypothesis. By looking at the p value, we can see that the probability of finding these results by chance with independent samples is 18.64%.

Kruskal–Wallis Test

kruskalwallis() is used when there are more than two *independent* groups. It is therefore similar to the anova1() function. Similarly to anova1(), it can be passed either a single matrix in which each column represents a variable, or two vectors, the data vector and the group vector. The latter method has to be used when the groups' sizes differ.

Table 7.12 Hypothetical data of three groups of ten participants each. BE occurrences are measured as a function of alcohol consumption (three levels: alcohol, no alcohol, and placebo)

Alcohol	6/10	4/10	5/10	6/10	3/10	3/10	6/10	7/10	8/10	2/10
No alcohol	1/10	3/10	3/10	6/10	3/10	2/10	5/10	6/10	6/10	3/10
Placebo	1/10	4/10	4/10	6/10	3/10	3/10	6/10	6/10	5/10	3/10

Kruskal-Wallis ANOVA Table

```
Source     SS        df   MS        Chi-sq   Prob>Chi-sq
------------------------------------------------------------
Groups     66.1458   4    16.5365   7.44     0.1143
Error      13.8542   5    2.7708
Total      80        9
```

Fig. 7.11 Kruskal–Wallis ANOVA table

`kruskalwallis()` returns the same arguments as `anova1()`. Hence, we can run a multicomparison test through the `multcompare()` function in the same way we did for `anova1()`.

Let's consider again the BE experiment, but now there is a third group, which has been given a placebo instead of alcohol.

Table 7.12 shows the data for the three groups.

The following code tests the hypothesis that alcohol assumption affects BE when there are three groups of participants and data are not parametric.

```
>> Alcohol = [6/10 4/10 5/10 6/10 3/10 3/10 6/10 7/10 8/10 2/10];
>> NoAlcohol =[1/10 3/10 3/10 6/10 3/10 2/10 5/10 6/10 6/10 3/10];
>> Placebo=[1/10 4/10 4/10 6/10 3/10 3/10 6/10 6/10 5/10 3/10];
>> [p table stats]= kruskalwallis (Alcohol, NoAlcohol, Placebo)
```

Figure 7.11 shows the output of this code.

Friedman's Test

`friedman()` is used when there are two balanced independent variables. It takes as first argument a matrix in which data in different columns represent changes in the first factor, while data in the rows represent changes in the second factor. If there is more than one observation for each combination of factors, an optional second argument can be passed to the function indicating the number of replicates in each position, which must be the same and a multiple of the number of rows. Hence, this function works exactly in the same way as `anova2()`. However, although the column effects are weighted for row effects, the effect of rows is not considered by the

Friedman's ANOVA Table

Source	SS	df	MS	Chi-sq	Prob>Chi-sq	▲
Columns	54.65	2	27.325	2.91	0.2338	
Interaction	6.65	2	3.325			
Error	465.2	24	19.3833			
Total	526.5	29				▼

Test for column effects after row effects are removed

Fig. 7.12 Friedman's ANVOA table

Friedman test, and they represent nuisance effects that need to be taken into account but are not of any interest.

To show its use, let's consider again the data presented in Table 7.12 but let assume that for each group, the first five participants are females and the other five are males. The following code runs the Friedman test on two variables: Alcohol consumption and Gender.

```
>> [p table stats]= friedman ([Alcohol' NoAlcohol' Placebo'], 5)
```

Figure 7.12 shows the output of this code.

As can be seen from Fig. 7.12, the results are different from those obtained with the Kruskal–Wallis test because the gender effects have been removed.

Signal-Detection Theory (STD) Indexes

In yes/no psychophysics experiments, data can be interpreted according to signal-detection theory (Green and Swets 1966; Stanislaw and Todorov 1999). In particular, participants' responses can be coded as hits and false alarms, and the signal-detection indexes d' (sensitivity index), β, and c (bias indexes) can be calculated. Of course, MATLAB allows this calculation. Again, the Statistics toolbox includes functions devoted to this, but we can derive some of these functions by working on the MATLAB built-in functions. In the next sections, we see the parametric indexes d', β, and c; in the following section we show how to calculate the nonparametric indexes A' and B''.

d′

d′ is found by subtracting the z score corresponding to the false-alarm proportion from the z score that corresponds to the hit proportion. The Statistics toolbox includes the `norminv()` function, which can be used to calculate the z scores. If the variable pHit contains the hits proportion and pFA contains the false alarms proportion, then d′ can be calculated[2] with the following code:

```
zHit = norminv(pHit) ;
zFA = norminv(pFA) ;
d = zHit-zFA;
```

However, we can obtain the same results using MATLAB built-in functions in the following way:

```
zHit = -sqrt(2)*erfcinv(2*pHit) ;
zFA = -sqrt(2)*erfcinv(2*pFA) ;
d = zHit-zFA;
```

β

β is the most-used index for estimating the subject's bias. Using the Statistics toolbox, it can be calculated as follows:

```
>> B= exp((norminv(pHit)^2 - norminv(pFA)^2)/2);
```

If you want to get the same result using the MATLAB built-in erfcinv function, then you can write the following command:

```
>> norminv (x) = -sqrt(2)*erfcinv(2*x);
```

c

Another useful index to estimate subjects' bias is c. It can be calculated as follows:

```
>> c= -(norminv(pHits) + norminv(pFA))/2;
```

A′ and B″

A′ and **B″** are the nonparametric indexes for the measure of sensitivity and bias (Pollack and Norman 1964; Grier 1971). They are very easy to calculate without using any specific function.

---

[2] Note that if the proportion of hits or false alarms is equal to 0 or 1, the calculation of the signal-detection indexes is undetermined. In these cases, the proportion of hits and false alarms has to be calculated in a particular way (see Hautus 1995 for further details).

The following `sensitivity_A` function takes Hits and False Alarms rates and returns the sensitivity measure A′. Here we have implemented the formula suggested by Snodgrass and Corwin (1988):

Listing 7.12

```
1   function A = sensitivity_A(pHit, pFA)
2
3   % A = sensitivity_A(pHit, pFA))
4   %
5   % The function returns the parametric index Ai.
6   %
7   % INPUT:   pHit is the hit rate
8   %          pFA is the false alarm
9   % OUTPUT:  Ai
10  % AUTHOR:  M. Borgo, A. Soranzo and M.Grassi  - 2009
11
12  if pHit>=pFA
13    A = 0.5 + ((pHit-pFA)*(1+pHit-pFA))/(4*pHit*(1-pFA));
14  else
15    A = 0.5 - ((pFA-pHit)*(1+pFA-pHit))/(4*pFA*(1-pHit));
16  end
```

The `bias_B` function shown in Listing 7.13 takes the Hit and False Alarm rates and returns the bias measure B″. Once again we have implemented the formula suggested by Snodgrass and Corwin (1988):

Listing 7.13

```
1   function B = bias_B(pHit, pFA)
2
3   % A = bias_B(pHit, pFA))
4   %
5   % The function returns the parametric index Bi.
6   %
7   % INPUT:   pHit is the hit rate
8   %          pFA is the false alarm
9   % OUTPUT:  Bi
10  % AUTHOR:  M. Borgo, A. Soranzo and M.Grassi  - 2011
11
12  B = (pHit*(1-pHit)-pFA*(1-pFA))/(pHit*(1-pHit)+pFA*(1-pFA));
13
14  if pHit<pFA
15    B=-B;
16  end
```

Summary

- MATLAB is a powerful tool for statistical analysis.
- Statistics can be implemented in MATLAB using the Statistics toolbox. (Nevertheless, keep in mind that any statistic can be implemented by writing a custom function.)
- Several custom functions can be found at the MATLAB central web site.

- MATLAB can be used to calculate descriptive statistics, bivariate statistics, multivariate statistics, and inferential statistics, either parametric or nonparametric.
- MATLAB can also be used to calculate all indexes of signal-detection theory.

Exercises

1. Calculate the standard deviation of n ($n = 2^1$, 2^2,... 2^{10}) random numbers taken from a normal distribution and plot the absolute value of the results. You should see how the standard deviation becomes closer to unity as n becomes larger.

   Solution:

   ```
   for i=1:10
       StdDev(i)=std(randn(2^i, 1));
   end
   plot(abs(StdDev))
   ```

2. Suppose your subject has a hit rate of .9 and a false alarm rate of .5. Calculate the d' and c indexes of signal-detection theory associated with proportions.

   Solution:

   ```
   d'=1.28, c=-.64
   dprime=norminv(.9)-norminv(.5);
   c=-(norminv(.9)+norminv(.5))/2
   ```

3. Calculate a one-sample *t*-test (against zero) for 20 random numbers generated from a normal distribution. Try also to have all possible results returned by the function.

   Solution:

   ```
   numbers = randn(20, 1);
   [H, p, CI, stats] = ttest(numbers);
   ```

4. Suppose three groups of subjects (named A, B, and C) have produced the following results: scoresA=rand(10, 1); scoresB=rand(20, 1)*3; scoresC=rand(15, 1); calculate a one-way analysis of variance and test whether the three groups were different from one another. Moreover, try to get all possible outputs of the function.

   Possible solution:

   ```
   scoresA = rand(10, 1);
   scoresB = rand(20, 1)*3;
   scoresC = rand(15, 1);
   GroupsCoding = zeros(length(scoresA)+length(scoresB)+length(scoresC), 1);
   GroupsCoding(1:10) = 1;
   GroupsCoding(11:30) = 2;
   GroupsCoding(31:45) = 3;
   [p, AnovaTab, Stats] = anova1([scoresA; scoresB; scoresC], GroupsCoding);
   ```

A Brick for an Experiment

In Chap. 2, we saw how to import a data file and how to calculate simple statistics on the data of our brick experiment. However, we need to perform a more complex statistical analysis to understand the real outcome of the experiment. The experiment described in the brick is a 2 by 2 within-subjects design experiment. We can therefore see whether there are differences in the number of bounce responses observed for the continuous vs. stopped motion display as well as for the silent vs. with sound display. We can do this with a two-way analysis of variance. To perform the analysis of the brick experiment we will use a function that is freely available from the MATLAB central web site (http://www.mathworks.com/matlabcentral/). This web site is a large community of MATLAB users who exchange function files as well as problems (and often the problems' solutions). The function can be found by searching "two way repeated measures ANOVA" in the search engine. The function's name is rm_anova2. This function expects five input parameters. The first four parameters are numbers, and they are all single-dimensional arrays. One array contains the dependent variable (i.e., the probability of bounce responses of each subject). The other three arrays contain the variables' coding and the number of repetitions (i.e., the subjects). All arrays must have identical lengths. Now we write a short code that stores and sorts all four arrays. Here we hypothesize that we have run ten subjects.

Listing 7.14

```
1  motion_cond = [1, 2];
2  snd_cond = [1, 2];
3  subjects = 1:10;
4
5  X = zeros(length(motion_cond)*length(snd_cond)*length(subjects), 1);
6  factor1 = X;
7  factor2 = X;
8  repetitions = X;
9
10 m=1;
11 for i = 1:length(motion_cond)
12     for j = 1:length(snd_cond)
13         for k = 1:length(subjects)
14             factor1(m)=i;
15             factor2(m)=j;
16             repetitions(m)=k;
17             X(m) = mean(data(data(:, 5)==motion_cond(i) &
   data(:,6)==snd_cond(j) & data(:, 1)==repetitions(k), 7));
18             m = m + 1;
19         end
20     end
21 end
```

Now data within the X array are sorted according to the variable codes contained within the f1, f2, and repetitions variables. We have now to run the analysis of variance.

```
>> stats = rm_anova2(X, repetitions, factor1, factor2, {'motion', 'sound'});
```

Note that motion and sound are two labels that later become useful for easily reading the results of the analysis returned by the function. These labels need to be passed to the function within a cell type variable. If you now type stats at the MATLAB prompt, you will see the results of the experiment.

References

Green DM, Swets JA (1966) Signal-detection theory and psychophysics. Wiley, New York

Grier JB (1971) Nonparametric indexes for sensitivity and bias: computing formulas. Psychol Bull 75:424–429

Hautus MJ (1995) Corrections for extreme proportions and their biasing effects on estimated values of d′. Behav Res Methods Instrum Comput 27:46–51

Intraub H, Richardson M (1989) Wide-angle memories of close-up scenes. J Exp Psychol Learn Mem Cogn 15:179–187

Pollack I, Norman DA (1964) A nonparametric analysis of recognition experiments. Psychon Sci 1:125–126

Simons DJ, Chabris CF (1999) Gorillas in our midst: sustained inattentional blindness for dynamic events. Perception 28:1059–1074

Snodgrass JG, Corwin J (1988) Pragmatics of measuring recognition memory: applications to dementia and amnesia. J Exp Psychol Gen 117:34–50

Stanislaw H, Todorov N (1999) Calculation of signal detection theory measures. Behav Res Methods Instrum Comput 31:137–149

Suggested Readings

The journals *Psychological Methods* and *Behavior Research Methods* often suggest statistical tools that are either implemented in that MATLAB environment or can be easily implemented in MATLAB.

Martinez WL, Martinez AR (2005) Exploratory data analysis with MATLAB. Boca Raton, FL: Chapman & Hall/CRC

Marques de Sa JP (2007) Applied statistics using SPSS, STATISTICA, MATLAB and R, 2nd edn. Springer

Chapter 8
The Charm of Graphical User Interface

In this chapter we introduce the use of GUIDE, which is the MATLAB Graphical User Interface Development Environment. This tool enables the user to create Graphical User Interfaces (GUI) that can be used to facilitate interaction with your programs.

Introduction

Nowadays we are used to interacting with programs through windows with menus, buttons, drop-down lists, etc. Such interaction tools constitute a graphical user interface (GUI). Graphical user interfaces are simple to use but relatively difficult to program. MATLAB provides a tool, called GUIDE, that helps you in programming a graphical interface.

GUIDE

The GUIDE Layout Editor makes it possible to design GUIs easily by clicking and dragging the GUI components—such as panels, buttons, text fields, sliders, menus, and so on—into the GUI Layout Area. When you create a GUI, GUIDE generates two files: a FIG-file and an application M-file. The FIG-file contains a description of the GUI appearance, whereas the M-file contains the code that controls the behavior of the GUI. FIG- and M-files need to be stored in the same folder. GUIs are governed by callback functions, which are routines within the M-file that are executed when a specific event occurs in any of the elements of the GUI (i.e., button, drop-down list, etc.). GUI's elements are called UiControls.

M. Borgo et al., *MATLAB for Psychologists*,
DOI 10.1007/978-1-4614-2197-9_8, © Springer Science+Business Media, LLC 2012

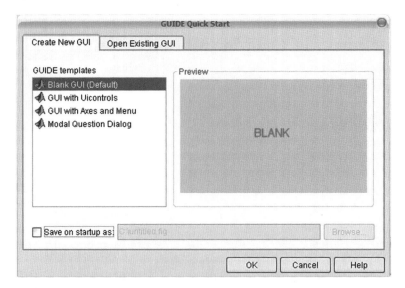

Fig. 8.1 GUIDE Quick Start dialog form

Starting GUIDE

Start GUIDE by typing `guide` at the MATLAB prompt or by selecting File -> New -> GUI from the menu bar. MATLAB displays the GUIDE Quick Start dialog box, as shown in Fig. 8.1. From the Quick Start dialog, you can choose from among four different GUIDE templates, that is, prebuilt GUIs that can be later modified at your convenience.

Choose the Blank GUI (Default) and ignore the 'Save on startup as' option at the bottom left corner of the box. A GUI is displayed in the Layout Editor, which is the control panel for all of the GUIDE tools. Figure 8.2 shows the Layout Editor for the blank GUI template. (If there are no names in your GUI component palette, don't panic, read the preferences for GUIDE section, later in this chapter.)

We can design the GUI by dragging components, such as panels, pushbuttons, pop-up menus, or axes, from the component palette on the left side of the Layout Editor into the layout area. Before going into the details of these components, we will go through the key menus, providing a short description of the main menu items.

The GUI Toolbar

GUIs come with a Toolbar with a number of shortcuts so that you can reach directly some of the options that are otherwise available from the Menu Bar. Figure 8.3 shows the icons in the GUI toolbar with their meanings.

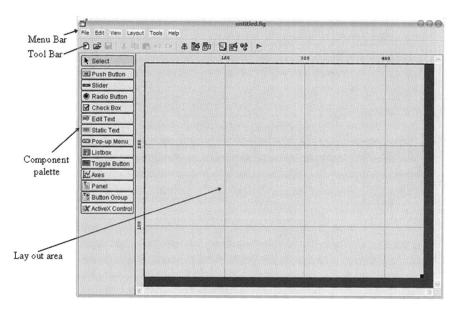

Fig. 8.2 Layout Editor for the blank GUI template

Fig. 8.3 The GUI toolbar

Adding UiControls to the GUI

Once we have created the GUI, it's time to insert the UiControls in the layout area
to implement the GUI's behavior. Table 8.1 shows what the GUI UiControls do:

In addition to the Callback functions associated to each component, GUIDE generates three further functions within the application M-file. The first has the name of
the GUI and we usually do not act on it. The other two functions are `nameOfFile_`
`OpeningFcn()` and `nameOfFile_OutputFcn()`; we need to operate on these
two functions to save users' inputs. Refer to the Saving users' inputs section to see
how this can be done.

Table 8.1 The component palette

Component palette	UiControl	Description
Select Push Button Slider Radio Button Check Box Edit Text Static Text Pop-up Menu Listbox Toggle Button Axes Panel Button Group ActiveX Control	Select	Restores the mouse pointer to selection mode
	Push button	This component creates a button that is used to take action in the GUI. Most of the GUIs you'll create will contain pushbuttons such as Cancel, OK, or Save
	Slider	This component creates a UiControl that can be manipulated with the mouse
	Radio button	A radio button together with an accompanying label is created by this component. Use this component if you need to choose one option within a pool of options. When two or more radio buttons are grouped within a button area, the selection of one of them causes the other to be automatically deselected.
	Check box	With this component you create a check box together with an accompanying label. You can select or clear the check box to turn on or off the behavior that has been programmed for this component
	Edit text	This component creates a text box into which the user can type text. You can also use a text box to display text to the user, or to provide text for the user to copy and paste elsewhere. A text box can contain either one line or multiple lines. In this latter case, a vertical scroll bar will also appear
	Static text	With this component you create a label, text used to identify a part of the GUI or to show information to the user
	Pop-up menu	With this component you create a box from which the user can choose from a list of options. They are much like the menus on the menu bar; except that they can be placed anywhere in the GUI
	List box	With this component you create a list box, which is a component that lists a number of values. The user can pick one value from the list, but can't enter a new value
	Toggle button	With this component you create a button that is used for taking action in the GUI. Unlike the pushbutton, the toggle button remains selected after being pressed, signaling whether the option is active
	Axes	With this component you create a box in which a plot can be inserted
	Panel	With this component you create a frame, an area of the GUI surrounded by a thin line together with an accompanying label. Use a panel to group related elements in the GUI
	Button group	With this component you create a frame as with the Panel component, but button groups manage *exclusive* selection for radio buttons and toggle buttons. That is, when a button group contains a number of radio buttons or toggle buttons, by selecting one of them all the others within its area are automatically deselected
	ActiveX	This control opens a select ActiveX control box in which you can select an ActiveX control to insert into your GUI (for Windows users only)

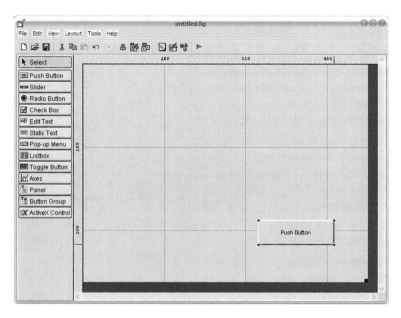

Fig. 8.4 Placing a Push Button

Closing the GUI

As a first example, let us implement a Cancel pushbutton; that is a UiControl that just closes the GUI. Run guide from the command line and chose Blank GUI (Default) from the GUIDE Quick Start box. The GUI is now opened in the Layout Editor. Select the pushbutton icon in the component palette and place it in the GUI layout area as shown in the Fig. 8.4.

By default, GUIDE names pushbuttons "`Push Button`". By double clicking on the pushbutton, the Properties Inspector box appears. Now change both the String and the Tag property to `Cancel` (Fig. 8.5).

This step needs to be commented. Do not confuse String and Tag properties. The String property is the string that will appear on the pushbutton. The Tag property, instead, is the actual name of the UiControl within the MATLAB code. In other words, when you need to refer to a UiControl, you have to call it with its Tag, not with its String.

To keep things simple, we can give to both the Tag and the String property the same name, but this is not always possible. For example, in the String property you can use any character you like (including periods, commas, and symbols). In contrast, in the Tag property you are restricted to letters of the alphabet.

There is another important thing to notice. After saving the GUI to the hard drive, the GUIDE automatically renames the Callback property from the default "`%auto-matic`" to `filename('Cancel_Callback',gcbo, [] ,guidata(gcbo))`.

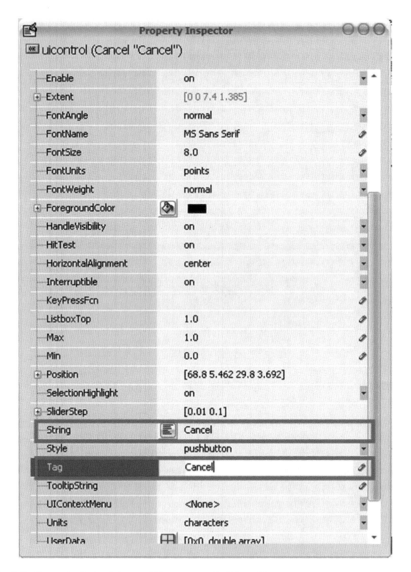

Fig. 8.5 Change both the String and Tag property in "Cancel"

Figure 8.6 shows what happens to the Property Inspector box after you save the GUI to the hard drive, naming it ClosingGUI.

This makes the finding of the Callback function for the Cancel pushbutton within the application M-file easier. The following lines of code were generated by GUIDE after saving the GUI.

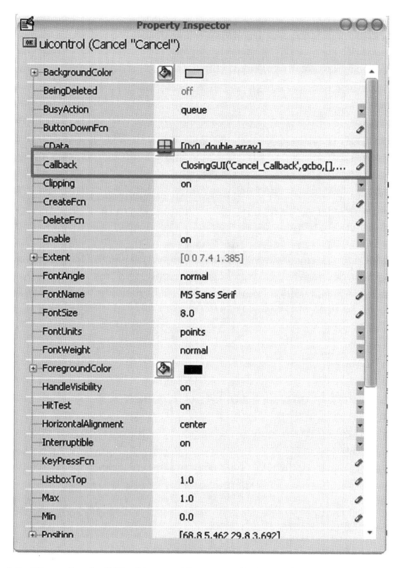

Fig. 8.6 After saving the GUI with a specific name and after naming the Tag property of the pushbutton, GUIDE automatically updates the callback function name accordingly

```
% --- Executes on button press in Cancel.
function Cancel_Callback(hObject, eventdata, handles)
% hObject handle to Cancel (see GCBO)
% eventdata reserved - to be defined in a future version of MATLAB
% handles structure with handles and user data (see GUIDATA)
```

Select the Cancel pushbutton and choose, from the View menu items, Callbacks->
Callback. You are directly pointed into the Cancel_Callback function in the
application M-file.

After the automatically generated comments, add `delete(gcf);` as shown:

```
% --- Executes on button press in Cancel.
function Cancel_Callback(hObject, eventdata, handles)
% hObject handle to Cancel (see GCBO)
% eventdata reserved - to be defined in a future version of MATLAB
% handles structure with handles and user data (see GUIDATA)
delete (gcf);
```

The `gcf` command returns the handle to the current figure (see Chap. 5), i.e., the
GUI image, and the delete function deletes the argument that is passed to it.

Now we are ready to run the GUI.

Select Tools -> run or press Ctrl+T, or click on the ▶ icon in the Tool Bar.
MATLAB will ask you to save the changes. Say yes, and your first GUI is running.
When you click on the Cancel button, the GUI closes!

This is not very exciting, but you should have now an idea on how GUIs work.
In the next sections we will see something more relevant, such as controlling the
appearance of UiControls from other UiControls, inserting figures and graphs in
the GUI, and saving participants' input.

Controlling UiControls from Other UiControls

In this section we see how to sum two numbers that have been typed by the user
using a pushbutton. This is a very instructive example because it shows how the
various components of the GUI communicate with one another.

The Sum-Two-Numbers Example

Create a GUI and place the Cancel button, as we have done before. (It is always a
good habit to insert a Cancel button into your GUIs. It might happen that you decide
not to run the program after all.) Proceed as in the previous section:

1. Run GUIDE from the command line;
2. Choose Blank GUI (Default) from the GUIDE Quick Start box;
3. Select the pushbutton icon from the component palette;
4. Change the name of both the Tag and the String property to 'Cancel';
5. Select the pushbutton and add `delete(gcf);` in the Cancel_Callback function
   in the application M-file.
6. Save and name the GUI SumTwoNumbers.

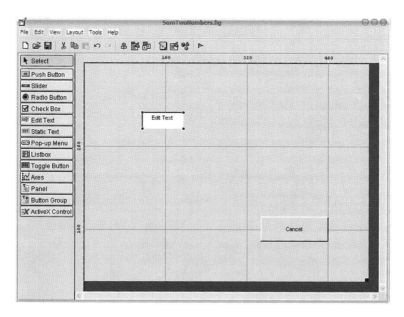

Fig. 8.7 Add an Edit Text component into the GUI Layout Editor

From the component palette select the Edit Text component and drag it into the GUI Layout Editor as shown in Fig. 8.7.

By default, "Edit Text" appears in the text box. We do not need that text. To delete the text, look at the properties of the text box within the Property Inspector box and cancel the "Edit text" value from the String property. You now have a blank Edit Text component in the GUI Layout Editor.

As you can see from the Property Inspector window, the default Tag for this component is "edit1". Because there will be more than one edit text component in this GUI, change the name to "FirstNumber" (Fig. 8.8).

From the Component palette select a Static Text component and drag it just below the FirstNumber component. Replace its String property from "static text" to "First Number". Since we are not going to work with this component, we can leave its Tag property as "text1". Select both the FirstNumber and the text1 components and use the Align Objects tool to horizontally align them (Fig. 8.9).

Repeat the procedure twice to add another Edit Text and Static Text component pair. From the Property Inspector box, delete the String property of the first Edit Text component and replace its Tag from "edit2" to "SecondNumber". Replace the Tag of the other Edit Text component from "edit3" to "Total". Select the first Static Text component so that the Property Inspector box shows its properties and replace its String property from "static text" to "SecondNumber". Replace the String property of the other Static Text component from "static text" to "Total". Use the Align Objects tool to vertically align and distribute these components. The GUI now should look similar to the one shown in Fig. 8.10.

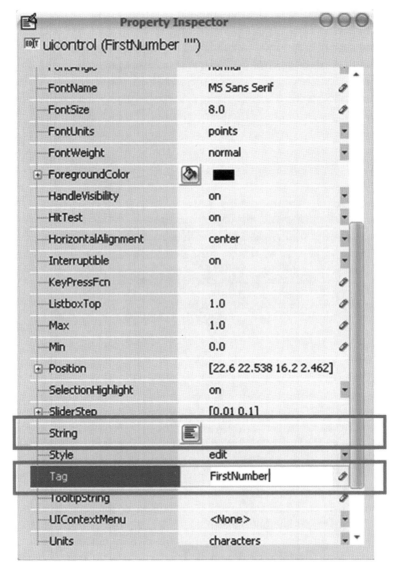

Fig. 8.8 Delete the default "Edit Text" in the String property and change the Tag property from "edit1" to "FirstNumber"

The last component we need is another pushbutton, and this will be biggest part of the job. Follow the same procedure that you followed to create the Cancel pushbutton. Name both its Tag and its String properties "Sum".

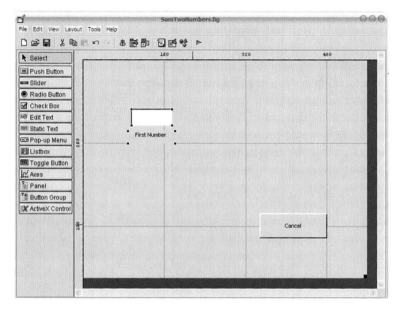

Fig. 8.9 Add a static text component and change its String property from edit1 to First Number

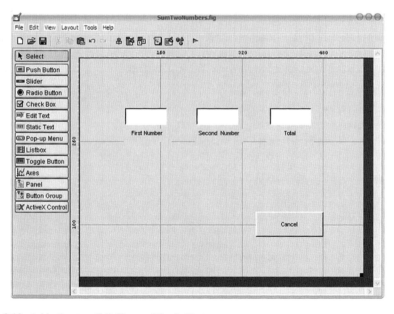

Fig. 8.10 Add other two Edit Text and Static Text components

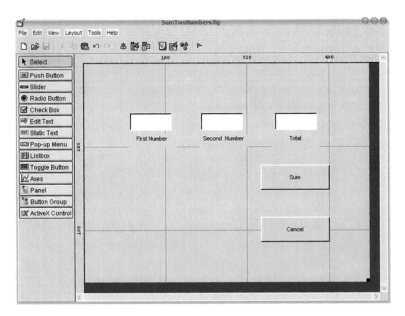

Fig. 8.11   The GUI Layout Editor with all the components you need for this task

The design of the GUI is now complete and should look similar to the one shown in Fig. 8.11.

You are now ready to program the GUI's behavior. Select the Sum button and from the View menu item choose View Callbacks -> Callback. You are directed to the application M-file, into the Move_Callback function.

After the comments, type the following line of code as shown:

```
function Sum_Callback(hObject, eventdata, handles)
% hObject handle to Sum (see GCBO)
% eventdata reserved - to be defined in a future version of MATLAB
% handles structure with handles and user data (see GUIDATA)

FirstNumber = str2double(get(handles.FirstNumber,'String') );
SecondNumber = str2double(get(handles.SecondNumber,'String') );
sum=FirstNumber+SecondNumber;
set(handles.Total,'String',sum);
```

FirstNumber and SecondNumber are variables that have been created to store user inputs. User input is character type; since we need numbers instead of characters, we change it by means of the str2double() function. The get() function, together with its counterpart set() function, is a very important one because it is used to get the values of the property that we are referring to. In this case, we want to get the 'String' values that have been typed in the FirstNumber and SecondNumber UiControls. Note that to refer to these components, we used the handles structure (which is passed to the callback function as argument), followed

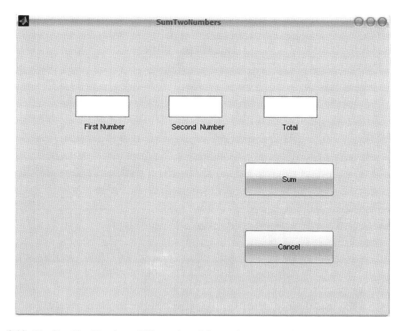

Fig. 8.12 The SumTwoNumbers GUI running. After typing two numbers, press the Sum button to display their sum in the Total edit box

by a dot and then the Tag. To refer to the property we need, we add a comma followed by the property name within quotation marks.

In the third line, we saved the sum of the numbers in the sum variable. Finally, in the last line we used the set() function to *set* the String property of the Total UiControl to the sum of the two numbers.

While running, this GUI should appear as in Fig. 8.12.

In this example we have seen how to *get* and *set* the properties of one component from the Callback function of another component. It is also possible to *set* and *get* the property of one component from *within* its own Callback function. In this case, instead of using the handles structure, we use hObject, which is the first argument that is passed to Callback functions.

We can improve the SumTwoNumber GUI by changing the background color of the Sum pushbutton when it is pressed. In this way, the user knows whether it has been pressed at least once.

Within the same Sum_Callback(hObject, eventdata, handles) add the following line of code:

```
set(hObject,'BackgroundColor','red')
```

Run the GUI again and press the Sum button. As you can see, besides summing the numbers, now the Sum button is turned to red (Fig. 8.13).

We could have done the same job using the handles argument of the same Sum_Callback function. However, when using the hObject argument, we do not need to specify the UiControl Tag.

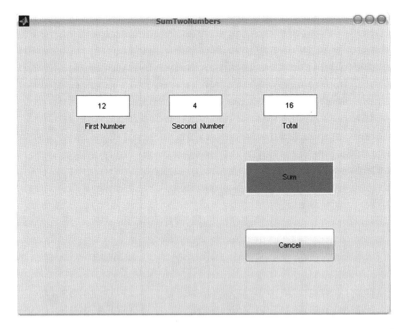

Fig. 8.13 The update SumTwoNumbers GUI. When the Sum button is pressed, it turns red

Displaying Graphs and Figures in the GUI

Among the components, it is the `axes` component that serves to display graphs and figures. Graphs are quite easy to understand. The following example shows how to plot a line in the axes component by pressing a button.

- Create a GUI and place the Cancel button.
- Save and name the GUI DisplayGraph.

From the component palette select the components and drag them into the GUI Layout Editor as shown in Fig. 8.14.

From the Property Inspector box, name the Tag for the upper Edit Text "To" and the bottom one "From". Name the first pushbutton "Display". Add the following lines of code in the `Display_Callback` function:

```
myfrom = str2double(get(handles.From,'String')) ;
myto = str2double(get(handles.To,'String'));
plot(myfrom:myto);
```

When the Display graph pushbutton is pressed, a line is plotted in the `axes` `component`.

This example is not very appealing. However, you get the picture now; you can plot any type of graph you like following these instructions. Displaying figures is another interesting feature of GUI. To explain how this works, in the following example we show how to display pictures representing visual illusion, into our GUI.

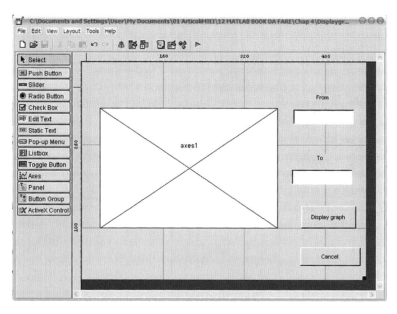

Fig. 8.14 GUI to display a graph

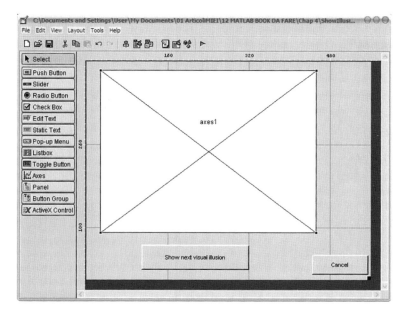

Fig. 8.15 GUI to show visual illusion saved in the current directory

Place your favorite visual illusion in the current directory in JPEG format (any other format will do). In MATLAB create a GUI and place a large axes component, the usual Cancel button, and a pushbutton whose tag is ShowNextIllusion (see Fig. 8.15).

In the ShowIllusions_OpeningFcn function add the following line of code that implements the variable count.

```
Global count;
```

In the `ShowNextIllusion_Callback` function add the following lines of code to display the JPEG figure that you have in your current directory.

```
global count
count=count+1;
illusions=dir(fullfile(cd,'*.jpeg'));
if count>size(illusions,1)
    msgbox('Sorry, no more illusions to show')
else
    illusionToshow=illusions(count).name;
    img=imread(illusionToshow);
    image(img)
end
```

Saving User Input

When running experiments, psychologists need to save participants' input. There are different ways of doing this. The simplest is to include a save() function within a pushbutton Callback function. You then retrieve participants' data using the load() (see Chap. 2) function from outside the GUI. However, you may want to save and retrieve participants' input while running the experiment, so you want to send participants' input to different M-files or to the MATLAB console. In these cases, there are a few steps to follow, and various functions of the application M-file have to be manipulated.

To show how this works, we consider the SumTwoNumbers GUI again, but now we want to store the numbers that have been typed by the user. We could do this within the Sum_Calback function, but to make it clearer, it is perhaps better to create another pushbutton and name both its Tag and its String "Save" as shown in Fig. 8.16.

The GUI design is now complete. Now we need to program its behavior.

There are three steps to follow:

Step 1
In the OpeningFcn function uncomment the %uiwait(handles.figure1); line as shown.

```
function SumTwoNumbers_OpeningFcn (hObject, eventdata, handles, varargin)
% This function has no output args, see OutputFcn.
% hObject handle editto figure
% eventdata reserved - editto be defined in a future version of MATLAB
```

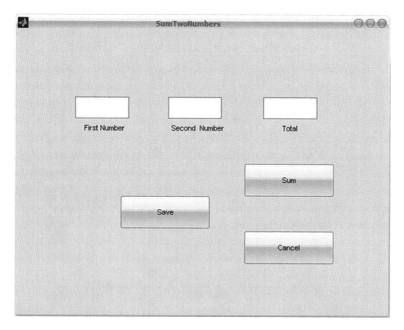

Fig. 8.16 Create a Save pushbutton into the SumTwoNumbers GUI Layout editor

```
% handles structure with handles and user data (see GUIDATA)
% varargin command line arguments editto SumTwoNumbers (see VARARGIN)

% Choose default command line output for SumTwoNumbers handles.output = hObject;
% Update handles structure
guidata(hObject, handles);

% UIWAIT makes SumTwoNumbers wait for user response (see UIRESUME)
uiwait(handles.figure1);
```

The `uwait()` function puts the GUI in standby mode. To understand what this means can be helpful in clarifying what happens when this command is commented. Without this command, MATLAB jumps directly into the `SumTwoNumbers_OutputFcn` function without waiting for the user's input. You do not want this to happen, because you want the OutputFcn function to be called only *after* the users have typed their numbers, so that this function "knows" what has been typed.

Step 2

In the SumTwoNumbers_OutputFcn function, replace `varargout{1} = handles.output;` with `varargout{1} =handles;` and add "`delete(gcf);`", as follows:

```
function varargout = SumTwoNumbers_OutputFcn(hObject, eventdata, handles)
% varargout cell array for returning output args (see VARARGOUT);
% hObject handle editto figure
% eventdata reserved - editto be defined in a future version of MATLAB
```

```
% handles structure with handles and user data (see GUIDATA)
```

```
% Get default command line output editfrom handles structure
varargout{1} = handles;
delete(gcf);
```

This code allows for saving different variables in a structure. By substituting `handles.output` with `handles`, we are instructing the OutputFcn function to output our own structure (we will come back to this point shortly). The `delete (gcf);` command is the same as the one within the `Cancel_Callback` function. By adding the command here as well, we are closing the GUI when the Save push-button is pressed.

Now the program is ready to save anything we want and to close the GUI after the save operation. The last step is to tell GUIDE what we want to save. In the `Save_Callback` function add the following lines of code:

Step 3

```
function Save_Callback(hObject, eventdata, handles)
% hObject handle to Save (see GCBO)
% eventdata reserved - to be defined in a future version of MATLAB
% handles structure with handles and user data (see GUIDATA)
handles.Number1 = get(handles.FirstNumber,'String');
handles.Number2 = get(handles.SecondNumber,'String');
guidata(hObject, handles);
uiresume(handles.figure1);
```

The `handles.Number1 = get(handles.FirstNumber,'String');` and `handles.Number2 = get(handles.SecondNumber,'String');` commands save the two numbers into the new `Number1` and `Number2` fields in the `handles` structure.

The `guidata(hObject, handles);` command updates the handles structure with the new field.

Finally, `uiresume()` reactivates the GUI so that the `OutputFcn` function can be executed. Note that if we close the GUI here, by means of the `delete()` function instead of using `uiresume()`, we do not save anything, because the `OutputFcn` function needs to get the updated handles structure to output it.

Let us now see how the program works. From the MATLAB command prompt type:

```
mystruct = SumTwoNumbers;
```

Now the program is running; type any number in the two edit box components and then press the Save pushbutton. When you do this, the GUI closes, and a structure named `mystruct` has been created in the MATLAB workspace. To retrieve the numbers that have been typed, just use the mystruct.Number1 and mystruct. Number2 variables.

Adding Your Own Functions

To conclude this chapter, it has to be noted that within the M-file you can insert any additional functions you want, and of course, you can pass to these functions both the hObject and the handles structures as arguments. Refer to Exercise 2 for an example.

Summary

- GUIDE generates two files that save and launch the GUI: a FIG-file and an application M-file.
- GUIDE owns a number of dedicated preferences that can be set from the Preferences dialog box in the File menu.
- GUIs are shaped by dragging components from the component palette into the layout area.
- A component's properties are set from the Properties Inspector box.
- GUIs benefit from Object Orienting Programming (OOP) technology, and their UiControls are governed by means of callback functions.
- Callback functions receive three arguments: hObject, eventdata, handles.
- The get() and set() functions are used to get and set, respectively, a component's properties.
- The uiwait() and uiresume() functions are used to stop and reactivate the GUI.
- The Filename_OutputFnc() function returns to MATLAB any input the user provides.

Exercises

Exercise 1

Using Radio Buttons grouped within a Button Group component, alter the visible property of two Static Text components so that they appear either to the left or to the right of the GUI.

Solution

Place the components as shown in Fig. 8.17.

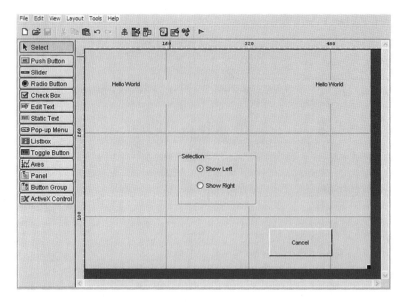

Fig. 8.17 Example of a GUI as required by Exercise 1

Assign the Tags to the Static text components "Left" and "Right". Assign the Visible property of both of them to "off". Name the Tags for the two radio buttons ShowLeft and ShowRight. Place the following lines of code within uipanel1_SelectionChangeFcn function:

```
function uipanel1_SelectionChangeFcn(hObject, eventdata, handles)
switch get(hObject,'Tag')
    case 'ShowLeft'
        set(handles.Left,'Visible', 'on')
        set(handles.Right,'Visible', 'off')
    case 'ShowRight'
        set(handles.Left,'Visible', 'off')
        set(handles.Right,'Visible', 'on')
end
```

Since the two Radio buttons are within the Button Group component, when the GUI is executing, selecting one Radio button automatically deselects the other.

Exercise 2

Suppose you are doing a memory experiment and that a participant has been presented with a sample of figures. Program a GUI to present a collection of figures (some of which where presented in the original sample and others that weren't) within the Axes component and add two pushbuttons. The participant has to press

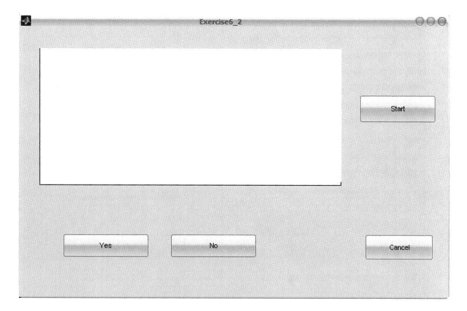

Fig. 8.18 GUI example as required by the exercise

one or the other pushbutton depending on whether the figure that is shown was present in the original sample or not. The participants' responses are to be collected and coded as right or wrong.

Solution

There are many different ways to solve this exercise. The one that we present here makes use of the handle structure created by GUIDE (but other solutions are possible) and creates a new function (named "savedata") in the application M-file that has been created by GUIDE, which takes as arguments both the handles and the answer that has been given by the participant.

Place the figures you want to present in the current directory and name them in such way that is easy for you to recall whether they were present in the original sample (for example, "A1.jpeg" for the first "Absent" figure and "P1.jpeg" for the first Present figure). Create a GUI like the following one (Fig. 8.18).

Here is the code for this GUI. Call this file from the MATLAB prompt and save the structure in the mystruct variable. mystruct.response and mystruct. figure are cell arrays containing participants' answers and figure names, respectively. We will then analyze these data by comparing participants' answers with the initials (either A or P) of the figure names.

Listing 8.1

```
1    function varargout = Exercise6_2(varargin)
2
3    % EXERCISE6_2 M-file for Exercise6_2.fig
4    % EXERCISE6_2, by itself, creates a new EXERCISE6_2
5    % or raises the existing singleton*.
6    %
7    % H = EXERCISE6_2 returns the handle to a new EXERCISE6_2 or the handle to
8    %the existing singleton*.
9    %
10   % EXERCISE6_2('CALLBACK',hObject,eventData,handles,...) calls the local
11   % function named CALLBACK in EXERCISE6_2.M with the given input arguments.
12
13   % EXERCISE6_2('Property','Value',...) creates a new EXERCISE6_2 or
14   % raises the existing singleton*.  Starting from the left, property value
15   % pairs are applied to the GUI before Exercise6_2_OpeningFunction gets
16   % called.  An unrecognized property name or invalid value makes property
17   % application stop.
18   % All inputs are passed to Exercise6_2_OpeningFcn via varargin.
19   %
20   % *See GUI Options on GUIDE's Tools menu.
21   % Choose "GUI allows only one instance to run (singleton)".
22   %
23   % See also: GUIDE, GUIDATA, GUIHANDLES
24   %
25   % Edit the above text to modify the response to help Exercise6_2
26   %
27   % Last Modified by GUIDE v2.5 18-Feb-2010 19:59:06
28   %
29   % Begin initialization code - DO NOT EDIT
30       gui_Singleton = 1;
31       gui_State = struct( 'gui_Name',        mfilename, ...
32           'gui_Singleton',  gui_Singleton, ...
33           'gui_OpeningFcn', @Exercise6_2_OpeningFcn, ...
34           'gui_OutputFcn',  @Exercise6_2_OutputFcn, ...
35           'gui_LayoutFcn',  [] , ...
36           'gui_Callback',   []);
37       if nargin && ischar(varargin{1})
38           gui_State.gui_Callback = str2func(varargin{1});
39       end
40       if nargout
41           [varargout{1:nargout}] = gui_mainfcn(gui_State, varargin{:});
42       else
43           gui_mainfcn(gui_State, varargin{:});
44       end
45       % End initialization code - DO NOT EDIT
46
47
48   % --- Executes just before Exercise6_2 is made visible.
49   function Exercise6_2_OpeningFcn(hObject, eventdata, handles, varargin)
50
51       % This function has no output args, see OutputFcn.
52       % hObject      handle to figure
53       % eventdata    reserved - to be defined in a future version of MATLAB
54       % handles      structure with handles and user data (see GUIDATA)
55       % varargin     command line arguments to Exercise6_2 (see VARARGIN)
56       % Choose default command line output for Exercise6_2
57       handles.output = hObject;
58       handles.count=0;
59       figures=dir(fullfile(cd,'*.jpeg'));
60       handles.response=cell(size(figures,1),1);
```

```
61          handles.myfigure=cell(size(figures,1),1);
62          % Update handles structure
63          guidata(hObject, handles);
64
65          % UIWAIT makes Exercise6_2 wait for user response (see UIRESUME)
66          uiwait(handles.figure1);
67
68
69          % --- Outputs from this function are returned to the command line.
70     function varargout = Exercise6_2_OutputFcn(hObject, eventdata, handles)
71
72          % varargout  cell array for returning output args (see VARARGOUT);
73          % hObject    handle to figure
74          % eventdata  reserved - to be defined in a future version of MATLAB
75          % handles    structure with handles and user data (see GUIDATA)
76
77          % Get default command line output from handles structure
78          varargout{1} = handles;
79          delete(gcf);
80
81
82          % --- Executes on button press in Yes.
83     function Yes_Callback(hObject, eventdata, handles)
84
85          % hObject    handle to Yes (see GCBO)
86          % eventdata  reserved - to be defined in a future version of MATLAB
87          % handles    structure with handles and user data (see GUIDATA)
88
89          savedata(hObject, 'Yes', handles)
90
91
92          % --- Executes on button press in No.
93     function No_Callback(hObject, eventdata, handles)
94
95          % hObject    handle to No (see GCBO)
96          % eventdata  reserved - to be defined in a future version of MATLAB
97          % handles    structure with handles and user data (see GUIDATA)
98
99          savedata(hObject, 'No', handles)
100
101         %-------------------------
102    function savedata(hObject,answer,handles)
103
104         handles.count=handles.count+1;
105         guidata(hObject, handles);
106         figures=dir(fullfile(cd,'*.jpeg'));
107
108         if handles.count>size(figures,1)
109             msgbox('End experiment')
110             guidata(hObject, handles);
111             uiresume(handles.figure1);
112         else
113             handles.myfigure(handles.count)={figures(handles.count).name};
114             handles.response(handles.count)={answer};
115             img=imread(handles.myfigure{handles.count});
116             image(img)
117             axis off
118         end
119         guidata(hObject, handles);
120
121         % --- Executes on button press in Start.
122    function Start_Callback(hObject, eventdata, handles)
123         % hObject    handle to Start (see GCBO)
124         % eventdata  reserved - to be defined in a future version of MATLAB
```

(continued)

Listing 8.1 (continued)

```
125    % handles    structure with handles and user data (see GUIDATA)
126    figures=dir(fullfile(cd,'*.jpeg'));
127    figureToshow=figures(1).name;
128    img=imread(figureToshow);
129    image(img)
130    axis off
131
132    % --- Executes on button press in Cancel.
133 function Cancel_Callback(hObject, eventdata, handles)
134    % hObject    handle to Cancel (see GCBO)
135    % eventdata  reserved - to be defined in a future version of MATLAB
136    % handles    structure with handles and user data (see GUIDATA)
137    delete(gcf)
```

A Brick for an Experiment

We just read how we can build a graphical interface. We may want to build a graphical interface to drive our experiment. For example, we may want to have a graphical interface that allows us to collect the subject's identifying information (e.g., the name, sex, age, as well as the number we assign to the subject) as well as an optional text note about the subject (e.g., is the subject naive or expert? right-handed or left-handed?). Additionally, we may want to have a button to "START" the experiment. We may want also to have the possibility to run instead of the complete experiment, only an abbreviated version of it with a few trials (one for each experimental condition) so that we can run a few practice trials if we need to. We may want/need to add further items to our graphical interface. For example, it could be useful to set within it the name of the file where we are going to save the data or the block number if the experiment we run is subdivided into more than one block. And we could insert other parameters as well, for example if we want stimuli to be presented in fixed or random order. Of course, the number of things you can control through a graphical interface has no limit.

The graphical interface we build is rather standard, so that we will set the following parameters: subject's number; subject's name; subject's sex; subject's age; subject's note; the block number; the datafile's name; the possibility to run the experiment in a fixed or random order; one "start experiment" button; one "start practice" button; one "cancel" button. Now launch the guide command and begin to draw a graphical interface that looks more or less like the following one:

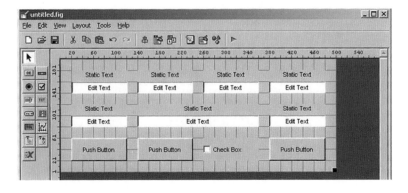

Now edit the text properties of the various objects you have created as follows, and in addition, change the bottom-right pushbutton background color to red:

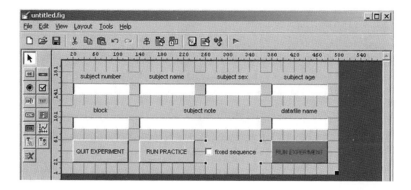

Now change the tag properties of your "Edit Text" slots and give them (more) meaningful names such as nsub, subname, subsex, subage, nblock, subnote, and filename. Now change the tag properties of your pushbuttons into QuitExp, RunPractice, and RunExp. Finally, change the tag property of your check box into isfixed.

The first thing we do is to activate the "QUIT EXPERIMENT" button. We saw how to do this above. Just insert the command line delete(gcf) into the QuitExp_ Callback function. Now activate the GUI for the user's input by uncommenting the uiwait(handles.figure1) command (see the Save user input section). In this way, the GUI now waits for user input. We now have to replace "varargout{1}=handles. output;" with "varargout{1}=handles;" so that we can get all the data we input each time we run the experiment within a structure called "handles". Immediately after this command, we write again the delete(gcf) command. In this way, we close the GUI if we press the "RUN EXPERIMENT" button. Do the same after the RunPractice_Callback function. Now we move to the end of the RunExp_Callback function. Here, after the comments, we have to add the following lines of code:

```
handles.nsub = str2num(get(handles.nsub,'String'));
handles.subname = get(handles.subname,'String');
handles.subsex = get(handles.subsex,'String');
handles.subage = str2num(get(handles.subage,'String'));
handles.nblock = str2num(get(handles.nblock,'String'));
handles.subnote = get(handles.subnote,'String');
handles.filename = get(handles.filename,'String');
handles.isfixed = get(handles.isfixed,'Value') == get(handles.
isfixed,'Max');
guidata(hObject, handles);
uiresume(handles.figure1);
delete(gcf)
```

Now save as "RunExp" your GUI. Note that we converted nsub and subage from strings to numbers, whereas subname and subsex are strings. Go to the command line and type the following command (remember to comment temporarily delete(gcf) first):

```
>> UserInputs = RunExp
```

Now input a set of hypothetical subjects' details and press the button "RUN EXPERIMENT". MATLAB should echo the contents of a structure. Within this content there are also the subject's number, the subject's name, the subject's sex, and so on.

Now that we have collected all the user's inputs, we have to pass them to the main program that runs the experiment. This program was introduced in Chap. 4 (Listing 4.19). To do this, we need to transform that script into a function that receives as input the data structure created through the graphical interface. So, add the following line at the top of that listing:

```
function SekulerExp(InputDataStruct)
```

Now let us return to the graphical interface. There, we need to add a further command line that will be executed when we press the "RUN EXPERIMENT" button at the end of the RunExp_Callback function (i.e., just after the lines of code we wrote previously):

```
SekulerExp(handles);
```

In practice, when we press the "RUN EXPERIMENT" button, we will launch the SekulerExp function, which receives a structure as input data. Within this structure will be all the subject's details, as well as the datafile name, the isfixed value, and so on. The last thing we do is to make the "run practice" button effective. Add the following lines after the RunPractice_Callback function:

```
handles.nsub = 0;
handles.isfixed = get(handles.isfixed, 'Value') == get(handles.isfixed, 'Max');
SekulerExp(handles);
```

You can see that here, rather than getting the data that the user inputs in the GUI, we directly set the nsub variable to zero. In the SekulerExp function, by convention, when the subject number is set to zero, the program runs a practice experiment, an experiment with one repetition for each of the stimuli.

The graphical interface is ready. Within the SekulerExp function, we can get the input data by adding the following lines at the beginning of the code.

```
% EXPERIMENT'S SETTINGS
% get input data from the structure passed through the interface
nsub = InputDataStruct.nsub;
subname = InputDataStruct.subname;
subsex = InputDataStruct.subsex;
subage = InputDataStruct.subage;
```

```
nblock = InputDataStruct.nblock;
subnote = InputDataStruct.subnote;
isfixed = InputDataStruct.isfixed;
filename = InputDataStruct.filename;
```

Let's now take a look at the renovated SekulerExp function:

Listing 8.2

```
1   function SekulerExp(InputDataStruct)
2
3   % M-script to realize a experiment based on the crossmodal perception
4   % The experiment first performed by Sekuler, Sekuler and Lau (1997)
5   % Author: Borgo, Soranzo, Grassi 2009
6
7   % EXPERIMENT'S SETTINGS
8   % get input data from the structure passed through the interface
9   nsub = InputDataStruct.nsub;
10  subname = InputDataStruct.subname;
11  subsex = InputDataStruct.subsex;
12  subage = InputDataStruct.subage;
13  nblock = InputDataStruct.nblock;
14  subnote = InputDataStruct.subnote;
15  isfixed = InputDataStruct.isfixed;
16  filename = InputDataStruct.filename;
17  % set the experiment details
18  conditions = [1, 1; 1, 2; 2, 1; 2, 2];
19  repetitions = 20;
20  if nsub == 0
21      repetitions = 1;
22  end
23  EventTable = GenerateEventTable(conditions, repetitions, isfixed);
24  TotalNumberOfTrials = length(EventTable(:, 1));
25  for trial = 1:TotalNumberOfTrials
26
27      % STIMULI (SELECTION)
28      VideoStimulusToPlay = EventTable(trial, 2);
29      SoundStimulusToPlay = EventTable(trial, 3);
30
31      % STIMULI (CREATION)
32      % STIMULI (PRESENTATION)
33      % COLLECT SUBJECT'S ANSWER
34  end
35
36  % STORE RESULTS
```

Appendix

Referring to Fig. 8.2, we give a short description of the remaining menu items that weren't previously defined. You can find the same information in the MATLAB help; we have given them here for quick reference.

The File Menu

As you might guess, the File menu provides commands for handling files. Here's a sketch of the items in the File menu.

New (Ctrl+N) Displays the GUIDE Quick Start dialog box again; that is, you can create more than one GUI at a time.

Open (Ctrl+O) Displays the usual open dialog box to open FIG-files you have already created.

Close (Ctrl+W) Closes the GUI.

Save (Ctrl+S) and Save as... save the current GUI to disk. This item will appear as Save and the name of the GUI, so you can clearly tell from the menu which open GUI it is being saved. It should be noted that when a GUI is saved, two files are automatically saved: The FIG-file and the M-file, both with the same name. However, once it is saved, to run our GUI we need only to prompt its name without any extensions (or you can double click in the FIG-file icon).

Export... This item is very helpful if you want to save one M-file only instead of both an M-file and a FIG-file. When you select this option, MATLAB first saves the current GUI to disk, that is, both the M- and FIG-files. Then it saves another M-file whose code creates the GUI from scratch. The default name for this M-file is the same as that of the saved M-file plus the "_export" suffix. You can change it according to your needs.

Preferences... displays the same dialog box that is displayed from the Preferences item in the MATLAB main windows (see the Preferences for GUIDE section in this chapter).

Print (Ctrl+P) Displays the Print dialog box for printing the GUI figure.

The Edit Menu

The Edit menu provides commands for working in the GUI. Most of these commands are standard to mainstream applications.

Undo (Ctrl+Z) undoes the previous action. GUIDE supports multiple undo operations; simply continue undoing to undo further actions.

Redo Redoes the last undone action. Again, GUIDE supports multiple redo operations, up to the number of undo operations that have been done.

Cut (Ctrl+X) Deletes the selected UiControl from the GUI and copies it into the Clipboard, allowing for pasting it in a different position of the same GUI or into another GUI.

Copy (Ctrl+C) Copies the selected UiControl to the Clipboard, allowing for pasting a copy of it in a different position of the same GUI or into another GUI.

Paste (Ctrl+V) Pastes the UiControl from the Clipboard into the current GUI.

Clear Deletes the selected UiControl.

Select All (Ctrl+A) Selects all the UiControls in the current GUI.

Duplicate (Ctrl+D) Duplicates the selected UiControl.

The View Menu

The View menu provides the means for displaying and moving the various windows of the GUI. Some of these windows are context sensitive, that is, the displayed window differs according to the selected UiControl. Here are the View menu items:

Property inspector Displays the Property inspector window. Property inspector is an interactive tool for exploring and modifying a UiControl's property values.

Object browser displays a hierarchical list of the UiControls in the GUI. You can select any UiControl from here.

M-File editor displays the application M-file connected with the GUI. If you haven't already saved the GUI, the Save as dialog box will first appear.

View Callbacks is similar to the previous one because it displays the application M-file connected with the GUI, but here you have the opportunity to jump directly into the callback function that you need. For example, if you need to change a callback function of a given pushbutton, you first select it and then, from the View Callback menu item, you jump directly into its callback function prototype.

The Layout Menu

The layout menu works on the selected UiControls by snapping them to the grid or by moving them backward and forward. We use this last feature when there are UiControls overlapping each other.

Snap to grid ties UiControls to the grid square borders when moved. (The Tools -> Grid and Rulers... menu item allows for displaying the grid and changing its size.)

Bring to Front (Ctrl+F) moves the selected UiControl(s) in front of the others.

Send to Back (Ctrl+B) moves the selected UiControl(s) to the back of the others.

Bring Forward moves the selected UiControl(s) forward by one level, that is, not in front of all UiControl, as Bring to Front does, but only in front of the one overlapping it. Hence, if you have three overlying uincontrols and you want to bring the last one in the second level, this is the item you need to use.

Send Backward moves the selected UiControl(s) back by one level, that is, behind the UiControl directly behind it, but not behind all UiControls, as Send to Back does.

Tools Menu

The Tools menu provides commands for running the GUI, to align UiControls, to display and regulate the grid and the ruler, to create Menus into the GUI, to display the Tab Order editor box, and to set the GUI options.

Run (Ctrl+T) starts running the current GUI.

Align Objects... displays the Align Objects box. This tool allows for aligning and distributing the UiControls within the GUI both vertically and horizontally. Facility with this tool will save considerable time. In practice, when you want to align or distribute two or more UiControls, you first to select them, you then click onto the self-explanatory icon in the Align Objects box, and finally you press the Apply button. The Align option aligns the selected UiControls to the same reference line, while the Distribute option spaces the selected UiControls uniformly with respect to each other. By default, the UiControls are spaced within the bounding box, but you can also space them to a specified value in pixels by selecting the Set spacing option and specifying the pixel value.

Grid and Rulers... displays the Grid and Rulers box. This tool allows for displaying the rulers and the grid in the GUI background. You can also regulate the Grid Size by selecting the desired pixel value for each square from the Grid Size pop-up menu. In this box there is also a duplicate of the snap-to-grid option that we have already discussed in the Layout Menu item. Of course, neither the ruler nor the grid will appear in run mode.

Menu Editor... displays the Menu Editor box. With this option you add Menus and menu items, in addition to context menus into your GUIs. Menus, menu items, and context menus work similarly to UiControls; that is, they perform the action defined in their Callback functions. As for the UiControls, for menus as well, prototype Callback functions are automatically created in the M-file by GUIDE.

Help

The help menu provides two items for help and information.

Using the Layout editor displays a starting guide on "Creating graphical user interfaces." It is a sort of index from which you can select many different subguides.

Creating GUIs displays a list of sections on how to create graphical user interfaces (GUIs) using GUIDE.

Preferences for GUIDE

There are a number of preferences that you can set for GUIDE. These preferences can be found in three different locations within the Preferences dialog box, which can be invoked from the File menu.

Confirmation preferences:
GUIDE can display a confirmation dialog box when "saving changes" is needed for GUIDE to proceed. Basically, before running (activating) the GUI and before exporting it, any change that has been done has to be saved. If you think that you may not want to keep these changes, then from the MATLAB file menu, select General -> Confirmation Dialogs to access the GUIDE confirmation preferences and tick on "prompt to save on activate" and/or "prompt to save on export" as shown in Fig. 8.19.

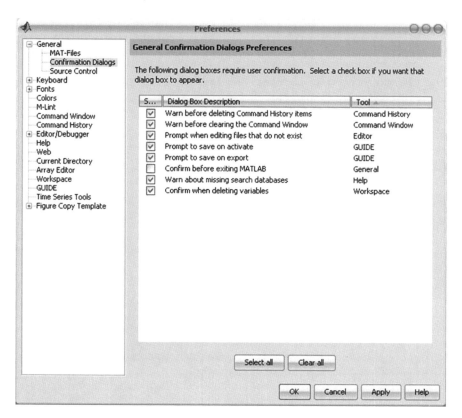

Fig. 8.19 Confirmation preferences

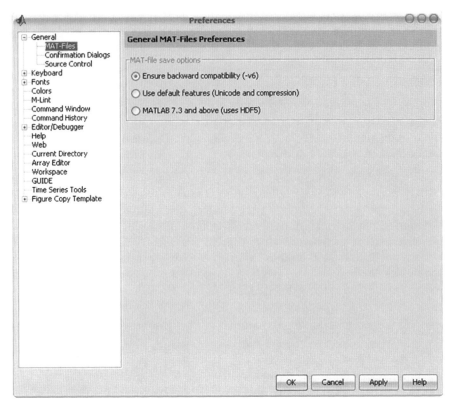

Fig. 8.20 Ensure backward compatibility (-v6)

Backward Compatibility

If you created a GUI with MATLAB 7.0 or an earlier version, and you need to run it also with older MATLAB versions, then this is the preference that you want.

From the MATLAB File menu, select Preferences and then click on Ensure backward compatibility (-v6) in the Preferences dialog box under General > MAT-Files (Fig. 8.20).

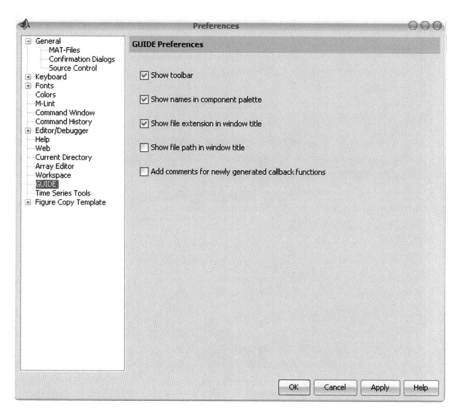

Fig. 8.21 GUIDE preferences

Other Preferences

Finally, five additional preferences for the Layout Editor interface and for M-file comments can be set from the Preferences dialog box, by selecting GUIDE in the left-hand panel. These preferences are self-explanatory. Unless you are already familiar with GUIs, it might be useful to click on "Add comments" for newly generated callback functions (Fig. 8.21).

Suggested Readings

Marchand P, Holland OT (2002) Graphics and GUIs with MATLAB. Boca Raton, FL: Chapman & Hall/CRC

Smith ST (2006) MATLAB: Advanced GUI development. Indianapolis, IN: Dog Ear Pub

Chapter 9
Psychtoolbox: Video

The Psychophysics Toolbox (PTB) is a package for psychophysics research developed by David Brainard and Denis Pelli (Brainard 1997; Pelli 1997) and recently by Mario Kleiner (Kleiner et al. 2007). The PTB toolbox can be freely downloaded from the follwing website http://psychtoolbox.org/PsychtoolboxDownload. This toolbox has been used extensively over the last decade (the first version was released in 1995), and it is very useful for running experiments needing audiovisual stimuli. PTB routines treat the computer (Linux, Mac, or Windows) as a display device, i.e., a frame buffer, a portion of memory generally placed within the graphics card where images are temporally stored. To do this, PTB interfaces MATLAB with a low-level computer language such as C. Hence, besides a number of .m functions, PTB includes low-level information included in MEX files. The most important MEX file is Screen.mex, which will be described in the current chapter.

PTB includes a great number of functions, whose documentation is displayed at http://docs.psychtoolbox.org/Psychtoolbox.

The Screen Function

As you may have anticipated, the core of PTB is the Screen function. It includes a number of subfunctions allowing for accurate control of the images presented on the computer screen. To see all the subfunctions of Screen (and a partial help), type "Screen" with no arguments at the MATLAB prompt (if you type "help Screen" you get a general introduction about the function). Each time you call the Screen function it outputs, at the MATLAB prompt, information about your graphics hardware. Before running any experiment it is important to read this information to make sure you are equipped for your needs. However, you may not want to have this information repeatedly prompted each time the Screen function is called. In this case, you can use the following code[1] to suppress it:

```
Screen('Preference','SuppressAllWarnings',1);
```

The general call of the Screen function is the following:

```
[v1, v2, …]=Screen('Sub-functionName', parameter1, parameter2, …)
```

The Screen function always needs the sub-function name together with the parameters of the sub-function. Moreover, the function returns a number of variables (from zero to many) according to the specific subfunction. The help of its subfunctions can be seen by typing `Screen('Sub-functionName?')` at the MATLAB prompt. For example:

```
Screen('OpenWindow?')
Screen('FillRect?')
```

Or equivalently

```
Screen OpenWindow?
Screen FillRect?
```

In the displayed help, optional input arguments are preceded by a comma, whereas nonoptional arguments are not. For example:

```
[VBLTimestamp StimulusOnsetTime FlipTimestamp Missed Beampos] = Screen('Flip',
windowPtr [, when] [, dontclear] [, dontsync] [, multiflip]);
```

Here `when`, `dontclear`, `dontsync` and, `multiflip` are optional arguments (i.e., they have default values), whereas `windowPtr` is not. Since the order of the function arguments cannot be modified, empty square brackets can be used to reach the desired position. Hence, in the above example, to change the `dontsync` default value, we need to write:

```
Screen('Flip', windowPtr, [], [], dontsync)
```

The following is an unsorted list of the things that can be done with `Screen`, which are usually done by a specific subfunction. `Screen` can be used to get information about the screen such as the refresh rate or the size in pixels. `Screen` can also be used to show strings (very useful in psycholinguistics experiments), to draw shapes such as lines, ovals, rectangles, or any other kind of geometrical shape you may want to draw. `Screen` can also import pictures from graphics files (such as .jpg, or .tif) saved on the hard drive and can be used to create video clips. But probably the most interesting feature of `Screen` is that everything is done with maximal timing accuracy. This is because the stimulus presentation is synchronized with the monitor refresh rate.

In the current chapter we first show how to use Screen to get information about the hardware and software characteristics. Then we show how to draw figures and

---

[1] Please note that the codes presented in this book works with Psychtoolbox from version 3.

text, and how to import pictures from external files. Finally, we show how to create a sequence of events and how to present them with great timing accuracy.

As anticipated, the Screen function, the main function of PTB, is written in a low-level computer language. Because of this, when you use Screen, if your code crashes it may be difficult to go back into your script or to the MATLAB prompt (for example, you might need to quit MATLAB from the task manager or, even worse, to switch off your computer!). To avoid this problem, we recommend writing all code within a try and catch block (see Chap. 3). This trick bypasses some of the problems that may arise if your program crashes. The following example shows how you should use the try–catch commands.

Listing 9.1

```
1  try
2     % write here the code written in the chapter
3  catch
4     Screen('CloseAll')
5     rethrow(lasterror)
6  end
```

Analysis

Lines: 1, 3–6 are to catch any error after a Screen has been opened.

Line 2: the script written in the chapter.

Lines 4–5: closes all screens in case the program written in the try section crashes. Moreover, it reports the last error found in the try section. This is useful for debugging the code.

Another option is to use an auxiliary monitor so to keep the MATLAB command window on one monitor and display the figures created with PTB on the other one. In this way, if the code crashes, it would be possible reading at the MATLAB prompt the error generating the crash and, in most of the cases, it would be possible to "close" the screen code.

How to Use Screen to Get Information

The function Screen can be used to get information about the PTB itself as well as the characteristics of the computer in use. In particular, the Screen subfunctions are useful for increasing a program's portability. For example, if you are displaying a video clip, it is important to get the screen refresh rate of the computer in use to produce the same visual effect in terms of timing when different machines are used. The following table explains some of these subfunctions.

Sub function	Command	Example
Version	`struct=Screen('Version');`	Return a structure with the characteristics of the PTB
Computer	`comp=Screen('Computer');`	Return a structure with the characteristics of the computer
Screen	`screens=Screen('Screens');`	Return an array of numbers (0, 1, 2, …). Each number identifies one screen connected to the computer. The default, 0, is the screen with the menu bar
Rect	`rect=Screen('Rect', screenNumber);`	Return an array with the top left corner (always 0, 0) and the bottom right corner (n, m) coordinates of the screen. The number of the bottom right corner coincides with the screen's resolution (e.g., 1,024×768). ScreenNumber is a pointer (i.e., the one returned by the Screens subfunction) that tells the function which screen-rect is to be returned
FrameRate	`hz=Screen('FrameRate', screenNumber);`	Returns the refresh rate of the screen identified by the pointer screenNumber
GetFlipinterval	`[monitorFlipInterval nrValidSamples stddev]=Screen('GetFlipInterval', windowPtr [, nrSamples] [, stddev] [, timeout]);`	Returns the flip interval (in seconds), i.e., the interval in seconds between two consecutive vertical retraces of the screen identified by the pointer. This subfunction has to be run after the OpenWindow subfunction

How to Use **Screen** to Draw Figures

Preliminary Notions: Drawing Figures in Three Steps—Opening, Drawing, and Closing

The main thing Screen is used for is to draw figures and to present them with maximal timing accuracy. Generally speaking, there are three main figure types: figures drawn with PTB, imported figures (e.g., .jpg, .tif, …) and text figures. Independently from the type of figure you are drawing, the drawing is done in three steps that we can call opening, drawing, and closing. These steps are normally found in any program that displays figures.

Opening the Window

The "opening" step is controlled by the subfunction 'OpenWindow':

```
[MyScreen, rect] = screen('OpenWindow', 0, [0, 255, 0]);
```

When the opening is done, we take control of the screen where we are going to draw the figure. The first argument of the 'OpenWindow' subfunction indicates the screen we want to refer to. Indeed, many screens can be connected to the same computer at the same time. The screen with the menu bar is identified with the default number "0".

Therefore, with the command line above, we get control of the screen with the menu bar. To this particular screen we also assign a name (i.e., the returned pointer MyScreen). Therefore, later in the code, every time we need to access this screen, we use screen's name (MyScreen) rather than 0. The above code paints the whole screen in green color using the RGB triplet [0, 255, 0]. In the Screen function, the color argument is passed either with a single gray value (i.e., 0–255) or with a RGB triplet. By default, if the color argument is omitted, the screen is white, i.e., the default value for this argument is [255 255 255]. Last but not least, 'OpenWindow' returns the screen size, which above we saved in the rect variable. The rect variable is an array of the screen coordinates in pixels. The first two coordinates are those of the top left corner; the second two coordinates are those of the bottom right corner. The top left coordinates are 0,0, whereas those of the bottom right depend on screen resolution.

The full list of arguments for the `OpenWindow` subfunction is the following:

```
Screen('OpenWindow',0[,color][,rect][,pixelSize][,numberOfBuffers]…
                    [,stereomode][,multisample][,imagingmode]);
```

The following table outlines the use of these arguments.

Opt. argument	Color
Description	Can be a scalar, if you want an achromatic screen or a 1×3 vector with the unnormalized RGB values (i.e. 1–256). For an RGB color description, refer to Chap. 5
Example	`Screen('OpenWindow', 0, [255,0,0])` `% it turns the screen red`

Opt. argument	Rect
Description	Specifies the size, in pixels, of your window (this option works better under Mac OS). This is a 1×4 vector with the coordinates of the window. The first two numbers refer to the x and y coordinates (in pixels) of the upper left corner, respectively; the last two numbers refer to the x and y coordinates of the bottom right corner of the window, respectively. Hence, there is the possibility to draw the stimuli even in a portion of your screen instead of the whole screen, although you'll probably never use it. The following example turns the screen red using the specified coordinates
Example	`Screen('OpenWindow', 0, [255, 0, 0],` `[250,250,450,650])`

Opt. argument	pixelSize
Description	Specifies the number of bits per pixel devoted to creating colors in the screen. Usual numbers of bits are 8, 16, or 32 per pixel, corresponding to 256, thousands, or millions of colors, respectively. This depends on the graphics card. If you do not know how many bits per pixel your graphics card can use, you can ask PTB using the Screen subfunction PixelSizes. By default, PTB works with 8 bits, and therefore colors are coded within the 0–255 (i.e., 2^8) range. If a different number of bits is used, the range defining the color also changes. For example, with 16 bits, the triplet for the red color is [65535, 0, 0]
Example	`Screen('Openwindow',0,[],[],16)`

Opt. argument	numberOfBuffers
Description	Determines the number of buffers to use. You normally use one or two buffers (see next chapter) to run your experiments, so you don't change this parameter except for testing or debugging reasons
Example	`Screen('Openwindow',0,[],[],[],2)`

(continued)

(continued)

Opt. argument	Stereomode
Description	PTB offers different stereo possibilities. The default value of this argument is 0, that is, Monoscopic viewing. If you are equipped with stereo hardware, such as shutter glasses, you can opt for values from 1 to 3 of stereomode according to where you want the images for the left and right eyes appearing on the screen
	If you want a stereogram, then set stereomode to 4. In this way you split the screen into two halves, where the left view is for the left eye; set stereomode to 5 for cross-fusion. If you are equipped with color glasses for anaglyph stereo vision, then set stereomode to 6, 7, 8, or 9 for different combinations of colors
	Finally, set stereomode to 10 if you have two monitors: you will have one image per monitor
Example	Screen('Openwindow',0,[],[],[],[],4)

Opt. argument	"multisample"
Description	This parameter enables an antialiasing procedure. In brief, when you design your stimuli for a screen, aliasing is a problem that occurs when the approximation due to pixel size is not good enough. When you draw a disc, for example, its smoothness can be very poor if the resolution of the screen in not high enough. Or, when you create video clips, you may have a temporal aliasing problem resulting from the limited frame rate. When multisample is greater than 0, PTB looks for the best antialiasing solution that can be obtained by your hardware. This will improve the quality of the stimuli; however, the downside in doing this is the increase of video memory use, leading to loss of precision in terms of time. You might not want this if you are collecting reaction times
Example	Screen('Openwindow',0,[],[],[],[],[],5)

Opt. argument	Imagingmode
Description	This parameter enables PTB's internal image-processing pipeline. The pipeline is off by default. By setting this parameter to 1, you enable this feature to perform image-processing operations that are executed on the graphics processor itself
Example	Screen('Openwindow',0,[],[],[],[],[],[],0)

Drawing: An Introduction

This is the step where we actually design the figures. We'll see later in the chapter how to program some figures that may be drawn directly within the PTB environment. But first, we have to introduce another subfunction. Indeed, in order for a drawing to be effective, it has to be followed by the subfunction Flip.

The figure is automatically drawn in the background memory (also called backbuffer), which is not visible. The Flip subfunction moves the previously drawn figure from the backbuffer to the foreground memory (the frontbuffer) so that it becomes visible on screen. This "flip" of the figure from the backbuffer to the frontbuffer occurs at a specific time, which is the first available vertical retrace of the screen. The flip action is performed on any figure found in the background memory. In other words, if you have drawn, let's say, a square, a circle, and a triangle and you want to show them on the screen, you do not need to flip each object, but instead, you can flip all objects at once. The `Flip` subfunction needs to be addressed to a particular screen (i.e., to a particular screen pointer). In everyday situations, the screen we address to is the only screen connected to the computer. However, if you are using two or more screens, you could decide on which screen the figure has to be flipped. When the `Flip` subfunction is executed, the background memory is cleared. Therefore, if you have nothing in the background and you call the `Flip` subfunction, everything that is currently in your foreground is deleted, because it is replaced with an empty object.

The complete Flip command is the following:

```
[VBLTimestamp StimulusOnsetTime FlipTimestamp Missed Beampos] = Screen('Flip',
 windowPtr [, when] [, dontclear] [, dontsync] [, multiflip]);
```

We will see later how to use some of the Flip options to control the timing of the stimuli.

Closing

Closing ends the code, and in the majority of cases may look simply like the following command:

```
screen('CloseAll');
```

The `CloseAll` subfunction closes all the figures created during code execution and sets the screen back to normality, returning control to MATLAB. It is important to close everything, otherwise, the control is not returned to MATLAB. In PTB, you can close all objects at once (for example, with the subfunction CloseAll) or close only specific objects (remember, however, that at the end of your code you need to close all the objects created). This can be done as follows:

```
screen('Close', objectPointer)
```

where objectPointer is the pointer to the object you want to close. The possibility of closing selected objects is particularly interesting if the code you are writing needs a lot of memory. Overall, the amount of memory you are using depends on the number of objects and on their size. If memory consumption becomes critical for your program, then it might be helpful closing the objects no longer in use.

Drawing: Reprise

Now that the preliminaries are out of the way, we can have a go at doing some drawing. Replace the text comment in the try–catch example (presented in Listing 9.1) as in Listing 9.2.

Listing 9.2

```
1    try
2        screens = Screen('Screens');
3        whichscreen = max(screens);
4        [myscreen,rect]=Screen('OpenWindow',whichscreen, [0, 255,0]);
5        KbWait;
6        screen('CloseAll');
7    catch
8        screen('CloseAll')
9        rethrow(lasterror)
10   end
```

Analysis

This short script does a few things:

On line 2: It looks for how many screens are connected to the computer.

On line 3: if there is more than one screen, it selects one of them without the menu bar and assigns an arbitrary name to it. Later, we'll open this screen and turn it green.

On line 4: the screen assumes the name myscreen (i.e., its pointer), and we save the coordinates of the screen in the variable rect. Moreover, we paint the full screen myscreen green.

On line 5: we make the program wait for a key-press event. This is done by means of the KbWait command, which stops the execution of the code until the user presses a keyboard key.

On line 6: The subfunction "CloseAll" returns control to MATLAB.
In the previous example, we did not draw any figures on the screen. In the next section we will extend the code by drawing some objects.

Drawing Shapes

To understand how to draw geometric shapes on the screen, we extend Listing 9.2 to make the stimulus for a color afterimage. To do this, we want to draw a red square (400 by 400 pixels) on a green background, and to do this we use the subfunction FillRect, which draws a filled rectangle; use the subfunction FrameRect to get a framed rectangle. Both the FillRect and FrameRect subfunctions take as parameters the screen pointer followed by the color (in RGB triplet form) and finally the coordinates of the rectangle we want to draw. When the FillRect or FrameRect subfunctions are called, a rectangle is drawn in the backbuffer. To actually see the rectangle on the screen, we need to call the Flip subfunction.

Listing 9.3

```
1   try
2       screens = Screen('Screens');
3       whichscreen = max(screens);
4       [myscreen, rect] = Screen('OpenWindow', whichscreen, [0, 255, 0]);
5       square_size = [0, 0, 400, 400];
6       square_rect = CenterRect(square_size, rect);
7       Screen('FillRect', myscreen, [255, 0, 0], square_size);
8       Screen('Flip', myscreen);
9       KbWait;
10      Screen('CloseAll');
11  catch
12      screen('CloseAll')
13      rethrow(lasterror)
14  end
```

Now if you look at the red square long enough (e.g., 20 s) and then move your eyes to a white sheet of paper, you can see the afterimage of the red color.

You may have noticed in the script above that we used the very handy function CenterRect. It calculates the coordinates to include one figure within the center of another one whose coordinates are known. In the example, the external figure is the entire screen; therefore, the function centers the figure within the screen.

CenterRect and the other functions for manipulating coordinates (type help PsychRets at the MATLAB prompt or see below) can also be used in a nested way. Let us now display a simultaneous lightness contrast display. We divide the screen into two sectors, one white and one black, and at the center of each sector we need to place a gray square. Everything is done in the following example.

Listing 9.4

```
1   try
2       screens = Screen('Screens'); % count the screens
3       whichscreen = max(screens); % select the screen
4       [myscreen, rect] = Screen('OpenWindow', whichscreen,
5       % create the black/white sectors
6       sector = [0, 0, rect(3)/2, rect(4)]; % set the size o
7       sector_l = sector;
8       sector_r = AdjoinRect(sector, sector_l, RectRight);
9       Screen('FillRect', myscreen, 255, sector_l);
10      Screen('FillRect', myscreen, 0, sector_r);
11      % create the left/right grey square
12      square = [0, 0, 100, 100];
13      square_l = CenterRect(square, sector_l);
14      square_r = CenterRect(square, sector_r);
15      Screen('FillRect', myscreen, 255/2, square_l);
16      Screen('FillRect', myscreen, 255/2, square_r)
17      Screen('Flip', myscreen);
18      KbWait;
19      Screen('CloseAll');
20  catch
21      screen('CloseAll')
22      rethrow(lasterror)
23  end
```

The script is very similar to Listing 9.3. In the example, we also introduced the `AdjoinRect` function which adds a rectangle at the right of the specified `sector`. Note also that here we used `CenterRect` in a nested way, because now "center" is the center of the defined sector, not the center of the screen. When you are drawing the stimuli for your experiment, our suggestion is to proceed as follows. First, set the size of the shape, regardless of its position on the screen, by setting its size starting from the top-left corner. Then use the `PsychRect` function to define the actual coordinates on the screen.

In the following table can be found a complete list of the functions that can be used to simplify your work that uses the rect coordinates. Please refer to the Psychtoolbox help for more complete information on how to use them.

Function	Description
AdjoinRect	Moves a rect next to another one
AlignRect	Aligns a rect over another one
ArrangeRects	Arranges an array of rects in a pleasant way
CenterRect	Centers a rect within a second one
CenterRectOnPoint	Centers a rect around given x,y coordinates
CenterRectOnPointd	Centers rect around an x,y coordinate pair
ClipRect	Returns the intersection of two rects
ClipRect	Returns the intersection of two rects
InsetRect	Shrinks/expands rect by additive insets
IsEmptyRect	Returns 1 if empty, returns 0 otherwise
IsInRect	Is the point inside a rect?
OffsetRect	Shifts rect vertically and horizontally
RectBottom	Returns index of yBottom entry of a rect
RectCenter	Returns the integer x,y coordinates of center
RectCenterd	Returns the exact x,y coordinates of center
RectOfMatrix	Accept an image as a matrix and returns a PTB rect specifying the bounds
RectHeight	Returns the height of a rect
RectLeft	Returns index of xLeft entry of a rect
RectRight	Returns index of xRight entry of a rect
RectTop	Returns index of yTop entry of a rect
RectWidth	Returns width of a rect
RectSize	Returns the width and the height of a rect
ScaleRect	Scales a rect by multiplicative factors
SetRect	Creates a rect (i.e., a vector) from four input coordinates
SizeOfRect	Accepts a Psychtoolbox rect [left, top, right, bottom] and returns the size [rows columns] of a MATLAB array (i.e. image) just big enough to hold all the pixels
UnionRect	Smallest rect containing two given rects

To draw filled ovals (including circles) we use the subfunction FillOvals instead of the subfunction FillRects. The counterpart of FrameRect is FrameOvals. In the following table, we present a list of the shapes that can be drawn with PTB. More-complex graphical shapes can be drawn by combining two or more figures.

Sub/Function	Command	Description
DrawLine	Screen('DrawLine', win-dowPtr [,color], fromH, fromV, toH, toV [,penWidth]);	draws a line
DrawArc	Screen('DrawArc',windowPtr ,[color],[rect],startAngle ,arcAngle)	draws a circular arc unfilled with color (i.e., a Pac-Man-like figure)
FrameArc	Screen('FrameArc',windowPtr ,[color],[rect],startAngle ,arcAngle[,penWidth] [,penHeight] [,penMode])	as above
FillArc	Screen('FillArc',windowPtr ,[color],[rect],startAngle ,arcAngle)	as above but filled with color
FillRect	Screen('FillRect', win-dowPtr [,color] [,rect]);	draws a rectangle filled with color
FrameRect	Screen('FrameRect', win-dowPtr [,color] [,rect] [,penWidth]);	draws a rectangle unfilled with color
FillOval	Screen('FillOval', win-dowPtr [,color] [,rect] [,perfectUpToMaxDiame-ter]);	draws a filled oval
FrameOval	Screen('FrameOval', win-dowPtr [,color] [,rect] [,penWidth] [,penHeight] [,penMode]);	draws a framed oval
FramePoly	Screen('FramePoly', win-dowPtr [,color], pointList [,penWidth]);	draws a framed polygon
FillPoly	Screen('FillPoly', win-dowPtr [,color], pointList [, isConvex]);	draws a filled polygon

Batch Processing: Drawing Multiple Figures at Once

It is often useful to be able to draw multiple figures at once. This operation is not only useful, but it is also an efficient operation to do with PTB 3. The repeated drawing is achieved using the functions that we have used so far. Instead of writing repeatedly the same drawing subfunctions:

```
Screen('FillRect', win, [red1 green1 blue1], [left1 top1 right1 bot1]);
Screen('FillRect', win, [red2 green2 blue2], [left2 top2 right2 bot2]);
...
Screen('FillRect', win, [redn greenn bluen], [leftn topn rightn
botn]);
```

you can write in the following:

```
mycolors = [red1, red2,... ; green1, green2,... ; blue1, blue2,...];
myrects = [xtop_1, xtop_2,...; ytop_1, ytop_2,...; xbottom_1, xbottom_2,...;
ybottom_1, ybottom_2,...];
Screen('FillRect', win, mycolors, myrects);
```

In other words, you first write a $3 \times n$ matrix for the RGB values, and then a $4 \times n$ matrix for the figures' coordinates. These matrices are then passed to the desired subfunction to draw the shapes. In the $3 \times n$ color matrix, each row identifies the RGB values for the corresponding figure. In the same way, in the $4 \times n$ matrix for the figures' coordinates, each column identifies the coordinates of the corresponding figure; odd rows are the x coordinates, and even rows are the y coordinates.

In the following example, we draw a setting that could be used for a Posner-like experiment by drawing three frames placed one after the other in the middle of the screen. The left and the right frames are gray, while the middle frame is black so that it cannot be seen. Note that colors and coordinates are transposed when they are passed to the FrameRect subfunction.

Listing 9.5

```
1  try
2      whichscreen = max(Screen('Screens')); % count the screens
3      [w, rect] = Screen('OpenWindow', whichscreen, 0); % open it
4      midsquare = CenterRect([0, 0, 100, 100], rect);
5      squares = [AdjoinRect(midsquare, midsquare, RectLeft); ...
6      midsquare; ...
7      AdjoinRect(midsquare, midsquare, RectRight)];
8      colors = [255/2, 255/2, 255/2; ...
9      0, 0, 0; ...
10     255/2, 255/2, 255/2];
11     Screen('FrameRect', w, colors', squares', 5);
12     Screen('Flip', w);
13     KbWait;
14     Screen('CloseAll');
15 catch
16     screen('CloseAll')
17     rethrow(lasterror)
18 end
```

Drawing Text

'DrawText' is the subfunction to draw text on the screen. The subfunction's options are the following:

```
[newX,newY]=Screen('DrawText', windowPtr, text [,x] [,y] [,color]
[,backgroundColor] [,yPositionIsBaseline]);
```

where windowPtr is the pointer to the screen, and text is the string of text you want to draw. Optional arguments are the x and y coordinates where the text starts (these coordinates refer to the top left corner) and the text color. Note that in this subfunction the color argument is passed after the coordinates, instead of before, as was the case for rectangles and ovals. Further optional arguments are backgroundColor and yPositionIsBaseline. backgroundColor is the color behind the text (It does not seem to work properly under Windows and Linux. However, this problem can be easily solved by drawing a colored rectangle before drawing the text.) yPositionIsBaseline is a logical value; if true, the y coordinate for the text refers to the bottom, instead of the upper, part of the text.

The Drawtext subfunction returns the x and y coordinates of the end of the text. This is useful because the strings you are writing could be of a different lengths, covering a different number of pixels. Therefore, knowledge of the ending coordinates of a string is important for arranging two or more strings of text. If you simply need to write one string in the middle of the screen, you can use the function DrawFormattedText:

```
[nx, ny, textbounds] = DrawFormattedText(win, tstring [, sx][, sy][, color]
[, wrapat][, flipHorizontal][, flipVertical][, vSpacing])
```

DrawText accepts not only coordinates expressed in pixels but also the option 'center', which can be used to center the text on the screen either on the horizontal or vertical axis. The following code writes a string starting from the middle of the screen.

Listing 9.6

```
1   try
2       screens = Screen('Screens');
3       whichscreen = max(screens)
4       [w, rect] =Screen('Openwindow', whichscreen);
5       mytext = 'MATLAB';
6       DrawFormattedText(w, mytext, 'center', 'center');
7       Screen ('Flip', w);
8       KbWait;
9       Screen('Close', w)
10  catch
11      Screen('Close',w)
12      rethrow(lasterror)
13  end
```

PTB provides additional writing subfunctions specifying the style, font, mode, and size of the text. To get these features the corresponding subfunctions have to be called before `DrawText` or `DrawFormattedText` is called. These subfunctions allow for *getting* and *setting* text features at the same time; that is, the same function *gets* the type of text that is currently on and *sets* the desired text type. Let us see how they work.

'TextStyle' specifies the text style. 0 is normal, 1 is bold, 2 is italic, 3 is bold and italic, 4 is underline, 5 is bold and underline, 6 is italic and underline, and 7 is italic, bold, and underline.

For example, the command:

```
previous_style = Screen('TextStyle', w, 2);
```

returns the style that was previously in use (0 is the default style) and sets the style to bold for next text.

'TextFont' specifies the text font; it can be invoked by passing the font name or via the font number. The subfunction returns two arguments, which are the number and name of the font that is currently in use (this is because to each font there also corresponds a number). Use the following syntax:

```
[previousFontName, previousFontNumber] = Screen ('TextFont',w, 'Verdana');
```

The function returns both previous name and number style and sets Verdana as the style for future text.

'TextMode' specifies the text mode; there are 16 different modes, ranging from normal to dashed, dot-dashed, and so on. It works only with Mac OS. Use the following syntax to get the previous mode and to set the new one:

```
previous_mode = Screen('TextMode', w,10);
```

'TextSize' specifies the text size. Use the following syntax to get the previous size and to set the new one:

```
previous_size=Screen('TextSize', w,40) ;
```

Finally, there is the 'TextWidth' subfunction, which returns the horizontal offset, that is, the change in the horizontal pen position that will be produced by the string. That is, if you are not sure how many bytes your string is, use 'TextWidth' to get it. Use the following syntax:

```
Width=Screen('TextWidth', w, mystring);
```

where `mystring` is the string that you are to type. It returns a negative number of bytes if you write from right to left. `Mystring` may include 2-byte characters (e.g., Chinese).

The following code listing shows how to use some of these subfunctions. Moreover, it provides an example of changing text. The word MATLAB is written three times in three different colors that are continuously changing. The word is also vertically and horizontally flipped using some of the options of DrawFormattedText.

Listing 9.7

```
1    try
2        screens = Screen('Screens');
3        whichscreen = max(screens);
4        [w, rect] =Screen('Openwindow', whichscreen, 0);
5        mytext = 'MATLAB';
6        Screen('TextSize',w, 50);
7        Screen('TextFont',w, 'Arial');
8        for r = [0:2:255, 254:-2:0]
9            DrawFormattedText(w, mytext, 'center', 'center', [r, 0, 0]);
10           Screen('Flip', w);
11       end
12       for g = [0:2:255, 254:-2:0]
13           DrawFormattedText(w, mytext, 'center', 'center', [0, g, 0], ...
14           [], 1, 0);
15           Screen('Flip', w);
16       end
17       for b = [0:2:255, 254:-2:0]
18           DrawFormattedText(w, mytext, 'center', 'center', [0, 0, b], ...
19           [], 0, 1);
20           Screen('Flip', w);
21       end
22       Screen('Close', w)
23   catch
24       Screen('Close',w)
25       rethrow(lasterror)
26   end
```

Importing Images

Screen can be used to import and to show images stored on the hard drive. Images are shown in three steps. First you need to load the image in the MATLAB workspace (see Chap. 5); then, you need to create a *texture* of the picture, and finally, you can show the texture on the screen. Let us analyze these steps by running the code in Listing 9.8.

Listing 9.8

```
1   try
2       load mandrill
3       [row, col] = size(X);
4       r = [0, 0, row, col];
5       [windowPtr, rect] = Screen('OpenWindow', 0);
6       r = CenterRect(r, rect);
7       X2=ind2rgb(X,map);
8       X2=X2*256;
9       pic = Screen('MakeTexture', windowPtr, X);
10      Screen('DrawTexture', windowPtr, pic, [], r, 45);
11      Screen('Flip', windowPtr);
12      KbWait;
13      Screen('CloseAll');
14  catch
15      Screen('Close',w)
16      rethrow(lasterror)
17  end
```

Analysis

On lines 2 and 3 we load the image, get its size, and store it in the MATLAB workspace.

On line 4 we set a rectangle as large as the picture, and change its coordinates so that it is set at the center of the screen.

On line 7 we change the indexed image format into an RGB format using the MATLAB function ind2rgb. We need to do this because PTB works with intensity matrices (i.e., gray-scale or RGB) instead of indexed matrices.

On line 8 we multiply the resulting RGB matrix by 256. This is because PTB expects integers ranging from 0 to 255, while the values returned by ind2rgb are in the 0–1 range.

On line 9 we transform the picture into a PTB texture. PTB uses OpenGL[2] commands, and a texture can be seen as a sort of image in OpenGL. A discussion of OpenGL technology is beyond the scope of the present text. However, it is important to know that we need to 'remap' every image into a *texture* element.

On line 10 we draw the texture image in the background memory.

On line 11 we show the picture on the screen.

It has to be stressed that the matrix of an image cannot be directly displayed: the matrix has to be converted into a texture before being displayed.

---

[2] OpenGL's main purpose is to render two- and three-dimensional figures into a frame buffer. These figures are described as sequences of vertices (which define geometric objects) or pixels (which define images). OpenGL performs several processing steps on these data to convert them into pixels to create the image in the frame buffer.

Video Clips

PTB functions can be used to create video clips such as a figure moving along the screen, where a video clip is a succession of static pictures. Each picture is called frame. The possibility of drawing video depends on the refresh rate and on the pixel size. These two factors affect the granularity of the motion. A displacement cannot be lower than the size of one pixel. Similarly, frames cannot be presented at a faster rate than the refresh rate.

In the majority of cases, video clips are drawn using for loops, as in the following example. Here, a black disc on a white background moves horizontally from left to right on the screen.

Listing 9.9

```
1    try
2       screens = Screen('Screens');
3       whichscreen = max(screens);
4       [w, rect] =Screen('Openwindow', whichscreen, 0);
5       discdiam = 20;
6       disc = [0, 0, discdiam, discdiam];
7       rectinrect = [0, 0, rect(3)/2, rect(4)/2];
8       rectinrect = CenterRect(rectinrect, rect);
9       disc = AlignRect(disc, rectinrect, 'center', 'left');
10      for i = 0:600
11         Screen('FillRect', w, 255, rectinrect);
12         Screen('FillOval', w, 0, [disc(1)+i, disc(2), disc(3)+i, disc(4)]);
13         Screen('Flip', w);
14      end
15      Screen('CloseAll'); % close all
16   catch
17       Screen('Close',w)
18       rethrow(lasterror)
19   end
```

Analysis

On line 6 we implement the variable disc, which is a quadruplet of coordinates for the disc; on lines 7 and 8 we implement rectinrect, which is a quadruplet of the coordinates for the frame within which the disc will move.

From line 10 to line 14 we implement the "for loop" in which the x coordinates of the disc change. At the first iteration (i = 0) the disc is placed at the left border of the frame. When i equals 1, the x coordinate of the disc is augmented of one unit; therefore the disc is drawn 1 pixel further to the right than the previous disc. When i equals 2, the shift of the discs becomes 2 pixels, and so on up to i = 600, when the discs disappear behind the frame.

In practice, every time you iterate a loop you need to redraw the object you want to move in a different position by specifying the new x and y coordinates where you want the figure to be drawn. Of course you can set into motion any figure you want. Moreover, motion can be done not only along a straight line but also with a certain fuzziness. Here the string "hello" moves from left to right in an "uncertain" way.

Listing 9.10

```
1   try
2       screens = Screen('Screens');
3       whichscreen = max(screens);
4       [w, rect] =Screen('Openwindow', whichscreen, 0);
5       frame = CenterRect([0, 0, rect(3)/2, rect(4)/2], rect);
6       x = frame(1);
7       y = rect(4)/2;
8       Screen('TextSize', w, 24);
9       for i = 0:600
10          Screen('FillRect', w, 255, frame);
11          Screen('DrawText', w, 'hello world!', x, y);
12          Screen('Flip', w);
13          x = x + (round(rand)*4)-1;
14          y = y + (round(rand)*2)-1;
15      end
16      Screen('CloseAll'); % close all
17  catch
18      Screen('Close',w)
19      rethrow(lasterror)
20  end
```

Analysis

In the current example, the x and y coordinates of the string "hello world!" are modulated by a random factor (using the function *rand* on lines 13 and 14). On line 14, y is made to change by either −1 (a displacement to the upper part of the screen), 0 (no displacement), or +1 (a displacement toward the bottom part of the screen). Therefore, on average, the figure oscillates along the y axis without progressing in any particular direction. However, on line 13, the x coordinate can change by −1, 0, +1, +2, or +3. Negative changes move the string toward the left, whereas positive changes move the string toward the right. Because the randomly generated number is more likely to be positive than negative, the string eventually moves toward the right of the screen.

Drawing Things at the Right Time

Up to now, we have not paid yet much attention to timing. However, on many occasions, timing is an important issue for our stimuli, because we need to be able to control their duration.

Timing is intrinsically connected to the screen refresh rate. For example, you cannot present objects whose duration lasts less than one refresh per cycle. By the same token, you cannot present a stimulus for a duration that is not an exact multiple of the screen refresh rate. The reason is the following. Let's suppose you are showing one stimulus (s1) and that this stimulus has to be replaced by the next stimulus (s2). If the duration of s1 on screen is not a multiple of the refresh rate, it may happen that the drawing of s2 begins when s1 is still on screen. Therefore, when you are deeply concerned about timing, always use durations that are multiples of the screen refresh rate.

Independently from the stimulus type, timing is controlled by two optional arguments of the subfunction Flip. These arguments are "when" and "VBLTimestamp". "when" tells the flip subfunction when the flip from foreground to background is to be done. "VBLTimestamp" is the time when the flip has actually been done. Both "when" and "VBLTimestamp" are expressed in seconds and refer to the system time, a timer that is switched on when you switch on your computer.

The following example illustrates how to control the timing. We first generate a fixation point which stays on the screen for 0.5 seconds and then a red square appears. After 0.75 seconds the red square is cleared, and after 1 seconds a green square appears for 0.6 seconds.

Listing 9.11

```
1  try
2      % general opening operations
3      whichscreen = max(Screen('Screens'));
4      [w, rect] = Screen('OpenWindow', whichscreen);
5      % get the flip interval
6      slack = Screen('GetFlipInterval', w)/2;
7
8      % draw the fixation dot in the backgound
9      Screen('FillOval', w, 0, CenterRect([0, 0, 10, 10], rect));
10     % present the fixation
11     fixation_onset = Screen('Flip', w); % get the onsettime of the fixation
12
13     % draw the first stimulus in the backgound
14     Screen('FillRect', w, [255, 0, 0], CenterRect([0, 0, 50, 50], rect));
15     % present the first stimulus 0.5 seconds after the onset of the fixation
16     firststimulus_onset = Screen('Flip', w, fixation_onset + 0.5 - slack);
17     % keep the stimulus on screen for 0.75 seconds
18     firststimulus_offset=Screen('Flip',w,firststimulus_onset + 0.75 -slack);
19
20     % draw the second stimulus in the backgound
21     Screen('FillRect', w, [0, 255, 0], CenterRect([0, 0, 50, 50], rect));
22     % draw the second stimulus 1 second after the offset
23     % of the first stimulus
24     secondstimulus_onset=Screen('Flip',w,firststimulus_offset+1.0-slack);
25     % keep the second stimulus on for 0.6 second
26     secondstimulus_offset=Screen('Flip',w,secondstimulus_onset+0.6-slack);
27     Screen('CloseAll'); % close all
28 catch
29     Screen('Close',w)
30     rethrow(lasterror)
31 end
```

Analysis

In the example, the timing is achieved by getting the onset/offset times of each stimulus. For example:

On line 15 we flip the first stimulus at a time that is the sum of the onset of the fixation point and 0.5 s.

On line 17 we flip again after a period of 0.75 s. However, because there is nothing in the background, the screen is cleared after such a period. In this way, the presence of the first stimulus on the screen is controlled by this second flip.

On line 24 the second stimulus is switched 1 s after the offset time of the first stimulus.

On line 26 the second stimulus is cleared after 0.6 s due to the second flip.

Note the use of the subfunction 'GetFlipInterval' on line 6. This subfunction returns an estimate of the monitor flip interval for the specified onscreen window. This allows for maximum control of the display time. We use such slack in the computation of the "when" time in the flip subfunction.

Finally, there is another operation you can do to obtain maximal timing accuracy. When we use the computer there are several software processes running at the same time. The CPU does calculations for all of them. These activities reduce the resources that are available to MATLAB and PTB. PTB, however, has a set of functions for redirecting all available CPU resources to MATLAB to improve timing accuracy. These functions will be presented in the next chapter.

Summary

- The Psychophysics Toolbox (PTB) is a package specifically developed for psychophysics research.
- The core of the PTB is the `Screen` function.
- PTB uses a double buffering system (back and front buffers = 'background and foreground memory') that provides great timing control for visual stimuli.
- PTB can be used to draw objects (geometric figures, figures imported from graphics files or text) onscreen. The drawing of objects onscreen is performed in three steps: opening, drawing, and closing.
- The spatial arrangements of objects can be manipulated with the PsychRects functions, and the drawing can be done in batch-processing mode.
- The Screen subfunction flip can be used to control the timing of your stimuli and to synchronize the drawing with the screen's vertical retrace.
- The Screen function can be used to create movies.

Exercises

Exercise 1

Draw the Kanizsa triangle by designing three Pac-Men shaping the illusory contour.

Solution 1

```
1   try
2       [w, rect] =Screen('Openwindow',0);
3       cx = rect(3)/2;
4       cy=  rect(4)/2;
5       size = 90;
6       displacement = 200;
7       coord1 = [cx-size,cy-size-displacement,cx+size,cy+size-displacement];
8       coord2 = [cx-size-displacement, cy-size+displacement/2,...
9   cx+size-displacement, cy+size+displacement/2];
10      coord3 = [cx-size+displacement, cy-size+displacement/2,...
11  cx+size+displacement, cy+size+displacement/2];
12      MystartAngle11 = 210;
13      MystartAngle2 = 90;
14      MystartAngle3 = 330;
15      MyarcAngle = 300;
16      Screen('FillArc', w, 0, coord1, MystartAngle, MyarcAngle);
17      Screen('FillArc', w, 0, coord2, MystartAngle2, MyarcAngle);
18      Screen('FillArc', w, 0, coord3, MystartAngle3, MyarcAngle);
19      Screen ('Flip',w)
20      mychar = KbWait;
21      Screen('Close',w)
22  catch
23      Screen('Close',w)
24      rethrow(lasterror)
25  end
```

Exercise 2

Draw a Kanizsa triangle equal to the previous one but "dishonestly" (by shaping a white triangle on a white background whose vertex covers three black discs). Besides reviewing how to draw polygons, the purpose of this exercise is to realize that depending on where in your code listing you put a function, it can give rise to different results. Indeed, to solve this exercise, the triangle has to be drawn after, instead of before, the discs.

Solution 2

```
1    try
2        [w, rect] =Screen('Openwindow',0);
3        cx = rect(3)/2;
4        cy= rect(4)/2;
5        size = 90;
6        displacement = 200;
7        coord1 = [cx-size, cy-size-displacement, cx+size, ...
8                    cy+size-displacement];
9        coord2 = [cx-size-displacement, cy-size+displacement/2, ...
10                   cx+size-displacement, cy+size+displacement/2];
11       coord3 = [cx-size+displacement, cy-size+displacement/2, ...
12                   cx+size+displacement, cy+size+displacement/2];
13       coordtriangle = [cx-displacement cy+displacement/2; ...
14                   cx cy-displacement; cx+displacement cy+displacement/2];
15       Screen('FillOval', w, 0, coord1);
16       Screen('FillOval', w, 0, coord2);
17       Screen('FillOval', w, 0, coord3);
18       Screen('FillPoly',w, 255,coordtriangle);
19       Screen ('Flip',w)
20       mychar = KbWait;
21       Screen('Close',w)
22   catch
23       Screen('Close',w)
24       rethrow(lasterror)
25   end
```

A Brick for an Experiment

The stimulus for our experiment is simple: two discs that move with identical motions (one rightward, one leftward) and that start from one position and each end at the other disc's starting point. A stimulus similar to this has been shown previously in this chapter. Here we just reduce the size of the frame within which the discs are moving so that is a square of 300 by 300 pixels. The following script (slightly optimized in comparison to that of the chapter) shows the motion display used by Sekuler et al. (1997). In the example, two discs move: disc1 moves from left to right, disc2 from right to left.

```
1    try
2        % opening operations
3        whichscreen = max(Screen('Screens'));
4        [w, rect] =Screen('Openwindow', whichscreen, 0);
5        % discs setting
6        frame = CenterRect([0, 0, 300, 300], rect);
7        disc1 = AlignRect([0, 0, 20, 20], frame, 'center', 'left');
8        disc2 = AlignRect([0, 0, 20, 20], frame, 'center', 'right');
9        Screen('Flip', w);
10       for i = 0:2:280
11           Screen('FillRect', w, 255, frame);
12           Screen('FillOval', w, 0, [disc1(1)+i,disc1(2),disc1(3)+i,disc1(4)
13           Screen('FillOval', w, 0, [disc2(1)-i,disc2(2),disc2(3)-i,disc2(4)
14           Screen('Flip', w);
15       end
16       Screen('FillRect', w, 255, frame);
17       Screen('Flip', w);
18       KbWait;
19       Screen('CloseAll'); % close all
20   catch
21       Screen('Close',w)
22       rethrow(lasterror)
23   end
```

A few comments about this script. First of all, please note how we set the starting coordinates of all objects in a nested way. The coordinates of the frame within which the movement takes place are calculated according to the screen coordinates. The starting coordinates of the discs are calculated according to the coordinates of the frame. Note also that we flipped once before the for loop showing the motion. This simple operation enables us to synchronize the subsequent for loop (thus the successive flips) with the refresh rate. In a certain sense, we could say that we are "getting the pace" of the refresh rate. Note also how the i index is changed: in 2-unit steps. This increases the velocity of the motion (2 pixels per frame) in comparison to that originally shown in the chapter. The x coordinates of disc1 are increased by i (so that the discs moves toward the right), whereas the x coordinates of discs2 are decreased by i (so that the disc moves toward the left). At the end of the for loop, we again flip the frame only (but not the disc) so that the frame does not disappear after the motion.

We have now to build the second motion display, where the discs at the overlap point stop the motion for a few frames. Here we will stop the motion for two frames. In order to do this, we need the i index to remain for more than one cycle at the value 140. When i is equal to 140, the discs overlap completely. Everything can be done simply by modifying the beginning of the for loop as follows:

```
for i=[0:2:140, 140, 140:2:280]
```

Now the i index, the variable that lets us move the discs, increases from 0 to 140 (when the discs overlap), then is equal to 140, then increases from 140 to 280.

We can now write everything into the scripts and the function we wrote for the previous bricks. The opening and closing operations will be written into the SekulerExp function. The generation/presentation of the motion display will be written in a separate script that will be called MakeVideoStimulus.m. In this way we will not overload the text content of the SekulerExp function.

This is the script:

```
1   % discs setting
2   frame = CenterRect([0, 0, 300, 300], rect);
3   disc1 = AlignRect([0, 0, 20, 20], frame, 'center', 'left');
4   disc2 = AlignRect([0, 0, 20, 20], frame, 'center', 'right');
5
6   if VideoStimulusToPlay == 1
7       Screen('Flip', w);
8       for i = 0:2:280
9           Screen('FillRect', w, 255, frame);
10          Screen('FillOval',w,0,[disc1(1)+i,disc1(2),disc1(3)+i,disc1(4)]);
11          Screen('FillOval',w,0,[disc2(1)-i,disc2(2),disc2(3)-i,disc2(4)]);
12          Screen('Flip', w);
13      end
14  elseif VideoStimulusToPlay == 2
15      Screen('Flip', w);
16      for i = [0:2:140, 140, 140:2:280]
17          Screen('FillRect', w, 255, frame);
18          Screen('FillOval', w,0,[disc1(1)+i,disc1(2),disc1(3)+i,disc1(4)]);
19          Screen('FillOval', w,0,[disc2(1)-i,disc2(2),disc2(3)-i,disc2(4)]);
20          Screen('Flip', w);
21      end
22  end
23  Screen('FillRect', w, 255, frame);
24  Screen('Flip', w);
```

The following is the modified SekulerExp function. Note that we have written the KbWait command after the presentation of the stimulus.

```
1   function SekulerExp(InputDataStruct)
2   % M-script to realize an experiment based on crossmodal perception
3   % The experiment first performed by Sekuler, Sekuler, and Lau (1997)
4   % Author: Borgo, Soranzo, Grassi 2009
5   % EXPERIMENT'S SETTINGS
6   % get input data from the structure passed through the interface
7   nsub = InputDataStruct.nsub;
8   subname = InputDataStruct.subname;
9   subsex = InputDataStruct.subsex;
10  subage = InputDataStruct.subage;
11  nblock = InputDataStruct.nblock;
12  subnote = InputDataStruct.subnote;
13  isfixed = InputDataStruct.isfixed;
14  filename = InputDataStruct.filename;
15  % set the experiment details
16  conditions = [1, 1; 1, 2; 2, 1; 2, 2];
17  repetitions = 20;
18  if nsub == 0
19      repetitions = 1;
20  end
21  EventTable = GenerateEventTable(conditions, repetitions, isfixed);
22  TotalNumberOfTrials = length(EventTable(:, 1));
23  % opening operations for the screen function
24  whichscreen = max(Screen('Screens'));
25  [w, rect] =Screen('Openwindow', whichscreen, 0);
26  refreshrate = Screen('FrameRate', w);
27  for trial = 1:TotalNumberOfTrials
28      % STIMULI (SELECTION)
29      VideoStimulusToPlay = EventTable(trial, 2);
30      SoundStimulusToPlay = EventTable(trial, 3);
31      % STIMULI (CREATION)
32      % STIMULI (PRESENTATION)
33      SoundToPlay = GenerateSound(SoundStimulusToPlay, w);
34      MakeVideoStimulus
35      % COLLECT SUBJECT'S ANSWER
36      KbWait;
37  end
38  % closing operation
39  Screen('CloseAll'); % close all
40  % STORE RESULTS
```

In the next chapter we will play the sound and substitute the command KbWait with a more appropriate command that will enable us to get the participant's response. Moreover, we will see how to get maximal priority before running a movie, and finally, we will see how to get rid of the mouse pointer, which is unnecessary (and perhaps annoying) in the current experiment.

References

Brainard DH (1997) The psychophysics toolbox. Spat Vis 10:433–436
Kleiner M, Brainard DH, Pelli DG (2007) What's new in psychtoolbox-3? Perception (ECVP Abstract Supplement) 14
Pelli DG (1997) The VideoToolbox software for visual psychophysics: transforming numbers into movies. Spat Vis 10:437–442
Sekuler R, Sekuler AB, Lau R (1997) Sound alters visual motion perception. Nature 385:308

Suggested Readings

Tutorials for the Psychtoolbox can be found at the following web pages:

http://psychtoolbox.org/wikka.php?wakka=HomePage
http://psychtoolbox.org/wikka.php?wakka=PsychtoolboxTutorial

Chapter 10
Psychtoolbox: Sound, Keyboard and Mouse

PTB has a number of functions that can be useful to program behavioral experiments. Although their number is high, there is a relatively small number of core functions that we need to know to program a large spectrum of experiments. These core functions are presented in this chapter.

Timing

PTB has many functions dedicated to timing issues; probably the simplest one is `WaitSecs()`, which waits the number of seconds specified in the input argument. `WaitSecs()` can be used to set the pauses within trials (or blocks of trials) of your experiment. By running the following script, the monitor will remain white for 10 s before returning to its normal appearance.

Listing 10.1

```
1  try
2      Screen('OpenWindow', 0);
3      WaitSecs(10);
4      Screen('CloseAll');
5  catch
6      Screen('Close',w)
7      rethrow(lasterror)
8  end
```

Another useful function to manage timing is `GetSecs()`, which returns the time (in seconds) elapsed between when you switched on the computer and when

M. Borgo et al., *MATLAB for Psychologists*,
DOI 10.1007/978-1-4614-2197-9_10, © Springer Science+Business Media, LLC 2012

GetSecs() has been called. In the following example, code listing 10.1 is extended
to calculate the time elapsed between the two GetSecs() calls.

Listing 10.2

```
1    try
2        Screen('OpenWindow', 0);
3        t0 = GetSecs;
4        WaitSecs(5);
5        t1 = GetSecs;
6        Screen('CloseAll');
7        t_elapsed = t1 - t0;
8    catch
9        Screen('Close',w)
10       rethrow(lasterror)
11   end
```

GetSecs() is useful in several contexts, for example when it is used together
with the functions controlling the keyboard and the mouse.

Priority

When we are running experiments, we want to allocate all the computer's resources
(e.g., memory and CPU) for the experiment only. PTB lets you do this thanks to the
priority functions. You should know that when you use a computer, although you
may have only one application open and visible on the monitor (e.g., MATLAB),
there are several applications running in the background. All these applications use
the CPU and computer memory, and therefore they reduce the available resources.
This might be a problem if we are interested in getting the exact time a participant
in our experiment has pressed a button. PTB allows for allocating the maximal priority to the event we want. However, this maximal priority can be kept for only a
few seconds. For this reason it is better to get it just before calling this event and
then setting the computer priority back to normal. The levels of priority are identified by integers, which depend on the operating system. To find out the number
corresponding to the maximum priority level in your system, use the MaxPriority
function. The following script shows its use.

Listing 10.3

```
1   try
2       whichscreen = max(Screen('Screens'));
3       [myscreen, screen_rect] = Screen('OpenWindow', whichscreen);
4       Screen('FillRect', myscreen, 0, CenterRect([0, 0, 100, 100],
    screen_rect));
5       priorityLevel=MaxPriority(window);
6       Priority(priorityLevel);
7       t0 = Screen('Flip', myscreen);
8       Screen('Flip', myscreen, t0 + 1);
9       Priority(0);
10      Screen('CloseAll');
11  catch
12      Screen('Close',w)
13      rethrow(lasterror)
14  end
```

Let us analyze the script. Before calling the flip subfunction, we have interrogated the system about the maximal priority available and stored the returned value in the priorityLevel variable. Then, we set the priority to its maximum level, and as soon as the flip is over we set the priority back to zero. Zero is the default priority that is normally attributed to all applications running on the computer. In other words, during normal usage, the priority of all application is equal to zero.

Sound Functions

PTB includes also some functions that can be used for synthesizing and playing sounds. These functions are particularly suitable for psychological experiments because they use drivers that are highly time-efficient in comparison to the native sound drivers of Windows or those of other operating systems. The main sound function in PTB is the PsychPortAudio function. This function can work both synchronically and asynchronically. The way you call this function is similar to the Screen function. The function name must be followed by the subfunction name and by a variable list of parameters that varies according to the subfunction. In the following table we present the most important PsychPortAudio subfunctions. In the table, the input parameters given within square brackets are optional:

Sub Function	Command	Explanation
Version	struct=PsychPortAudio ('Version')	return the version of PsychPortAudio in a struct
Verbosity	oldlevel=PsychPortAudio ('Verbosity' [,level]);	Set level of verbosity for error/warning/ status messages

(continued)

(continued)

Sub Function	Command	Explanation
GetOpenDeviceCount	count = PsychPortAudio ('GetOpenDeviceCount');	Return the number of currently open audio devices
Open	pahandle = PsychPortAudio ('Open' [, deviceid] [, mode] [, reqlatencyclass] [, freq] [, channels] [, buffersize] [, suggestedLatency] [, selectchannels]);	Open a PortAudio audio device and initialize it. Returns a 'pahandle' device handle for the device
Close	PsychPortAudio ('Close' [, pahandle]);	Close a PortAudio audio device
FillBuffer	[underflow, nextSampleStart Index, nextSampleET-ASecs] =PsychPortAudio ('FillBuffer', pahandle, bufferdata [, streamingrefill = 0] [, startIndex = Append]);	Fill audio data playback buffer of a PortAudio audio device. 'pahandle' is the handle of the device whose buffer is to be filled
CreateBuffer	bufferhandle=PsychPortAudio('CreateBuffer' [, pahandle], bufferdata);	Create a new dynamic audio data playback buffer for a PortAudio audio device and fill it with initial data
DeleteBuffer	result = PsychPortAudio ('DeleteBuffer'[, bufferhandle] [, waitmode]);	Delete an existing dynamic audio data playback buffer
Start	startTime = PsychPortAudio ('Start', pahandle [, repetitions = 1] [, when = 0] [, waitForStart = 0] [, stopTime = inf]);	Start a PortAudio audio device
GetStatus	status = PsychPortAudio ('GetStatus', pahandle);	Returns 'status', a struct with status information about the current state of device 'pahandle'
Stop	[startTime endPositionSecs xruns estStopTime] = PsychPortAudio ('Stop', pahandle [, waitForEndOfPlayback = 0] [, blockUntilStopped = 1] [, repetitions] [, stopTime]);	Stop a PortAudio audio device. The 'pahandle' is the handle of the device to stop

The help of each subfunction can be viewed in the same way you can view the help of the Screen function, i.e., by typing a question mark at the end of the subfunction name (e.g., PsychPortAudio ('Open?')). For an overview of the function, type PsychPortAudio() or "help PsychPortAudio".

The usage of PsychPortAudio is the following. First, you need to open the audio device. Second, you need to fill a sound buffer with your sound. Third, you need to play the sound. Moreover, PTB developers suggest that you call

InitializePsychSound before the first invocation of PsychPortAudio. If you omit this call, the initialization of the driver may fail, and MATLAB may return some "Invalid MEX file" error.

Here we present an example showing another useful sound function: MakeBeep(). Makebeep synthesizes a pure tone of a given frequency, duration, and sample rate. Note that in the following example, PsychPortAudio works synchronically. To effect this, we use the subfunction "Stop", which has an optional parameter. This parameter enables us to specify when to stop the beep's playback. Therefore, in the example this parameter is set equal to "d", i.e., the overall duration of the beep.

Listing 10.4

```
1   try
2       f = 1000; % frequency in Hz
3       d = 1; % duration in sec
4       sr = 44100; % sample rate in Hz
5       beep = MakeBeep(f, d, sr); %synthesis of the beep
6       InitializePsychSound;
7       pahandle = PsychPortAudio('Open', [], [], [], sr, 1);
8       PsychPortAudio('FillBuffer', pahandle, beep);
9       PsychPortAudio('Start', pahandle);
10      PsychPortAudio('Stop', pahandle, d);
11  catch
12      Screen('Close',w)
13      rethrow(lasterror)
14  end
```

Getting Participants' Inputs: Keyboard and Mouse Functions

When we run behavioral experiments we usually collect responses from our participants. In the majority of these experiments the response is collected through either the keyboard or the mouse.

Keyboard Response

There are two classes of functions for capturing keyboard events. The first class is *keypress*-oriented. The second is *character*-oriented. The former fulfill the majority of an experimental psychologist's needs; hence we describe this set of functions only. Kbwait() and KbCheck() are the main keypress-oriented functions. They work in a similar way; however, KbWait waits for user input, whereas KbCheck does not. In other words, KbWait stops the script until the user presses a key on the keyboard, whereas `KbCheck` checks whether a key-press event has occurred when the function is called. Therefore, if at that moment no key is been pressed, the script continues. Because of the different characteristics of these functions we recommend using `KbCheck` for collecting responses such as high-accuracy response times, and to use `KbWait` for other kinds of responses.

"Press Any Key to Proceed"

In many circumstances, we need the participant to press a key to proceed with the experiment. For example, the key press can follow the presentation of instructions. `KbWait` can be used in such circumstances when it is called with no input argument.

Listing 10.5

```
1   try
2       screens = Screen('Screens');
3       whichscreen = max(screens);
4       [myscreen,rect]=Screen('OpenWindow',whichscreen);
5       DrawFormattedText(myscreen, 'PRESS ANY KEY TO PROCEED','center',
    'center');
6       Screen('Flip', myscreen);
7       KbWait;
8       screen('CloseAll');
9   catch
10      Screen('Close',w)
11      rethrow(lasterror)
12  end
13
```

"Press the Spacebar to Proceed"

In other circumstances, we want the participant to press a specific key to proceed. For example, we may want the participant to press the spacebar to go further with the experiment. To do this, we need to know something more about the keyboard. Both `KbWait` and `KbCheck` return as output the argument `keycode`. `keyCode` is a 256-element array in which every key is mapped to a number. The key that has been pressed is identified by the fact that its corresponding position in the array turns from the default 0 to 1. For example, in the Mac OS, the "return" key is mapped to the 40th position and the spacebar to the 44th. In contrast, the same keys are mapped to positions 13 and 32, respectively, under Windows. To know the position of a specific key in the array, use the KbName function. The following table outlines this function:

Usage	Explanation
KbName('s')	Return the keycode of the indicated key (inputted as a string). Special keys such as spacebar, return, and so on, are also passed as a string (e.g., 'space', 'return')
KbName(keyCode)	Return the label of the key identified by keyCode
KbName	Waits 1 s and then calls KbCheck. KbName then returns a cell array holding the names of all keys that were down at the time of the KbCheck call
KbName('KeyNames')	Print out a table of all keycodes->keynames mappings
KbName('KeyNamesOSX')	Print out a table of all keycodes->keynames mappings for MacOS-X
KbName('KeyNamesOS9')	Print out a table of all keycodes->keynames mappings for MacOS-9
KbName('KeyNamesWindows')	Print out a table of all keycodes->keynames mappings for MS-Windows
KbName('KeyNamesLinux')	Print out a table of all keycodes->keynames mappings for GNU-Linux, X11

Now that we have mastered keyboard events, let's deal with the case in which the program waits the participant to press the spacebar.

Listing 10.6

```
1   try
2       screens = Screen('Screens);
3       whichscreen = max(screens);
4       [myscreen,rect]=Screen('OpenWindow',whichscreen);
5       DrawFormattedText(myscreen, 'PRESS THE SPACEBAR TO PROCEED', 'center',
    'center');
6       Screen('Flip', myscreen);
7       space = KbName('space');
8       [secs, keyCode] = KbWait;
9       while keyCode(space)==0
10          [secs, keyCode] = KbWait;
11      end
12      screen('CloseAll');
13  catch
14      Screen('Close',w)
15      rethrow(lasterror)
16  end
```

The core of this script lies in the while loop. Before the loop we check the keyboard. Furthermore, we store the key pressed by the participant in the variable keyCode. As long as the participant presses any key on the keyboard other than the spacebar (or presses no key at all), the while loop is repeated. However, as soon as the participant presses the spacebar, the loop quits. In the script, the number corresponding to the spacebar is taken using KbName. Because keyCode is the second output argument returned by KbWait, we need to save the secs argument first.

"Press Any Key to Respond"

In many tasks, we ask the participants to produce a binary response. The following example extends the previous one to allow for a binary response.

Listing 10.7

```
1   try
2       screens = Screen('Screens');
3       whichscreen = max(screens);
4       [myscreen,rect]=Screen('OpenWindow',whichscreen);
5       DrawFormattedText(myscreen, 'PRESS ANY KEY TO PROCEED', 'center',
    'center');
6       Screen('Flip', myscreen);
7       KbWait;
8       y = KbName('y');
9       n = KbName('n');
10      words={'home', 'bank', 'nose', 'dog', 'car'};
11      responses = zeros(length(words), 1);
12      for i=1:length(words)
13          WaitSecs(1);
14          DrawFormattedText(myscreen, char(words(i)), 'center', 'center');
15          Screen('Flip', myscreen);
16          [secs, keyCode] = KbWait;
17          while keyCode(y)==0 && keyCode(n)==0
18              [secs, keyCode] = KbWait;
19          end
20          if keyCode(y) == 1;
21              responses(i) = 1;
22          end
23      end
24      screen('CloseAll');
25  catch
26      Screen('Close',w)
27      rethrow(lasterror)
28  end
```

This script first opens a PTB window with 'OpenWindow', then echoes "press any key to proceed". After the participant presses any key, the function KbName gets the "y" and "n" key progressive numbers. Next, we present the stimulus (the words) within a for loop. Note that we use WaitSecs to pause the experiment when passing from one trial to the next. Then we check the keyboard within the for loop, by means of a while loop. The check is done as in the previous example, with the difference that by means of the AND logical condition, the program stops until the participant presses either "y" or "n". Finally, we store the response in a numeric array in which 1 stands for y and 0 for n. This might be useful for later statistical analysis.

Reaction-Time Detection

The simplest reaction time to implement is that of detection (aka simple reaction time). In the detection reaction time, the participant has to press a key as soon as s/he detects something (e.g., a visual stimulus is presented on the screen). We recommend using KbCheck rather than KbWait. This is because KbWait checks the keyboard every 5 ms. Therefore, it adds an 5 extra ms of uncertainty to measurements. The same problem does not occur with KbCheck.

In the following example, we ask the participant to press the spacebar as soon as a stimulus appears on the screen.

Listing 10.8

```
1    try
2        screens = Screen('Screens');
3        whichscreen = max(screens);
4        [myscreen,rect]=Screen('OpenWindow',whichscreen);
5        DrawFormattedText(myscreen, 'PRESS ANY KEY TO PROCEED', 'center',
     'center');
6        Screen('Flip', myscreen);
7        KbWait;
8        space = KbName('space');
9        ntrials = 5;
10       rt = zeros(ntrials, 1);
11       stimulus duration = zeros(ntrials, 1);
12       for i=1:ntrials
13           WaitSecs(1);
14           Screen('FrameOval', myscreen, 0, CenterRect([0, 0, 10, 10], rect));
15           onset_fixation = Screen('Flip', myscreen);
16           Screen('FillRect', myscreen, [255, 0, 0], CenterRect([0, 0, 50,
     50], rect));
17           random_delay = rand+0.5;
18           onset_stimulus = Screen('Flip', myscreen, onset_fixation +
     random_delay);
19           t0 = GetSecs;
20           [keyIsDown, secs, keyCode] = KbCheck;
21           while keyCode(space)==0
22               [keyIsDown, secs, keyCode] = KbCheck;
23           end
24           rt(i) = secs - t0;
25           stimulus_offsettime = Screen('Flip', myscreen);
26           stimulus_duration(i) = stimulus_offsettime - t0;
27       end
28       screen('CloseAll');
29   catch
30       Screen('Close',w)
31       rethrow(lasterror)
32   end
```

This script is similar to the previous examples in that it waits until the a keypress event occurs. We then run five trials in a for loop. In each trial, the program first waits for 1 s, then, by means of the FrameOval subfunction, a fixation point appears. Then a red square, the target stimulus, appears at a random time interval after the fixation point has disappeared. As soon the target stimulus flips, GetSecs stores the onset time of the stimulus in the t0 variable. KbCheck checks the keyboard until the participant presses the spacebar. At that time, the reaction time is stored. It should be kept in mind that KbCheck registers the time in seconds from when the computer has been switched on. Hence, to get the actual reaction time we need to calculate the difference between secs and t0, i.e., the difference between the moment the spacebar has been pressed and the stimulus onset. Finally, note that when calling `KbCheck` we collect also the variable `keyIsDown`. `keyIsDown` is the first output argument of `KbCheck`, and it is a logical value (i.e., 0–1) that is equal to 1 when the user presses one key at the moment `KbCheck` is called.

Choice Reaction Time

A second kind of reaction time is called *choice*. The participant has to press one button in response to a particular stimulus and another button in response to another stimulus. In the following example, the participant has to press "r" for a red and "g" for a green square. Furthermore, we save the participant's response to check its accuracy.

Listing 10.9

```
1   try
2       screens = Screen('Screens');
3       whichscreen = max(screens);
4       [myscreen,rect]=Screen('OpenWindow',whichscreen);
5       DrawFormattedText(myscreen, 'PRESS ANY KEY TO PROCEED', 'center',
    'center');
6       Screen('Flip', myscreen);
7       KbWait;
8       g = KbName('g');
9       r = KbName('r');
10      ntrials = 6;
11      colorsequence = [1, 2, 2, 2, 1, 1];
12      rt = zeros(ntrials, 1);
13      response = zeros(ntrials, 1);
14      stimulus_duration = zeros(ntrials, 1);
15      for i=1:ntrials
16          WaitSecs(1);
17          Screen('FrameOval', myscreen, 0, CenterRect([0, 0, 10, 10], rect));
18          onset_fixation = Screen('Flip', myscreen);
19          if colorsequence(i) == 1
20              stimuluscolor = [255, 0, 0];
21          else
22              stimuluscolor = [0, 255, 0];
23          end
24          Screen('FillRect', myscreen, stimuluscolor, CenterRect([0, 0, 50,
25  50], rect));
            random_delay = rand+0.5;
26          onset_stimulus = Screen('Flip', myscreen, onset_fixation +
    random_delay);
27          t0 = GetSecs;
28          [keyIsDown, secs, keyCode] = KbCheck;
29          while keyCode(g)==0 && keyCode(r)==0
30              [keyIsDown, secs, keyCode] = KbCheck;
31          end
32          rt(i) = secs - t0;
33          response(i) = find(keyCode==1);
34          stimulus_offsettime = Screen('Flip', myscreen);
35          stimulus_duration(i) = stimulus_offsettime - t0;
36      end
37      screen('CloseAll');
38  catch
39      Screen('Close',w)
40      rethrow(lasterror)
41  end
```

As a difference from the previous script, here the color of the square has to be monitored trial by trial; hence we save the color in the `colorsequence` variable. Moreover, we declare the `response` variable where we store the response of the participant. In the `if` function, embedded in the for loop, the color of the square that will appear in the trial is set. Finally, in the while loop that collects the participant's response we include as valid response both the "`r`" and the "`g`" keys. When the response is collected, we store both the reaction time, as in the previous example, and the key that has been pressed by the participant.

Go/No-Go Reaction Time

In some cases, a participant has to react selectively to different stimuli. The following example shows the go/no-go reaction-time paradigm by modifying the previous example. The participant's task is to press the spacebar when a red square appears and to do nothing when a green square appears.

Listing 10.10

```
screens = Screen('Screens');
whichscreen = max(screens);
[myscreen,rect]=Screen('OpenWindow',whichscreen);
DrawFormattedText(myscreen, 'PRESS ANY KEY TO PROCEED', 'center', 'center');
Screen('Flip', myscreen);
KbWait;
space = KbName('space');
ntrials = 6;
colorsequence = [1, 2, 2, 2, 1, 1];
rt = zeros(ntrials, 1);
stimulus_duration = zeros(ntrials, 1);
for i=1:ntrials
    WaitSecs(1);
    Screen('FrameOval', myscreen, 0, CenterRect([0, 0, 10, 10], rect));
    onset_fixation = Screen('Flip', myscreen);
    if colorsequence(i) == 1
        stimuluscolor = [255, 0, 0];
    else
        stimuluscolor = [0, 255, 0];
    end
    Screen('FillRect', myscreen, stimuluscolor, CenterRect([0, 0, 50, 50],
rect));
    random_delay = rand+0.5;
    onset_stimulus = Screen('Flip', myscreen, onset_fixation + random_delay);
    t0 = GetSecs;
    [keyIsDown, secs, keyCode] = KbCheck;
    while keyCode(space)==0 && (secs - onset_stimulus) < 2
        [keyIsDown, secs, keyCode] = KbCheck;
    end
    rt(i) = secs - t0;
    stimulus_offsettime = Screen('Flip', myscreen);
    stimulus_duration(i) = stimulus_offsettime - t0;
end
screen('CloseAll');
```

The main difference between this example and the previous one is the condition that has to be satisfied to exit from the while loop in which the response is collected. Here, the while loop is exited in two cases: either when the user presses the spacebar or when the stimulus stays on screen for more than the 2 s. This second condition is controlled by the `onset_stimulus` and `secs` variables. The first variable is the square onset time; the second is a time value that continuously updates every time the keyboard is checked.

Reaction Times Within a Video Clip

So far, we have seen how to collect a reaction time for static stimuli. How can we collect reaction times when a video clip is being played? This is a particular case, and it requires a different technique to collect the reaction time. Indeed, in previous examples, the `while` loop where `kbCheck` gets the timing stopped the execution of any other command. Therefore, if we were inserting the while loop within a `for` cycle used to create a video clip, we would stop the clip until a key is pressed. To solve this problem we need to call `KbCheck` once every refresh cycle. The limit of this approach is that the accuracy of the reaction time is linked to the refresh rate: the higher the refresh rate, the greater the accuracy of the response time. Of course, we need to call `GetSecs` just before showing the video clip so that the reaction is calculated as a difference between the motor reaction and the moment the video starts. The following example shows how to do it.

Listing 10.11

```
1  t0 = GetSecs;
2  for i = 1:number_of_frames
3      % draw the video clip
4      % flip the video clip
5      [keyIsDown, t_press, keyCode] = KbCheck;
6      if keyCode(responsekey) == 1
7          t_press = t_press-t0;
8      end
9  end
```

However, this technique has a problem. When the participant presses the key, the participant' s finger stays on the key for a certain time, and obviously the key-touch is not instantaneous. We do not exactly know the duration of this time, but let's assume that the finger stays on the key for about 50 ms. Let's suppose we are work-ing at a refresh rate of 100 Hz and therefore `KbCheck` checks the keyboard every 10 ms. When the user first presses the response key, the reaction time is calculated. Then, the next iteration of the for loop occurs. Because the finger is still on the key, the reaction time is calculated twice, and then there is a new iteration of the for loop; the video clip continues, and the finger is still on the key and the reaction time is calculated once again, and so on. In practice, if we were using the script above we would be calculating the reaction time based on the key-release motor action instead of the key strike motor action. Therefore, when you are measuring the reaction time within a video clip, the conditional if has to be written differently:

Listing 10.12

```
1   t0 = GetSecs;
2   firsttouch = 0;
3   for i = 1:number_of_frames
4       % draw the movie
5       % flip the movie
6       [keyIsDown, t_press, keyCode] = KbCheck;
7       if keyCode(responsekey) == 1 && firsttouch == 0
8           t_press = t_press-t0;
9           firsttouch = 1;
10      end
11  end
```

In the example, we added the variable firsttouch, which is set to 0 and becomes equal to 1 when the participant first touches the keyboard. In this way, in the following for loop the response time is not recalculated because the variable firsttouch is now 1.

Now let's combine everything into a working example. A disc is placed in the middle of the screen and the participant has to detect when the disc starts its motion. In order to prevent anticipations due to fixed timing, the start of the disc's motion is controlled by a random parameter.

Listing 10.13

```
1   try
2       screens = Screen('Screens');
3       whichscreen = max(screens);
4       [w, rect] =Screen('Openwindow', whichscreen);
5       disc = CenterRect([0, 0, 20, 20], rect);
6       Screen('FillOval', w, 0, disc);
7       Screen('Flip', w);
8       space = KbName('space');
9       firsttouch = 0;
10      WaitSecs(1)+rand*2;
11      t0 = GetSecs;
12      for i = 1:200
13          Screen('FillOval', w, 0, [disc(1)+i, disc(2), disc(3)+i, disc(4)]);
14          Screen('Flip', w);
15          [keyIsDown, secs, keyCode] = KbCheck;
16          if keyCode(space) == 1 && firsttouch == 0
17              rt = secs-t0;
18              firsttouch = 1;
19          end
20      end
21      Screen('CloseAll');
22  catch
23      Screen('Close',w)
24      rethrow(lasterror)
25  end
```

Mouse Input

The mouse is not used as often as the keyboard to collect the participant's response. However, PTB is provided with functions enabling for this possibility. Before describing these functions, let us present two very simple (but extremely useful) functions: HideCursor and ShowCursor. These functions can be called with no input argument. They hide the mouse pointer and show it, respectively. Here is an example of how to use them.

Listing 10.14

```
1    try
2        Screen('Openwindow', 0);
3        HideCursor;
4        WaitSecs(5);
5        ShowCursor;
6        WaitSecs(5);
7        Screen('CloseAll');
8    catch
9        Screen('Close',w)
10       rethrow(lasterror)
11   end
```

The most important functions contained in PTB to deal with the mouse are GetMouse, GetClick, and SetMouse. SetMouse places the mouse cursor at the desired x and y coordinates. Therefore, the function waits for at least two input parameters (i.e., the desired x and y positions of the mouse). A third optional parameter can be passed to the function which is a screen pointer. In the current example, the mouse cursor is placed in the middle of the screen every 2 s. Try to move the mouse while the example is running:

Listing 10.15

```
1    try
2        screens = Screen('Screens');
3        whichscreen = max(screens);
4        [mainscreen, rect] = Screen('Openwindow', whichscreen);
5        for i = 1:5
6            SetMouse(rect(3)/2, rect(4)/2, mainscreen);
7            WaitSecs(2);
8        end
9        Screen('CloseAll');
10   catch
11       Screen('Close',w)
12       rethrow(lasterror)
13   end
```

GetMouse() returns three arguments: The firsts two are the x and y mouse coordinates in pixels. The third is a logical vector whose length corresponds to the number of mouse buttons. When a button is pressed, the corresponding bit in the vector is set to 1, so it is easy to start a procedure when a specific button is pressed. This function receives, as optional argument, the pointer to the screen (in case you have more than one screen).

GetClicks() is similar to GetMouse() and takes three arguments. The first is the number of mouse clicks that the user performed within a time interval. The time interval is set by the variable ptb_mouseclick_timeout. The other two are the x and y current positions in pixel coordinates, respectively, of the cursor position when the first click has been executed.

In the following example we capture the position of the mouse click with GetClicks, and each time we display the x-y coordinates of the click.

Listing 10.16

```
1   try
2       screens = Screen('Screens');
3       whichscreen = max(screens);
4       [myscreen,rect]=Screen('OpenWindow',whichscreen);
5       DrawFormattedText(myscreen, 'PRESS THE SPACEBAR TO PROCEED', ...
6                        'center', 'center');
7       Screen('Flip', myscreen);
8       KbWait;
10      Screen('Flip', myscreen);
11      for i = 1:5
12          [clicks, x, y, whichButton] = GetClicks;
13          while ~clicks
14              [clicks, x, y, whichButton] = GetClicks;
15          end
16          Screen('DrawText', myscreen,sprintf('This is the coordinate: X=%i,
    Y=%i ', x, y), x, y, 0);
17          Screen('Flip', myscreen);
18      end
19      Screen('CloseAll');
20  catch
21      Screen('Close',w)
22      rethrow(lasterror)
23  end
```

Note that GetClicks is called in a similar way to KbCheck. The function returns four output arguments. The first is a logical value informing whether any click occurred. We call GetClicks with a while loop as well as KbCheck. Here, however, we proceed (i.e., the program continues) as soon as the user presses the mouse.

Using Participants' Input to Manipulate Shape Characteristics

In chapter 9 we saw how to design simple figures using PTB, how to write text into the destination window, while in this chapter we have seen how to capture participant input. The aim of this section is to combine these things to allow the user to manipulate the characteristics of shapes. This may be useful, for example, when you adopt the adjustment method as the psychophysics method for your experiments. In this case, you want the participants to adjust a shape characteristic to match the same characteristic of another shape. The following code listing shows how to use the participants' inputs to manipulate the color of a rectangle.

Keyboard Manipulations

As stated in Chap. 6, the simultaneous lightness contrast is probably the most studied phenomenon in lightness perception [see Kingdom (1997) for a historical review]. Listing 10.17 shows how to measure, in RGB values, this phenomenon through the adjustment method using the keyboard.

Listing 10.17

```
1   try
2       HideCursor;
3       [w, rect] = Screen('Openwindow',0);
4       grey= 128;
5       black =0;
6       adjustable = 90;
7       cx = rect(3)/2;
8       cy = rect(4)/2;
9       size=60;
10      displacement = cx/2;
11      coordLeft =[cx-displacement-size cy-size cx-displacement+size cy+size];
12      coordRight=[cx+displacement-size cy-size cx+displacement+size cy+size];
13      coordBlack = [0 0 cx rect(4)];
14      Screen('TextSize', w,12) ;
15      Instructions = 'Press the Up and Down arrow keys to adjust the' +
        'of the square to your right to match the color of the other.';
16      Instructions2 = 'Press Esc when you are satisfied with your match.';
17      while 1
18          Screen('FillRect',w,  black,coordBlack);
19          Screen('DrawText',w, Instructions, 10, 20,grey);
20          Screen('DrawText',w, Instructions2, 10,40,grey);
21          Screen('FillRect',w,  grey,coordLeft);
22          Screen('FillRect',w,  adjustable,coordRight);
23          Screen('Flip', w);
24          [ keyIsDown, s, keyCode ] = KbCheck;
25          if keyCode(38)
26              adjustable=adjustable+1;
27          elseif keyCode(40)
28              adjustable=adjustable-1;
29          elseif keyCode(27)
30              break;
31          end
32      end
33      Screen('DrawText',w, sprintf('Your final RGB was %d, press any key to
    exit.', adjustable),10,60);
34      Screen('Flip', w);
35      while kbcheck end
36          KbWait;
37          ShowCursor;
38          Screen('Close',w)
39  catch
40      screen('Close',w)
41      rethrow(lasterror)
42  end
```

Analysis

Line 2 hides the cursor to avoid any unwanted interference.

Lines 4–6 implement the variables for `color` They are scalar because only achromatic colors will be used. The variable `adjustable` is the color for the adjustable patch.

Lines 7–13 implement variables for the positioning and coordinates of the shapes. Please read these lines carefully to familiarize yourself with screen coordinates and shape positioning.

Line 14 sets the text size to 12.

Lines 15, 16 implement the instructions that will be displayed in the destination window.

Lines 17, 32 implement the while loop in which the user will adjust the color of a patch.

Lines 18–22 draw in the backbuffer shapes and texts.

Line 23 flips from backbuffer to frontbuffer to display the shapes and texts.

Line 24 implements the `KeyCode` and `KeyIsDown` variables that will be used to manipulate the color of the right-hand square.

Lines 25–31 implement the conditional loop to change the color of the right-hand square. Note that the variable `adjustable` increases or decreases its value by 1 depending on `KeyCode`. You can use larger values than 1 for quicker changes. These lines are very important, since they are commonly used to manipulate shape characteristics. In this code we used `KeyCode`. As outlined above, this is a logical array containing all zeros except for the bit corresponding to the key that has been pressed. Each time the code runs to line 23, all `KeyCode` bits are set to zero until a `keypress` event occurs. In this code listing we have used the ASCII code corresponding to the left, right, and esc keys. If you do not want to remember these numbers, you can get the same code behavior using `KbName(KeyCode)`. For example, line 28 can be replaced with the following:

```
if strcmp(KbName(keyCode), 'esc')
```

Of course, this option takes more time, but if time is not an issue for your experiment, then use it to increase readability.

Line 33 writes to the backbuffer the last RGB value that has been assigned by the user.

Line 35 clears the buffer from any `keypress`. This trick is necessary because otherwise, the following `Kbwait` doesn't work, since the keyboard has been pressed to adjust the square color.

Line 36 waits for the user to press a key to display the string.

Line 37 shows the cursor again.

Placing Discs with the Mouse

In this section we see how to place a disc on the screen and use the mouse to indicate where the disc is to appear. To do this, we will measure the Müller-Lyer illusion (Müller-Lyer 1889). It is one of the best-known geometric optical illusions consisting of two arrows, one with ends pointing in, and the other with ends pointing out. The next code is aimed at measuring the illusion magnitude in the arrows with ends pointing out, taking the participants' mouse button press.

Listing 10.18

```
1   try
2       [w, rect] = Screen('Openwindow',0);
3       cx = rect(3)/2;
4       cy = rect(4)/2;
5       myWidth = 2;
6       mylength  = 200;
7       arrowsize = 40;
8       displacement = cx/2;
9       myx = cx+displacement;
10      Instructions= 'Click any mouse button to create a dot in correspondence
    of the upper and lower limit of the line to your right.';
11      Instructions2 = 'Click another time any mouse button when you are
    satisfied with your match';
12      Screen('TextSize', w,12} ;
13      ShowCursor ('CrossHair')
14      SetMouse (myx,cy)
15      count=0;
16      clicks=0;
17      Usery=0;
18      Userdata=zeros(2,1);
19      while count<2
20          Screen('DrawText',w, Instructions, 10, 20);
21          Screen('DrawText',w, Instructions2, 10, 40);
22          Screen('DrawLine',w,0,cx-displacement,cy+mylength,cx-displacement,cy-
    mylength,myWidth);
23          Screen('DrawLine',w,0,cx-displacement-arrowsize,cy-mylength-
    arrowsize,cx-displacement,cy-mylength,myWidth);
24          Screen('DrawLine',w,0,cx-displacement+arrowsize,cy-mylength-
    arrowsize,cx-displacement,cy-mylength,myWidth);
25          Screen('DrawLine',w,0,cx-displacement-
    arrowsize,cy+mylength+arrowsize,cx-displacement,cy+mylength,myWidth);
26          Screen('DrawLine',w,0,cx-displacement+arrowsize,cy+mylength+arrowsize,
    cx-displacement,cy+mylength,myWidth);
27          UserOval = [myx,Usery,myx+6,Usery+6];
28          if clicks
29              count=count+1;
30              Screen('FillOval',w,0,UserOval);
31              Userdata(count ,1)= Usery;
32          end
33          Screen('Flip',w );
34          [clicks,Userx,Usery] = GetClicks;
35      end
36      Screen(w,'DrawText', sprintf('Your final length  was %d, press any key
    to exit\n', Userdata(2,1)-Userdata(1,1)),10,60);
37      Screen('Flip', w);
38      while kbcheck end
39          KbWait;
40          ShowCursor;
41          Screen('Close',w)
42  catch
43      screen('Close',w)
44      rethrow(lasterror)
    end
```

Analysis

Lines 3–4 use the `rect` argument to determine the screen-center pixel coordinates.

Lines 5–8 implement the variables for shaping the standard line. Please read these lines carefully to familiarize yourself with screen coordinates and shape positioning.

Line 9 implements the variable `myx` for mouse positioning.

Lines 10, 11 implement the instructions that will be displayed in the destination window.

Line 12 sets the text size to 12.

Line 13 sets the cursor to the cross-hairs shape.

Line 14 places the mouse in the right-hand side of the screen, in the middle y position.

Lines 15–18 implement variables to collect user button press.

Lines 19, 31 implement the while loop during which the user will click the mouse buttons.

Lines 20–26 draw in the backbuffer shapes and texts.

Lines 28–32 if the user has clicked the mouse, then draw the disc at the clicked position and save the y position in the `Userdata` variable to be displayed at the end of the experiment.

Line 33 flips from backbuffer to frontbuffer to display shapes and texts.

Line 34 gets user mouse click.

Line 36 writes in the backbuffer the length that has been assigned by the user.

Line 37 flips from backbuffer to frontbuffer.

Line 38 clears the buffer from any `keypress`. This trick is necessary because otherwise the following `Kbwait` doesn't work, since the keyboard has been pressed to adjust the square color.

Summary

- PTB has many subsidiary functions that are useful in programming behavioral experiments.
- PTB makes it possible to get participants' responses from the keyboard.
- The keyboard response can be speeded up or not.
- PTB enables you to get the participants' responses from the mouse.
- Mouse and keyboard functions can also be used for letting the participant interact with the stimulus.

Exercises

Exercise 1

In Listing 10.18 we have programmed a code to measure the Müller-Lyer illusion in the condition in which the arrow's ends point out and it was presented to the left. Program a code in which the arrow's ends point in and it is presented to the right.

Solution

```
1   try
2       [w, rect] = Screen('Openwindow',0);
3       cx = rect(3)/2;
4       cy= rect(4)/2;
5       myWidth = 2;
6       mylength  = 200;
7       arrowsize = 40;
8       displacement = cx/2;
9       myx = cx-displacement;
10      Instructions= 'Click any mouse button to create a dot in correspondence
    of the upper and lower limit of the line to your left.';
11      Instructions2 = 'Click another time any mouse button when you are
    satisfied with your match';
12      Screen('TextSize', w,12) ;
13      ShowCursor ('CrossHair')
14      SetMouse (myx,cy)
15      count=0;
16      clicks=0;
17      Usery=0;
18      Userdata=zeros(2,1);
19      while count<2
20          Screen('DrawText',w, Instructions, 10, 20);
21          Screen('DrawText',w, Instructions2, 10, 40);
22          Screen('DrawLine',w,0,cx+displacement, cy+mylength,
    cx+displacement, cy-mylength,myWidth);
23          Screen('DrawLine',w,0,cx+displacement-arrowsize,cy-
    mylength+arrowsize, cx+displacement,cy-mylength,myWidth);
24          Screen('DrawLine',w,0,cx+displacement+arrowsize,cy-
    mylength+arrowsize, cx+displacement,cy-mylength,myWidth);
25          Screen('DrawLine',w,0,cx+displacement-arrowsize,cy+mylength-
    arrowsize, cx+displacement,cy+mylength,myWidth);
26          Screen('DrawLine',w,0,cx+displacement+arrowsize,cy+mylength-
    arrowsize, cx+displacement,cy+mylength,myWidth);
27          UserOval = [myx,Usery,myx+6,Usery+6];
28          if clicks
29              count=count+1;
30              Screen('FillOval',w,0,UserOval);
31              Userdata(count ,1)= Usery;
32          end
33          Screen('Flip',w );
34          [clicks,Userx,Usery] = GetClicks;
35      end
36      Screen(w,'DrawText', sprintf('Your final length  was %d, press any key
    to exit\n', Userdata(2,1)-Userdata(1,1)),10,60);
37      Screen('Flip', w);
38      while kbcheck end
39      KbWait;
40      Screen('Close',w)
41  catch
42      Screen( 'Close',w)
43      rethrow(lasterror)
44  end
```

Analysis

Lines 1, 9–12: are to catch any error after a Screen has been opened.

Line 2: implements the two arguments returned by the `Screen Openwindow` subfunction: `w` is the pointer to the window; `rect` is a vector containing the coordinates in pixels of the screen.

Line 3: implements the vector `col` having the three RGB values to get the red color.

Line 4: implements the variable `myWidth` that will be used to supply the line width to the `DrawLine` subfunction.

Lines 5–6: draw in the backbuffer a wide red line running diagonally across the screen.

Line 7: flips from backbuffer to frontbuffer to display the line.

Line 8: `Kbwhait` waits for user's input.

Line 9 closes the `w` window.

A Brick for an Experiment

In our experiment, during each trial, the subject reports whether s/he perceived the discs as streaming or bouncing. Here in the brick this will be done using the function `KbWait` (because the response is not a reaction time). The first thing you need to do is to check how your response keys are coded. In the brick experiment the participant will press "b" if s/he sees the discs as bouncing and "s" if s/he sees the discs as streaming.

```
% set the keys we use in the experiment
bKey = KbName('b');
sKey = KbName('s');
```

Now we can get the subject's response with a while loop as we have seen previously in the chapter.

```
[secs, keyCode] = KbWait;
while keyCode(bKey)==0 && keyCode(sKey)==0
    [secs, keyCode] = KbWait;
end
```

Moreover, once the subject has pressed the key, we have to code the response. We could, for example, keep the response as is and have in the final data a long list of "r" and "s" values associated with each stimulus to which the subject has responded. However, it may be more convenient to code the subject's response as "probability of bounce response" as in the original paper (Sekuler et al. 1997). If we decide to do this, we can encode the response as '1' (i.e., the probability of bounce response is '1') when the subject presses "b". As an alternative, and there is only one possible alternative, i.e., when the subject presses "s", we encode the response as '0' (i.e., the probability of bounce response is '0'). Therefore:

```
if keyCode(bKey) == 1
    pbounce = 1;
else
    pbounce = 0;
end
```

Now let's write everything into our SekulerExp function. Note that the rows of code we just wrote will be distributed in different places in the SekulerExp function. For example, the response keys variables sKey and bKey are declared at the beginning of the function. There is, in fact, no need to declare them during each trial before the response is collected. Note also that we have added the variable "response" to store the participant's response (i.e., pbounce) during the trials of the experiment.

Listing 10.19

```
1  function SekulerExp(InputDataStruct)
2  % M-script to realize an experiment based on crossmodal perception
3  % The experiment first performed by Sekuler, Sekuler, and Lau (1997)
4  % Author: Borgo, Soranzo, Grassi 2009
5  % EXPERIMENT`S SETTINGS
6  % get input data from the structure passed through the interface
7  nsub = InputDataStruct.nsub;
8  subname = InputDataStruct.subname;
9  subsex = InputDataStruct.subsex;
10 subage = InputDataStruct.subage;
11 nblock = InputDataStruct.nblock;
12 subnote = InputDataStruct.subnote;
13 isfixed = InputDataStruct.isfixed;
14 filename = InputDataStruct.filename;
15 % set the experiment details
16 conditions = [1, 1; 1, 2; 2, 1; 2, 2];
17 repetitions = 20;
18 if nsub == 0
19     repetitions = 1;
20 end
21 % set the keys we use in the experiment
22 bKey = KbName('b');
23 sKey = KbName('s');
24 EventTable = GenerateEventTable(conditions, repetitions, isfixed);
25 TotalNumberOfTrials = length(EventTable(:, 1));
26 response = zeros(TotalNumberOfTrials, 1);
27 % opening operations for the screen function
28 try
29     whichscreen = max(Screen('Screens'));
30     [w, rect] =Screen('Openwindow', whichscreen, 0);
```

(continued)

Listing 10.19 (continued)

```
31      refreshrate = Screen('FrameRate', w);
32      for trial = 1:TotalNumberOfTrials
33          % STIMULI (SELECTION)
34          VideoStimulusToPlay = EventTable(trial, 2);
35          SoundStimulusToPlay = EventTable(trial, 3);
36          % STIMULI (CREATION)
37          % STIMULI (PRESENTATION)
38          SoundToPlay = GenerateSound(SoundStimulusToPlay, w);
39          MakeVideoStimulus
40          % COLLECT SUBJECT'S ANSWER
41          [secs, keyCode] = KbWait;
42          while keyCode(bKey)==0 && keyCode(sKey)==0
43              [secs, keyCode] = KbWait;
44          end
45          if keyCode(bKey) == 1
46              pbounce = 1;
47          else
48              pbounce = 0;
49          end
50          response(trial) = pbounce;
51      end
52      % closing operation
53      Screen('CloseAll'); % close all
54      % STORE RESULTS
55  catch
56      Screen( 'Close',w)
57      rethrow(lasterror)
58  end
```

We now further modify the script to play the sound (rows 32–33, 42–43, 59) hide/show the cursor (rows34, 60) and save the data (rows 62–64):

Listing 10.20

```
1   function SekulerExp(InputDataStruct)
2   % M-script to realize an experiment based on crossmodal perception
3   % The experiment first performed by Sekuler, Sekuler, and Lau (1997)
4   % Author: Borgo, Soranzo, Grassi 2009
5   % EXPERIMENT'S SETTINGS
6   % get input data from the structure passed through the interface
7   nsub = InputDataStruct.nsub;
8   subname = InputDataStruct.subname;
9   subsex = InputDataStruct.subsex;
10  subage = InputDataStruct.subage;
11  nblock = InputDataStruct.nblock;
12  subnote = InputDataStruct.subnote;
13  isfixed = InputDataStruct.isfixed;
14  filename = InputDataStruct.filename;
15  % set the experiment details
16  conditions = [1, 1; 1, 2; 2, 1; 2, 2];
17  repetitions = 20;
18  if nsub == 0
19      repetitions = 1;
20  end
```

(continued)

Listing 10.20 (continued)

```
21  % set the keys we use in the experiment
22  bKey = KbName('b');
23  sKey = KbName('s');
24  EventTable = GenerateEventTable(conditions, repetitions, isfixed);
25  TotalNumberOfTrials = length(EventTable(:, 1));
26  response = zeros(TotalNumberOfTrials, 1);
27  % opening operations for the screen function
28  try
29      whichscreen = max(Screen('Screens'));
30      [w, rect] =Screen('Openwindow', whichscreen, 0);
31      refreshrate = Screen('FrameRate', w);
32      InitializePsychSound;
33      pahandle = PsychPortAudio('Open', [], [], 0, 44100, 1);
34      HideCursor;
35      for trial = 1:TotalNumberOfTrials
36          % STIMULI (SELECTION)
37          VideoStimulusToPlay = EventTable(trial, 2);
38          SoundStimulusToPlay = EventTable(trial, 3);
39          % STIMULI (CREATION)
40          % STIMULI (PRESENTATION)
41          SoundToPlay = GenerateSound(SoundStimulusToPlay, w);
42          PsychPortAudio('FillBuffer', pahandle, SoundToPlay);
43          PsychPortAudio('Start', pahandle);
44          MakeVideoStimulus
45          % COLLECT SUBJECT'S ANSWER
46          [secs, keyCode] = KbWait;
47          while keyCode(bKey)==0 && keyCode(sKey)==0
48              [secs, keyCode] = KbWait;
49          end
50          if keyCode(bKey) == 1
51              pbounce = 1;
52          else
53              pbounce = 0;
54          end
55          response(trial) = pbounce;
56      end
57      % closing operation
58      Screen('CloseAll'); % close all
59      PsychPortAudio('Close', pahandle);
60      ShowCursor;
61      % STORE RESULTS
62      results = [EventTable, response];
63      save(filename, 'results', 'nsub', ...
64      'subname', 'subsex', 'subage', 'subnote')
65  catch
66      Screen( 'Close',w)
67      rethrow(lasterror)
68  end
```

References

Kingdom F (1997) Simultaneous contrast: the legacies of Hering and Helmholtz. Perception 26(6):673–677

Müller-Lyer FC (1889) Optische Urteilstäuschungen. Archiv für Physiologie, Supplement Volume, 263–270

Sekuler R, Sekuler AB, Lau R (1997) Sound alters visual motion perception. Nature 385:308

Suggested Readings

Tutorials on the Psychtoolbox can be found at the following web pages:

http://psychtoolbox.org/wikka.php?wakka=HomePage
http://psychtoolbox.org/wikka.php?wakka=PsychtoolboxTutorial

About the Authors

Mauro Borgo received his B.A. and his Ph.D. in Electronic and Telecommunication Engineering in 1999 and in 2003 respectively, both from the University of Padova, Italy. His interests are in signal and data processing for wireless communication. He adapted his skills in signal processing to multisensor/multiactuator cellular systems. He has an international patent on "multisite–single-cell electroporation." He was a lecturer in electrical communication and in MATLAB at the University of Padova (Italy).

Alessandro Soranzo received his B.A. in experimental P\psychology in 1999 and his Ph.D. in experimental psychology in 2004, both from the University of Trieste, Italy. He also completed a postdoc in vision sciences at Glasgow Caledonian University (Glasgow, UK). He is senior lecturer in cognitive psychology at Teesside University in Middlesbrough (UK). His research interests are in color perception and psychophysical methods.

Massimo Grassi received his B.A. in experimental psychology in 1997 and his Ph.D. in experimental psychology in 2003, both from the University of Padova (Italy). He has also been a visiting scientist at the University of Sussex (UK). He is a lecturer in sensation and perception at the University of Padova (Italy). His research interests are in sound perception, cross-modal perception, and psychophysical methods.

Index

Printed by Printforce, the Netherlands